P9-BZW-608

Noah's Ark
and the Ziusudra Epic

Abstract

This is a reconstruction of a lost legend about Ziusudra (Noah) who was king of the Sumerian city-state Shuruppak at the end of the Jemdet Nasr period about 2900 BC. A six-day thunderstorm caused the Euphrates River to rise and flood Shuruppak and a few other cities in southern Sumer. The ark was a commercial river barge that was hauling grain, beer, and other cargo including a few hundred animals when the storm began. The runaway barge floated down the river into the Persian Gulf where it grounded in an estuary at the mouth of the river. Ziusudra then offered a sacrifice at the top of a hill which storytellers misunderstood as mountain. This led them to assume that the nearby barge had grounded on the top of a mountain. The flood myth is demythologized with emphasis on what was physically possible, technologically practical, and consistent with archaeological facts.

Short abstract

A reconstruction of a lost legend about Ziusudra (Noah) a Sumerian king whose cattle barge got caught in a local river flood about 2900 BC.

About the author

Robert MacAndrew Best was born in Pennsylvania and received a BS degree in physics from Carnegie–Mellon University. Comments and criticisms of *Noah's Ark and the Ziusudra Epic* are welcome. Please e-mail suggestions and criticisms to: comments@noahs-ark.cc

Cover

The cover scene is an artist's conception of the flood hero's sacrifice after the flood as described in Genesis 8:20 and line 156 of tablet XI of the Epic of Gilgamesh: "I placed an offering at the top of a hill-like ziggurat." This was an animal sacrifice on a fireplace, a primitive altar, at the top of a ziggurat at the temple of Enki in the city of Eridu. A high priestess is holding up her lapis-lazuli "large flies" amulet of power and is blessing the food before giving permission to the priests to eat the sacrificial offering. The priests have shaved heads and wool skirts as shown in Sumerian art. Noah in the foreground also has a shaved head and wool skirt because he was made an honorary priest after the flood. Noah's hands are folded in reverence. As seen from the top of the ziggurat, the city of Eridu is artistically depicted in the distance next to a branch of the Euphrates River. This imagery is inferred from a mythical part of the flood story and may or may not have happened.

Noah's Ark

and the Ziusudra Epic

Sumerian Origins of the Flood Myth

Robert M. Best

Enlil Press
5100 S. Cleveland Ave. 318–325
Fort Myers, Florida 33907
USA

1999

Published by Enlil Press, 5100 S. Cleveland Ave. 318–325, Fort Myers, FL 33907.

Cover art by Robert M. Best, adapted from sacrifice scene painted by Eric Buckingham, Copyright © 1999 by Robert M. Best.

Sacrifice scene (p. 63) painted by Eric Buckingham, Pencil Neck Studio, Fort Myers, Florida from sketches by the author. Copyright © 1999 by Robert M. Best.

Boatbuilding scene (p. 93) by Daisy De Puthod, Daisy Illustrations, Hopewell Junction, New York. Copyright © 1999 by Robert M. Best.

Maps, line drawings, and archaic and cuneiform characters were drawn by the author, Copyright © 1999 by Robert M. Best. Body text and heading fonts are Baskerville.

Printed in the United States of America on alkaline paper, library binding.

First edition, printing 9 8 7 6 5 4 3 2 1

Library of Congress Catalog Card Number: 98-93918

Publisher's Cataloging-in-Publication Data

Best, Robert M., 1937–
    Noah's ark and the Ziusudra epic : Sumerian origins of the flood myth / Robert M. Best. – 1st ed.
      p. cm.
    Includes bibliographical references and index.
    LCCN: 98-93918
    ISBN: 0-9667840-1-4 (hardcover)

    1. Noah's ark.   2. Noah (Biblical character)   3. Mythology, Sumerian.
4. Sumerian literature.   5. Mythology, Assyro–Babylonian.
6. Sumerians–History.   I. Title.

BL325.D4B47   1999   291.1′3
                    QBI98–1460

Contents

97831

11   Expanded Theory

This chapter retells the story as a narrative without evidence or arguments. Additional conjectures are included.

12   Answers to Objections

Illustrations and Maps

Tables

Acknowledgments

I would like to express my appreciation to the following professors who helped me with different parts of this book and to those who read the manuscript and offered constructive criticisms. Lloyd R. Bailey at Duke University offered continual encouragement, sent me several pages of criticisms, and helped me with Hebrew questions. Scott B. Noegel at the University of Washington (Seattle) sent me several pages of criticisms and taught me with numerous e-mail messages much of what I know about the Akkadian language. Walter Farber at the University of Chicago, David Marcus at Jewish Theological Seminary, and David I. Owen at Cornell answered numerous questions about Akkadian and suggested corrections. Åke Sjöberg at the University of Pennsylvania and John L. Hayes at UCLA gave me important information about the Sumerian language. Robert K. Englund at UCLA told me several facts about archaic numbers that were essential for my theory of Genesis 5. James F. Strange at the University of South Florida helped me with Hebrew. James J. Clauss at the University of Washington helped me with Greek. David MacDonald at Illinois State University and Davis A. Young at Calvin College offered several important suggestions. These professors should not be held accountable for my interpretation of their advice or for any of my errors, but without the facts they provided me, this book could not have been written. RMB

Credits

The author and publisher gratefully acknowledge permission for use of the following materials:

Genesis 6–9 text unless otherwise noted, is from the Revised Standard Version of the Bible, copyright 1946, 1952, 1971, 1973 by the National Council of the Churches of Christ in the U.S.A.

The text of the Gilgamesh flood story is adapted from *The Gilgamesh Epic and Old Testament Parallels* by Alexander Heidel, copyright 1946, 1949, 1963 by The University of Chicago.

The Egyptian Khufu boat drawing is from *Ships of the Pharaohs* by Björn Landström, translated by Keith Bradfield, Translation copyright © 1970 by International Book Production, Stockholm. Used by permission of Doubleday, a division of Bantam Doubleday Dell Publishing Group, Inc.

A paragraph from the article *The Impossible Voyage of Noah's Ark* by Robert A. Moore, copyright 1983 by Robert A. Moore.

Summary of the article *Problems with a Global Flood* by Mark Isaak, copyright 1998 by Mark Isaak.

Preface

Of all the stories in the Hebrew Bible, the story of Noah's Ark is one of the most famous. More than a hundred books have been written about Noah, the flood, the ark, the animals, and Mount Ararat, and several movies have been based on the flood story. The Noah's Ark story holds a fascination for people of all ages and has enjoyed discussion and popular story telling for more than three millennia.

A continuing controversy exists between various groups of people regarding the Noah's Ark story and the Genesis flood. Mythologists and skeptics believe the flood story is entirely fiction, because many of the reported or implied events, such as a global flood, would have been physically impossible. Ark-searching mountain climbers and young-earth creationists believe that Noah's flood was global because only a global flood could cover high mountains. Biblical and Ancient Near East scholars generally reject the creationist fantasies, but some scholars consider the flood story worthy of serious study.

Much of the flood story is mythical and the entire story may have been fiction, but some of the plausible details may have been based on real events that were mythologized by later poets and story tellers. This book attempts to separate the legendary parts from the mythical parts and to reconstruct some of the events that may have occurred during a local flood that inspired the mythical stories that survived to the present.

After removing the myth from the Sumerian, Babylonian, Genesis, and Berossus versions of the story, I have combined the remaining legendary fragments into one coherent story, while emphasizing what would have been physically possible, technologically practical, and consistent with archaeological facts.

Each legendary story element is checked for possible scribal errors, mistranslations, misunderstandings, exaggerations, and other distortions of the text, because these are the kinds of distortions usually found in orally transmitted legend. Each detail is interpreted in the context of what witnesses of a local flood could have seen with their own eyes from their limited perspective. Subjective opinions of the narrators are replaced with more plausible explanations for alleged events.

Writing a book that rationalized the Genesis flood story was not initially my intent. Instead, as a pastime I was attempting to decipher the numbers in Genesis 5, an effort that was finally successful (see Chapter 7 herein). Having a physical science background, I initially had no interest in the flood story, because I knew it was impossible for the ocean to cover "Mount Ararat" only 5000 years ago. But to decipher the numbers in Genesis 5, I needed to understand the numbers in Genesis 7:6 and 9:28 and that got me involved in the flood story. Under the conventional notion that the ark landed on a mountain, the story did not make sense. But I kept inventing alternative theories and eventually the pieces began to fit together like the pieces of a jigsaw picture puzzle. This led me to thoroughly research the remaining holes in the puzzle. As more and more of the pieces fit together, a new picture emerged that was surprisingly different than anything I had ever seen or read, before or since. This book is the result and provides a fresh viewpoint for understanding the flood myth that was not previously available.

I am not presuming that there was a historical basis for the major elements in the Noachian flood myth. Even if the original legend was based on an actual river flood, the boatload of animals may have been fiction. And even if an actual cattle barge got caught in an actual river flood, the story elements linking the barge owner to the king of Shuruppak may have been fiction. There is no way to determine how much of the flood legend was fiction and how much was fact. Therefore, my objective is not to prove the historicity of the flood myths; rather it is my objective to reconstruct as much as possible the original legend, regardless of what percentage was fiction or fact.

Several ambiguous words in the flood myths can be given physically possible and plausible meanings, but are usually given impossible meanings because of ancient mistakes, centuries of tradition, and uncritical storytelling. To clear away the misunderstandings and mistranslations that have grown like barnacles on the original legend, it is essential to focus on what was physically possible and practical in the early third millennium BC. Facts about the Euphrates River annually rising and falling provide a chronological foundation for reconstructing the events on which the flood legend was based. Archaeological evidence provides essential facts for linking legendary story elements to the real world. I have filled some of the gaps in the story with conjecture, but this conjecture may be disregarded without weakening the basic theory. Some of these conjectures lead to hypotheses that were confirmed by other data in the sources or by archaeological facts.

This book is for people who would like to know the historical basis of Noah's flood story, but who know the story is mostly myth. The historicity of the flood story remains unproven, but the events reconstructed here would have been physically possible and some may have happened, although under circumstances that were different than what is commonly believed.

Robert M. Best

Summary of Conclusions

The Ancient Near East flood myths, including the one in Genesis, were adaptations of one archetype flood myth that was first written in clay about 2600 BC. This archetype flood myth was based on legends about a local flood of the Euphrates River that occurred about 2900 BC in southern Sumer (now southern Iraq). The flood hero in the archetype myth was based on Ziusudra, who was king of the Sumerian city-state of Shuruppak at the time of the river flood, at the beginning of the Early Dynastic period. The ark was based on a commercial river barge used for transporting cargo on the Euphrates River. This river barge was about 200 feet long and held less than 280 animals along with thousands of baskets of grain and jars of beer and wine that were being transported to market.

A six-day thunderstorm caused the river to rise about 15 cubits above the levees and resulted in local flooding of Shuruppak and a few other Sumerian cities. The swollen river carried the runaway cattle barge downriver into the relatively deep water of the Persian (Arabian) Gulf. The cattle barge drifted about the Gulf for several months and finally grounded in the mud of an estuary "at the mouth of the rivers" at sea level. After disembarking, the flood hero Ziusudra (Noah) offered a sacrifice at the top of a nearby hill which story tellers mistranslated as mountain. This led them to erroneously assume that the barge had grounded on the top of a mountain. There were many survivors of the river flood and Ziusudra met some of them after the barge grounded.

About three hundred years later, orally transmitted mythical versions of the flood story were written in clay and included several mistranslations and misunderstandings of the original local flood legends. In the original legends, Ziusudra did not know a flood was coming until rain began to fall, the cattle barge never came close to a mountain, the so-called "Mount Ararat" was not involved, and there was no global deluge. The impossibly large numbers in Genesis 5 and the Sumerian King List resulted from ancient mistranslations of the original numbers.

1

Myths, Legends and History

Introduction

*"The knavery and folly of men are such common
phenomena, that I should rather believe the
most extraordinary events to arise from their
concurrence, than admit of so single a violation
of the laws of nature."*

David Hume (1748)

Every year in December, millions of otherwise rational people speak and
sing about an overweight man in a red and white suit who some say is pulled
through the air by flying reindeer and who reportedly slides down narrow
chimneys with a sack of toys. A foreign visitor who had never heard of this
Santa Claus and his alleged method of transportation, would quickly
recognize in this story the characteristics of a myth. The superhuman hero
of this myth has magical abilities, does impossible things, distributes gifts to
deserving people and is a kindly but judgmental grandfather figure who
nobody ever sees.

Interwoven with this Santa Claus myth are unconfirmed legends from
which the myth is said to have evolved. Suppose we explained to our foreign
visitor that Santa Claus was originally known as Saint Nicholas who was a
real person and lived seventeen centuries ago in Myra, Turkey.[1] In view of
the many impossible things that Santa Claus is said to have done, our skeptical
visitor would probably dismiss the Saint Nicholas legend as fiction.

The problem of separating the myth from the legend in Noah's flood
story is similar to the problem of separating the Santa Claus myth from the
legend of Saint Nicholas. Without pushing the analogy too far, Santa Claus
is mentioned here because it is well known that the myth and the legend are
separable. It is easy to discuss the legend of archbishop Nicholas without
getting entangled in the Santa Claus myth, because the names are different
and much of the myth was created recently. The modern image of Santa
Claus was largely invented or compiled by writer Washington Irving, poet
Clement Moore, and cartoonist Thomas Nast during the nineteenth century.[2]

If we were to prepare a plausible case that Saint Nicholas really existed, we would first have to remove the myths about flying reindeer and chimney climbing. If the remaining legendary material could be confirmed, a history of Saint Nicholas might be developed. But developing reliable history is not always possible from surviving legends. Historians require documentation for alleged historical facts that can stand up to various tests and proofs for accuracy. Unsubstantiated folklore, saga, epic poetry, etc. do not qualify as history. Unless we could find contemporaneous documents, such as church records, that attest to essential details of Nicholas's life, we would not be able to prove the historicity of Saint Nicholas. The best we could hope for would be a plausible but unconfirmed legend.

Separating myth from legend

Separating the myth from the legend (if any) in the Ancient Near East flood story is more difficult, because thousands of years have passed since the original flood legends were first written down, during which time many of the details have become garbled. From a comparison of various versions of the flood story it is clear that several poets, story tellers, writers, and editors have altered details and added new material during transmission of the stories. Moreover, we have no way of knowing whether the original flood stories were partly fictional or entirely fictional and based only on general knowledge of the original authors.

Myths usually involve physically impossible supernatural events because miracles are entertaining and memorable. Story tellers who want to entertain rather than report facts add mythical material to their received story whenever it suits their needs. In myths animals talk, gods intervene, people or things get magically transformed, super heroes do impossible things and have knowledge they could not possibly have. Physical details such as distances, forces, strengths, velocities, heights, and sizes are exaggerated to impossible degrees and physical objects and forces are given humanlike emotions. The story teller who is not interested in historical accuracy substitutes fantasy for anything he does not understand or cannot remember. Usually the impossible and exaggerated parts of the story are easy to recognize, but there is no guarantee that the remaining plausible details are factual, even if the legendary parts of the story were based on actual events.

A legend is a story about a subject that is believed to have been historical[3] but cannot be verified. Legends concern named heroes, specific places, and possible events in the past, but some or all of a legend may be fiction. For example, some of the stories about King Arthur such as the battle of Camlan where Arthur was said to have been fatally wounded could have happened,[4] although many other Arthurian tales could not have happened. Even though the battle of Camlan seems possible, it is also possible that Arthur was not at the battle or the battle was fiction.[5] Until a contemporaneous document or artifact is found that provides details about the battle of Camlan, this story that seems true but may be fiction will remain legendary.

The Trojan War is another familiar example of a legendary event for which there is no proof. Troy was a real place and the Greeks probably fought the Trojans at some time, but there is no historical evidence that the Greeks ever used a wooden horse to gain entry to a city or that a beautiful Greek queen named Helen ever lived with a Trojan prince.[6]

When legendary characters possess superhuman or divine qualities, or when supernatural beings interact with them, then the legend becomes a myth.[3] Myth and legend are often interwoven in the same stories and are sometimes falsely attached to provably historical events, people or places. Also, as with the legends and myths of Santa Claus and King Arthur, the legendary portion is often only a small part of the surviving texts, especially because each generation of story tellers alters details and adds another layer of myth.

Even though legends can quickly become myths through fantasy and inaccurate transmission, certain details of a legend may continue to be retold by generations of story tellers exactly as they heard them, because some of their listeners have heard the story before and expect the details to be repeated accurately. The details that are found in two or more versions of the flood story, such as the bird scene and the altar scene, identify these stories as variations of the same story and increase the probability that these stories have a common origin. But as we shall see, some of the common details in different versions of the story were mistakes made during oral transmission or during translation from Sumerian to Akkadian.

Legendary stories can quickly become historical if and when credible documents or artifacts are found. Searching for such evidence is therefore a legitimate activity, although it is understandable that historians do not want to waste their time on myth-tainted legendary stories that are probably fiction. Even when a physical or historical basis is found for a mythical legend (for example, excavated flood strata in cities where Noah may have lived) scholars tend to dismiss as myth any story that has a major part that is clearly mythical. Joseph Campbell[7] stated this emphatically when referring to Noah's age and other excessively large numbers in Genesis 5 and the Sumerian King lists: "all are of the same mythological order and could not possibly be read today by anybody in his right mind as referring accurately to historical events." Most historians and many biblical scholars believe that nothing historical or legendary can be found in the Genesis flood story. If the events or numbers in a story are impossible or very improbable, it would seem foolish as well as futile to look for historical or legendary material in such stories.

However, apparent impossibilities of the events and numbers may be the result of words being mistranslated, events being misunderstood, places being incorrectly identified, facts being exaggerated or omitted, and erroneous amendments, inferences, and overgeneralizations being added many years after the original stories were created. Hence, classifying a story as totally mythical before such errors are removed or corrected may be premature.

But removing the overburden of myth to uncover a buried vein of legend is not easy, especially as each sentence of the story does not have a tag attached that says: "this is myth" or "this is misunderstood legend." And if we amend the story to "correct" apparent errors, how do we know they were really errors? How do we know that we are not deceiving ourselves when we "correct" errors that were really fiction from the original author's imagination? Simply put, we can't. That is the nature of legend. In such cases, it may be impossible to establish the historicity of the legendary part of the story which will therefore continue to be unconfirmed legend that may never have happened. But what we can do is reorganize the received story material into a sequence of physically possible events tied together with physical facts and plausible conjectures, so that details in the reinterpreted and reorganized story can be verified or falsified if someone in the future chances upon ancient records that attest to details in the story.

This technique cannot be used with all legend/myth stories because not all legendary stories would have contemporaneous records and many lack details that are potentially verifiable or falsifiable. For example, it is futile to demythologize the Adam and Eve story. After the mythical portions are removed, no usable legend remains. The absence of who, what, when and where details label this story as totally mythical. Even the name of the hero is missing. Adam is a generic Hebrew word for man. Eve being formed from Adam's rib was a pun on the Sumerian word for rib.[8] Eden was a generic Sumerian word meaning a 'plain' or 'steppe' and was a common Aramaic word meaning 'enriches, gives abundance'.[9] There is no hope of finding any usable legend in the Adam and Eve story.

However, in the case of the flood story, there is usable legend and a better chance of finding near contemporaneous records. Building of large boats often leaves a trail of administrative, financial and legal records, especially if high government officials are involved.

In addition to the mythology already present in the ancient texts, modern versions of the flood story add additional details that are not supported by and often conflict with the plain meaning of the ancient texts. Most books on Noah's Ark picture a parade of giraffes, lions, elephants and other exotic animals marching in pairs up a ramp into a rounded-hull deep-keel boat under the watchful eyes of Noah who is pictured with white hair and a long white beard. The ark usually has a small deck house with a sloping gabled roof and the ark is often shown resting on a sharp rocky peak. None of this imagery is supported in the ancient texts.

It is ironic that people who accept the Genesis flood story but ignore the Babylonian flood myths, are usually unaware that their own views have been affected by recently-invented mythology. This recent mythology has been compounded by modern proponents of pseudo-scientific theories based on a supposed worldwide flood.[10] If we are to determine how the notion of a global flood originated, we need more than just popular mythology built on vague sentences in Genesis. The Babylonian and Sumerian myths provide additional clues about the origins of the story of the flood, and therefore analysis of these myths is essential for separating the legendary material (if any) from the mythical material.

Demythologizing a myth

Three methods of demythologizing the flood story are used here to uncover underlying legend. The first method is to disregard every phrase that contains obvious mythical material or conflicts with known facts. The phrases that remain are the legend, although this method yields only a few disconnected fragments of legend.

The second method is to reinterpret each impossible or improbable phrase as a mistake and seek alternative interpretations that conform to what would have been physically possible and plausible before rejecting the phrase as myth. Excluding the supernatural, some reported events that are impossible or improbable can be corrected for mistranslations, exaggerations, misunderstandings, mistaken identifications, and similar errors, if plausible causes can be found for such errors.

The third method is to reinterpret phrases that are clearly mythical as a story teller's mythical interpretation of legendary events. This third method is clearly unreliable, because new interpretations of mythical material may be only the fantasy of the interpreter. Such reinterpreted myth is not used here to develop the basic theory, but is used sparingly to flesh out the story when constrained by a theory based on the non-myth legend. The first and second methods provide the essential evidence from which a basic framework of the theory is built. This theory then guides interpretation of the mythical material.

Phrases and sentences that cannot be rationalized with these three methods are disregarded. Even with this cautious approach, the best we can hope for is a plausible theory. There is no way of proving such a theory beyond a reasonable doubt. The reinterpreted flood legend, as presented in this book, should therefore be read with the same tentative but critical attitude in which it was written and all of the reinterpreted myth may be disregarded, if necessary.

Demythologizing a myth is like deciphering a cryptogram in which one starts with the most frequent constant parts and defers the variable parts until later. Personal names, place names, and mental states are the most variable parts of a myth. Story tellers routinely adapt myths to local audiences by changing the names to familiar local names. Story tellers also imagine what gods and people were thinking and such fantasy varies between versions of the story. We should disregard such names, mental states, and agendas of the gods and focus instead on the constant parts of the story which are:

> the hero builds a boat;
> a storm occurs, accompanied by a flood;
> the hero and his family are on the boat during the flood;
> the boat grounds on a mountain; and
> the hero offers a sacrifice to a god.

The key to demythologizing the flood myth is the mountain, because grounding on a mountain is the one constant story element that could not have happened. Although most commentators focus on identifying and locating the mountain, this is futile because a worldwide ocean flood rising above any mountain for a year would be physically impossible. Either this constant part of the story is fiction or it was a misunderstanding or a mistranslation. As will be shown in Chapter 3, the reported grounding of the ark on the top of a mountain was both a misunderstanding and a mistranslation. The ark, if it existed, never came close to a mountain.

Reported facts imply other facts

Some facts can be inferred from the received text, because one fact follows from another fact. For example, the received statement that the Sumerian Noah (Ziusudra) was a king or chief executive of Shuruppak implies several things about his personality and activities. Being a king implies he was probably wealthy, he controlled many people, he delegated responsibility, he was involved in diplomatic relations with foreign states, he was interested in increasing the wealth of Shuruppak, he had rivals, he did not build boats with his own hands, etc. Although these inferences are conjecture, they are more plausible than guesses about an ancient story teller's agenda.

We cannot escape the physical implications of the purported facts. The ark reportedly carried Noah's family and animals for a year and therefore there would have to be enough food and water on board and these supplies would have occupied more space on the ark than the animals. The number of animals could not have been more than the people on the boat could feed and water. However, such possible inferences and conjectures are dependent on the legendary story elements which may be partly or wholly fictional.

The criteria for deciding what parts of a story to disregard or reinterpret as myth and what parts to consider as legend should be based on whether each event would have been possible and probable under the circumstances and whether parts of the reorganized story fit together, i.e. does the reorganized story make sense. If we force the details of a story to conform to what would have been possible and join the pieces together in a plausible way, of course we will not be surprised that the reorganized story is possible and plausible. But then are we not adding more myth to the story by distorting the received details to conform to our preconceptions?

In the present instance the answer is no. When I began this reconstruction of the flood story, my preconception was that Noah's flood, if it occurred, could have been the result of an earthquake or meteor impact[11] that created a tsunami in the Persian Gulf that lifted a boat up into the foothills of the Ararat mountains. I resisted the notion that the boat might have washed down into the Persian (Arabian) Gulf during a storm, because then it would have been even more difficult for the boat to rise up into the mountains of Ararat. Under this preconception, the pieces of the story did not fit together well. Only after I considered the possibility that the boat entered the Persian Gulf and the word for mountain was mistranslated, then the pieces began to fit together much better like the pieces of a jigsaw picture puzzle.

Regardless of how well the pieces fit together, there is still a real possibility that Noah was a fictional character and the flood story was a fictional biography based on a local flood and perhaps a historical king, especially as fictional Akkadian[12] and Sumerian[13] biography was an established genre in the Old Babylonian period. We may never know how much of the flood story was fiction and how much was distorted fact. But this is also true of other legends. Even if the Trojan War was an actual war, Hector, Achilles, and Helen may have been fictional characters cast in a historic setting by Homer or by anonymous bards whose combined works were first written down in the sixth century BC, about six centuries after the Trojan War.

Ark story is myth and legend, not history

It is not my objective in this book to prove the historicity of Noah's Ark. That is not possible without confirmation from contemporaneous artifacts. But it is also not my objective to dismiss the flood myths as entirely fictional. Rather my objective is to present a demythologized legend, an alternative version of the story that is based on archaeological, geological, and meteorological facts and therefore would have been physically possible and may have happened. Or if some of the reconstructed legend was fiction, the legend may approximate some fictional biographies about the Sumerian Noah that were mythologized by ancient story tellers and epic poets.

In most instances my statements express probability and plausibility, not certainty. The arguments and conclusions presented in this book should be viewed as hypotheses to be revised as additional evidence is discovered.

References

1.   Charles W. Jones, *Saint Nicholas of Myra, Bari, and Manhattan*, (Chicago: University of Chicago Press, 1978), pp. 7–9, 46–47.

2.   ibid, pp. 344–353.

3.   Donna Rosenberg, *Folklore, Myths, and Legends*, (Lincolnwood, Illinois: NTC Publishing Group, 1997), pp. xxvi–xxvii.

4.   Norma Lorre Goodrich, *King Arthur*, (NY: Harper Collins, 1986), pp. 257–265.

5.   Richard Barber, *King Arthur: Hero and Legend*, (New York: Boydell Press, 1986), pp. 10–16.

6.   J. B. Hainsworth, "The Fallibility of An Oral Heroic Tradition" in *The Trojan War: its Historicity and Context*, Lin Foxhall and John K. Davies, editors, (Bristol, England: Bristol Classical Press, 1981), pp. 111–135.

7.   Joseph Campbell, *The Masks of God: Oriental Mythology*, (New York: Penguin Books, 1962), pp. 119–130.

8.   Samuel Noah Kramer, *The Sumerians*, (Chicago: University of Chicago Press, 1963), p. 149. The Sumerian word for rib was TI but TI also meant "to make live." The name NIN–TI, literally "lady of the rib" came to mean "lady who makes live" which makes Genesis 3:20 understandable, although the Hebrew words for rib and live have nothing in common.

9.   A. R. Millard, "The Etymology of Eden", *Vetus Testamentum*, 34, 1 (January 1984), pp. 103–106.

10.   Stephen Jay Gould, "Creationism: Genesis vs. Geology" in *The Flood Myth* by Alan Dundes (editor), (CA: University of California Press, 1988), pp. 427–437.

11.   Isaac Asimov, *Asimov's Guide to the Bible*, (NY: Doubleday, 1968), pp. 40–42.

12.   Tremper Longman III, *Fictional Akkadian Autobiography: A Generic and Comparative Study*, (Winona Lake, Indiana: Eisenbrauns, 1991).

13.   Scott B. Noegel, "Fictional Sumerian Autobiographies," *Journal of the Association of Graduate Near Eastern Students*, 4/2 (1993), pp. 46–55. The flood myths were not autobiographies in the sense used by Longman or Noegel.

2

Versions of the Flood Story

*"Nobody ever sees truth
except in fragments."*

Henry Ward Beecher (1887)

Six versions of the flood story are analyzed here and combined into one coherent story. Although numerous flood stories exist from around the world,[1] the six selected here are the most ancient, are from a geographically small area (the Ancient Near East) and share many common story elements.

1. The Ziusudra Epic[2] was written in the Sumerian language and only one fragmented copy of this text survives. These fragments, which include only about one-third of the original text, were found at the site of the ancient Sumerian city of Nippur in the southern valley of the Euphrates River in what is now Iraq. The fragments were part of a large library in the temple of Enlil and have been dated to around 1600 BC.[4] Ziusudra was the flood hero in this abridged version of the flood myth.

2. The Atrahasis Epic[3] was written in Akkadian and only about two-thirds of the original text survives. It was found in two different editions at the site of the ancient Assyrian city of Nineveh in the library of Ashurbanipal, king of Assyria (669–633 BC). Nineveh was in the northern end of the Tigris River valley. The earlier and most complete edition was copied during the reign of Ammizaduga, the next to the last king of the Old Babylonian Period (about 1636 BC) during a period when Sumerian literature was being collected and translated into Akkadian by scribes in Babylonia. Atrahasis was the flood hero in this version of the flood myth.

3. In the Epic of Gilgamesh,[5] the flood story forms a major part of tablet eleven, usually labeled XI in modern translations. The Gilgamesh epic consists of twelve poems of about 300 lines each. Each poem was written on a separate tablet. The flood story was added to an earlier edition of the Epic of Gilgamesh about 1200 BC by an editor (perhaps Sin-liqi-unninni). The most complete copy was written in Akkadian and was also found in the library of Ashurbanipal. Several fragmented copies survive in the Akkadian, Middle Babylonian, Hittite and Hurrian languages. Quotations used here are from various English translations of Tablet XI unless otherwise specified. The hero of the flood was named Utnapishtim in this version of the flood myth.

4. Genesis 6–9 (in Hebrew). The Genesis version of the flood story reached its present form during the post-exilic period before 400 BC. The Revised Standard Version is used herein except where noted. This is a modern English translation from the Masoretic Text, the standard Hebrew text. The Septuagint (ancient Greek translation from Hebrew) version of the Genesis 5 genealogy is analyzed in Chapter 7.

5. The Berossus version[6] (in Greek). Berossus was a Babylonian priest of the god Marduk and wrote a history of Babylonia that was published about 281 BC. This history has not survived, but excerpts of his version of the flood story were preserved by a few later writers including Josephus, Polyhistor, Eusebius and Syncellus. The flood hero is named Xisuthros.

6. The Moses of Khoren[7] version of the flood story was published in his History of Armenia (in Armenian) about the eighth century CE.[8] He cited a legend from Olympiodorus regarding "a book about Khsisuthros [Ziusudra the Sumerian Noah] and his sons, which has not survived to the present." Although the legend about the flood that Moses of Khoren recorded does not mention events before grounding of the boat, he does mention some events after the grounding.

In addition, the Sumerian King List WB-62 mentions the flood and the flood hero Ziusudra. The King List has impossibly large numbers of years for each king, but these numbers are deciphered in Chapter 7.

Numerous other ancient versions of the flood story were studied in preparing the present book, including Old Testament apocrypha, pseudepigrapha, Rabbinic traditions, Muslim traditions, Greek myths, Hindu myths, etc. These do not appear to add any usable legend to the Sumerian–Babylonian flood story.

Common phrases imply common origin

Distinctive story elements and phrases that are common to two or more of these six stories indicate a common origin. Parallel quotations make it obvious that these six flood stories did not originate independently:

"Side-wall...pay attention" Ziusudra iv,155
"Wall, listen to me." Atrahasis III,i,20
"Wall, pay attention" Gilgamesh XI,22

"the decision that mankind is to be destroyed" Ziusudra iv,157–158
"The gods commanded total destruction" Atrahasis II,viii,34
"The great gods decided to make a flood" Gilgamesh XI,14
"God...decided to make an end of all flesh" Genesis 6:13

"Destroy your house, spurn property, save life" Atrahasis III,i,22
"Tear down house, abandon property, save life" Gilgamesh XI,24–26

"Enki...over the capitals the storm will sweep" Ziusudra iv,156
"He [Enki] told him of the coming of the flood" Atrahasis III,i,37
"God said to Noah...I will bring a flood" Genesis 6:13,17
"Kronos...said...mankind would be destroyed by a flood" Berossus

"...the huge boat" Ziusudra v,207
"Build a ship" Atrahasis III,i,22
"Build a ship" Gilgamesh XI,24
"Make yourself an ark" Genesis 6:14
"build a boat" Berossus

"who protected the seed of mankind" Ziusudra vi,259
"Bring into the ship the seed of all life" Gilgamesh XI,27
"to keep their seed alive" Genesis 7:3 (KJV)

"Like the apsu you shall roof it" Atrahasis III,i,29
"Like the apsu you shall roof it" Gilgamesh XI,31
"Make a roof for the ark" Genesis 6:16

"coming of the flood on the seventh night" Atrahasis,III,i,37
"after seven days the waters of the flood came" Genesis 7:10

"...and addressed the elders" Atrahasis III,i,41
"I answer the city people and the elders" Gilgamesh XI,35

"This is what you shall say to them..." Gilgamesh XI,38
"If asked where he was sailing he was to reply..." Berossus

"I cannot live in [your city]" Atrahasis III,i,47
"I cannot live in your city" Gilgamesh XI,40

"An abundance of birds, a profusion of fishes" Atrahasis III,i,35
"[an abundance of] birds, [a profusion of] fish" Gilgamesh XI,44

"pitch I poured into the inside" Gilgamesh XI,66
"cover it inside and out with pitch" Genesis 6:14
"some people scrape pitch off the boat" Berossus

"your family, your relatives" Atrahasis DT,42(w),8
"he sent his family on board" Atrahasis III,ii,42
"into the ship all my family and relatives" Gilgamesh XI,84
"Go into the ark, you and all your household" Genesis 7:1
"he sent his wife and children and friends on board" Berossus

"animals which emerge from the earth" Ziusudra vi,253
"all the wild creatures of the steppe" Atrahasis DT,42(w),9
"The cattle of the field, the beast of the plain" Gilgamesh XI,85
"clean animals and of animals that are not clean" Genesis 7:8
"and put both birds and animals on board" Berossus

"Enter the boat and close the boat's door" Atrahasis DT,42(w),6
"Pitch was brought for him to close his door" Atrahasis III,ii,51
"I entered the boat and closed the door" Gilgamesh XI,93
"And they that entered...and the Lord shut him in" Genesis 7:16

"Ninurta went forth making the dikes [overflow]" Atrahasis U rev,14
"Ninurta went forth making the dikes overflow" Gilgamesh XI,102

"One person could [not] see another" Atrahasis III,iii,13
"One person could not see another" Gilgamesh XI,111

"to Puzur-Amurri the boatman" Gilgamesh,XI,94
"the boatman shared the same honor" Berossus

"the storm had swept...for seven days and seven nights" Ziusudra 203
"For seven days and seven nights came the storm" Atrahasis III,iv,24
"Six days and seven nights the wind and storm" Gilgamesh XI,127
"rain fell upon the earth forty days and forty nights" Genesis 7:12

"consigned the peoples to destruction" Atrahasis III,iii,54
"All mankind was turned to clay" Gilgamesh XI,133
"And all flesh died...and every man" Genesis 7:21

"Ziusudra made an opening in the large boat" Ziusudra vi,207
"I opened the window" Gilgamesh XI,135
"Noah opened the window of the ark" Genesis 8:6
"he pried open a portion of the boat" Berossus

"On Mount Niṣir the boat grounded" Gilgamesh XI,140
"the ark came to rest upon the mountains" Genesis 8:4
"the boat had grounded upon a mountain" Berossus
"After Khsisuthros...landed...a long mountain" Moses of Khoren

"The dove went out and returned" Gilgamesh XI,147
"sent forth the dove and the dove came back to him" Genesis 8:10
"let out the birds and they again returned to the ship" Berossus

"The king slaughtered...bulls and sheep" Ziusudra vi,211
"He offered [a sacrifice]" Atrahasis III,v,31
"And offered a sacrifice" Gilgamesh XI,155
"offered burnt offerings on the altar" Genesis 8:20
"built an altar and sacrificed to the gods" Berossus

"[The gods smelled] the savor" Atrahasis III,v,34
"The gods smelled the sweet savor" Gilgamesh XI,160
"And the Lord smelled the sweet savor..." Genesis 8:21

"the lapis around my neck" Atrahasis III,vi,2
"the lapis lazuli on my neck" Gilgamesh XI,164

"That I may remember it [every] day" Atrahasis III,vi,4
"I shall remember these days and never forget" Gilgamesh XI,165
"I shall remember my covenant...I may remember" Genesis 9:15-16

"How did man survive the destruction?" Atrahasis III,vi,10
"No man was to survive the destruction" Gilgamesh XI,173

"[on the criminal] impose your penalty" Atrahasis III,vi,25
"On the criminal impose his crimes" Gilgamesh XI,180
"Who sheds the blood of man, by man his blood be shed" Genesis 9:6

"he touched our foreheads to bless us" Gilgamesh XI,192
"And God blessed Noah" Genesis 9:1

"elevated him to eternal life, like a god" Ziusudra vi,257
"they shall be like gods to us" Gilgamesh XI,194

"I lived in the temple of Ea, my lord" Atrahasis RS 22.421,7
"go down to dwell with my lord Ea" Gilgamesh XI,42
"he had gone to dwell with the gods" Berossus
"Noah walked with God." Genesis 6:9c

Flood story originated about 2900 BC

The above parallels are so numerous and unmistakably similar that it should be obvious that these versions have literary affinity if not dependency. Directly or indirectly, these six stories had a common source or sources and are surviving editions of the same story. According to archaeologist Max Mallowan, this flood story originated in the Early Dynastic I period about 2900–2800 BC.[9] After that, hundreds of years passed before the art of syllabic writing was sufficiently developed for this archetype flood story to be written in narrative form. After the oral tradition was written in clay, this written archetype story was reedited into at least six written versions in which the same mundane events were mythologized and interpreted differently.

Although the hero in these six versions was given different names (Ziusudra, Atrahasis, Utnapishtim, Noah, Xisuthros and Khsisuthros), they are the same person because it is the same story. Therefore, the name Noah or the "Babylonian Noah" or the "Sumerian Noah" will be used for the flood hero throughout this book, regardless of the source of the story element being discussed, although the name Ziusudra is usually implied. This is done for convenience and is not intended as an endorsement of every fanciful action attributed to the Biblical Noah or his Babylonian counterparts. It has been suggested[10] that the name Noah (n-w-h) originally meant "long" as in "long life" the literal meaning of Ziusudra. Xisuthros and Khsisuthros are grecized forms of Ziusudra.

Each of the six versions of this flood story includes details that are not found in the other versions, thus indicating that each version is not wholly derived from one of the other versions. The following are examples of significant details found in one version that are not found in the other versions:

Ziusudra vi,260:
"Ziusudra...settled in the eastern country of Dilmun."

Atrahasis III,i,30
"So that the sun shall not see inside it."

Atrahasis III,ii,40–41:
"He invited his people to a banquet."

Gilgamesh XI,94:
"caulking of the boat I gave to Puzur-Amurri, the boatman."

Gilgamesh XI,196:
"Utnapishtim lives far away at the mouth of the rivers."

Genesis 8,14:
"In the second month, on the twenty-seventh day of the month..."

Berossus:
"His wife, his daughter, and the boatman shared the honor."

Berossus:
"Recover the writings at Sippar and publish them to men."

Moses of Khoren:
"Shem moved northwest to explore the land."

Moses of Khoren:
"He arrived at a small plain at the foot of a long mountain."

A thunderstorm caused flooding in the Euphrates Valley

According to Gilgamesh XI,97–109: "there arose a black cloud from the horizon…thundering within it… For one whole day the south wind blew, gathering speed…tore out the dam posts…made the dikes overflow." These lines clearly indicate that Noah's flood was caused by a heavy thunderstorm that caused flooding which breached the dams and levees. This flood was probably unusual in the Tigris–Euphrates valley, but need not have been unique or even rare. Torrential floods are endemic to the Tigris–Euphrates valley and an overflow of the Tigris in 1954 submerged the low-lying plain for hundreds of miles, threatening Baghdad with destruction.[11]

In the Sumerian King List[12] for cities in the southern Euphrates valley, after the name of the flood hero and his city Shuruppak are the words "The flood swept thereover" followed by the names of more kings in the southern valley. In Gilgamesh XI,35 the flood hero was also placed at Shuruppak, the modern Fara in the southern Euphrates valley. This suggests a specific historical flood that took place in the southern Euphrates River valley.

Mallowan[9] discussed several historical floods in the Tigris–Euphrates valley and unusual alluvial strata that were deposited in various cities. Mallowan also discussed the question of which of these strata can be identified with the King list flood and the Genesis flood. Further discussion of this issue can be found in Raikes[14] and Bailey.[15]

Criticisms of attempts to identify Noah's flood with one or another of these historical floods have focused on the fact that none of these local floods affected all of the excavated cities at the same time. But if Noah's flood did not submerge all of the Tigris–Euphrates valley, then the story may have been inspired by one of the local historical floods that submerged some but not all of the cities in the valley.

Unusual alluvial strata were found at nearly contemporaneous levels during excavations of Shuruppak, Uruk, the earliest level at Kish, and possibly Lagash. These strata were deposited about 2900 BC and according to Mallowan[9] may have resulted from the flood of the "King list and Genesis flood." This flood deposited about 60 cm of yellow sediment in Shuruppak, a city where Utnapishtim (Noah) lived according to Gilgamesh XI,35. The alluvial stratum from this flood was found directly above a polychrome jar, seal cylinders, and stamp seals from the Jemdet Nasr period (= Uruk III) and directly below plano-convex bricks from the Early Dynastic period which followed the Jemdet Nasr period. According to radiocarbon dating, the Early Dynastic period began about 2900 BC.[16]

A similar stratum of sterile alluvial sediment five feet deep was excavated at Uruk by Jordan[17] who dated it to the beginning of the third millennium

BC, or about the same time as the Shuruppak stratum. The flood of 2900 BC that deposited sediment at Uruk and Shuruppak was the flood most likely to have inspired the Genesis story. This was at the beginning of the Early Dynastic I period and was about the same time as the first dynasty of Egypt, two hundred years before the pyramid builders.

Unusual alluvial strata have also been found at Ur and Nineveh, but these sediments were deposited more than 600 years earlier, about 4000–3500 BC and interrupted the Ubaid period. Woolley[18] who excavated Ur, thought he had discovered evidence of Noah's flood, but he was mistaken about this according to Mallowan.

At Kish, four flood strata were found. The earliest of these, identified with the King List flood, lay directly above the Jemdet Nasr stratum.[19] The yellow flood stratum at Shuruppak was also directly above the Jemdet Nasr stratum. The archeological record supports a dating of the flood mentioned in the Sumerian King List, Noah's flood, at the end of the Jemdet Nasr period about 2900 BC. Some scholars[20] date the King List flood at the end of the Early Dynastic I period (ED I about 2750 BC), because, according to the King List, the flood was followed by a new dynasty at Kish which is accepted as beginning the Early Dynastic II (ED II) period. However, the Kish dynasty need not have come immediately after the King List flood, especially as the ED I kings are unknown[21] and may have been missing in the King List.

The Early Dynastic I period lasted only 100–150 years and cannot be easily distinguished from the Early Dynastic II period. According to Martin,[22] "ED II, when judged by its pottery, does not stand out as a distinct period in its own right; it is much more a period of gradual transition from ED I to ED III" at Shuruppak. This is in contrast to the distinct "culture break" between the Jemdet Nasr period and ED I period, in the words of Schmidt[23] who excavated Shuruppak (Fara).

It would not be surprising if a major river flood destroyed kilns, potter's wheels, tools, and supplies used by producers of polychrome pottery (see example on front cover), thereby providing an opportunity for competitors, whose manufacturing operations were left undamaged by the flood, to take over the pottery market with a different design after the flood. A major river flood is more consistent with the culture break at the end of the Jemdet Nasr period than with a gradual transition between ED I and ED II.

According to Mallowan[9] the Genesis flood "was based on a real event which may have occurred in about 2900 B.C., or perhaps a century or more after, at the beginning of the Early Dynastic period."

A Sumerian document known as "The Instructions of Shuruppak" dated by Kramer[11] about 2500 BC, refers in a later version to Ziusudra (Noah). Kramer concluded that "Ziusudra had become a venerable figure in literary tradition by the middle of the third millennium B.C." Kramer agreed with

Mallowan that the Mesopotamian flood story "was inspired by an actual catastrophic but by no means universal disaster" that occurred in "the early third millennium B.C."

It is widely assumed that Noah's flood must have been of great magnitude to have survived in the world's literature for thousands of years. But it was not the magnitude of the flood that made the story memorable. Noah's flood was remembered primarily because a man and his family happened to survive it in a way that made an interesting story that people retold to their friends and relatives. For thousands of years story tellers repeated this flood story because their listeners wanted to hear about the flood hero. Early Sumerian and Babylonian literature frequently referred to this flood and the man who built a boat in which he saved some animals and his family.

Noah king of Shuruppak

Noah lived at a time when most of the population was involved with agriculture and farm animals. Noah probably had many years of experience with animals, but he was not a mere shepherd or cattle rancher. In the Ziusudra version of the flood story[2] the Sumerian Noah is repeatedly called a king or chief (*lugal*). According to the Weld–Blundell[13] king list WB–62, Ziusudra (Noah) was king of the city-state Shuruppak.[24] *Lugal* literally means great man and was "normally a young man of outstanding qualities from a rich landowning family".[25] The flood hero was a respected leader who spoke to "the city people and the elders" of Shuruppak according to Gilgamesh XI,35 and Atrahasis III,i,39–41. In the WB–62 king list, Ziusudra (Noah) succeeded his father SU.KUR.LAM as king of Shuruppak.[26] SU.KUR.LAM was probably Lamech, Noah's father (Genesis 5:28–31).[27]

The flood of 2900 B.C. deposited sediment in Shuruppak directly above artifacts from the Jemdet Nasr period.[9] Hence, the flood hero was probably chief executive of Shuruppak during the end of the Jemdet Nasr period and the flood story began to circulate during the Early Dynastic I period that followed the flood.

Shuruppak was then a capital city and a commercial center located on the Euphrates River. As head of the Shuruppak city-state government, Noah was probably a wealthy land owner. Wealthy people then invested in cattle and so apparently did Noah. A clue to what he did with these animals is found in Gilgamesh XI, 81–82: "All I had of silver I loaded, all I had of gold I loaded...into the boat." In earliest records, silver was used as an index of value for other commodities. But prior to minting of standard-weight coins in the seventh century BC, silver and gold were not a common medium of exchange, and were used largely by professional merchants and those involved in caravan trade.[28] Most people in Sumer used cups or bowls of barley as the common medium of exchange.

Possessing gold and silver, Noah was probably a merchant or government trade official before becoming chief executive of Shuruppak. Perhaps he owned a private merchanting business or managed foreign trade for his father, king of Shuruppak. Early in his career, Noah may have controlled large numbers of workers who transported livestock and other commodities in overland caravans and on small river barges and quffas to nearby cities. His workers may also have grown grain, hay and other crops near Shuruppak to feed the animals and to have surplus fodder and food to sell. Noah also had a vineyard (Genesis 9:20) which suggests he had a winery business.

A commercial river barge

If we remove supernatural explanations for Noah having a boat with a herd of animals and grain in it, we do not have to reach very far for an alternative explanation. The Euphrates River was used and is still being used for transporting cargo. As a merchant or trade official living near the Euphrates River, Noah was probably closely involved with transporting cargo in barges on the river. Noah's Ark was a commercial river barge for hauling cargo between cities on the river, including Shuruppak, Uruk, and Ur.

By 2100 BC river barges were routinely used for transporting flour and grain.[29,30] Several hundred years earlier, in Noah's time, a few river barges were probably already being used for transporting cargo. River barges substantially reduced the number of man-days and costs of transporting cargo compared to overland caravans. Towing a barge downriver from Shuruppak to Ur took about three days.[31] Upriver from Ur to Shuruppak took about ten days. Barges also provide economies of scale, i.e. a large barge is cheaper per ton of cargo than several small barges that are operated separately.

Profitable operation of small barges by Noah or other merchants would give Noah credibility when he proposed building a large commercial barge to expand the trade he and other merchants had established. Although Atrahasis DT,42(W),13 has the flood hero admitting that "I have never built a boat," it does not seem likely that he would propose building a large expensive river barge unless small barges were already being built and successfully operated on the Euphrates River. Noah's barge was built using to the technology of his time. Large barges would make use of technology perfected on smaller barges (see Chapter 6).

As a wealthy leader of the city-state Shuruppak, Noah would have had access to the labor and materials needed to build a large commercial barge. Although popular versions of the story have Noah being ridiculed by the townspeople, actually the elders of Shuruppak probably encouraged and supported building of the barge under control of their own leader Noah, because they may have envisioned that the barge would substantially increase their own personal wealth and the wealth of Shuruppak. Noah promoted this vision and told the elders that the gods would "shower plenty on you, an abundance of birds, a profusion of fish" when the new barge became operational, according to Atrahasis III,i,34–35.

Normally, Noah's servants and slaves would do the work and supervision of the workers would be done by other servants, although there is little mention of these servants in the received texts. Noah was a chief executive and executives delegate responsibility to subordinates. According to Berossus,[6] a boatman was on board during the flood. Gilgamesh XI,94 gives his name as Puzur–Amurri. Although Puzur is mentioned in connection with menial tasks: caulking the boat (line 94) and stowing jars of oil (line 69), the Babylonian Noah also "entrusted the great structure including its contents" to Puzur (line 95). Puzur was probably Noah's general manager in charge of the entire barge operation. Among his many responsibilities, Puzur probably managed the supervisors of the workers who steered the barge through the channels of the river while servants or slaves hauled or drove oxen hauling the barge. Puzur probably also managed loading and unloading of cargo at port cities where the barge docked and may have managed the scribes who kept detailed records on clay tablets of each shipment.

Although surviving versions of the flood story suggest that the flood hero rode on the barge only once, and that the barge made only one voyage, it is not likely that the storm and flood happened at exactly the right moment to interrupt the barge's maiden voyage. It is more likely that the barge was used many times to transport cargo, but without Noah on board. Kings have better things to do with their time than to ride on cattle barges. Only the final voyage was mentioned in the story, because that may have been one of the few times or the only time that Noah rode on the barge.

For several weeks each year, Noah's barge probably hauled cargo to cities on the Euphrates River including port cities near the Persian Gulf. The ancient city Eridu was then "on the shore of the sea"[32] as was nearby Ur,[33] i.e. on the shore of the Persian Gulf. The Tigris–Euphrates valley was much shorter at the time of the Sumerians[34] than it is now and the head of the Persian Gulf was about 140 miles northwest of its present location. The present delta around the modern cities of Basrah and Abadan was subsequently built up from silt deposited by the Karun, Euphrates and Tigris rivers. Lake Hammar and the marshes west of Lake Hammar were then part of an arm of the Gulf. Eridu was then near the mouth of the Euphrates River on or near the Gulf coast. The large body of water near Eridu was called the *apsû* and was then known for its great depth[35] compared to rivers and swamps.

According to Gilgamesh XI,42, the flood hero went "down [the river] to the *apsû*". Although *apsû* was the name of an underworld ocean god and a mythical primeval sea sometimes translated 'abyss', the word *apsû* also had mundane meanings, that of underground fresh water (aquifers), and a marshy area at the north end of the Persian Gulf[36] in the vicinity of Eridu. Eridu was built on the *apsû*[37] on the shore of the Persian Gulf. At Eridu there was also a temple of the god Enki called the *apsû*-house.[38]

Twelve miles north of Eridu was the port city of Ur which may have been the terminus of the barge's annual river voyage, where cargo for export was unloaded from barges, and where imported cargo was registered and unloaded from sailing ships and reloaded onto barges for the return trip up the river.

The phrase "Make yourself an ark" in Genesis 6:14 does not imply that Noah built or financed the barge all by himself. When people today say "I built a new house," they mean they hired a contractor with borrowed money. Noah or Puzur probably hired master shipwrights and numerous skilled workmen to design and build the barge. According to Gilgamesh XI,50–51, 70–76: "The carpenter carried his hatchet. The reed worker carried his stone... I butchered bulls for the people and killed sheep every day. Beer, oil and wine I gave the workmen to drink...[until] the boat was completed."

Noah may have financed purchase of the timber and the split and hewn lumber (including imported cedar) and other construction costs with loans from other wealthy men of Shuruppak who would benefit from new trade the barge would make possible. With financial support from investors, Noah could build a much larger barge than the Shuruppak budget or his personal wealth would allow. His foreign supplier of cedarwood (probably from the trading port of Dilmun)[39] may have helped finance the barge, because the barge would be used to transport imported lumber and other cargo upriver from gulf ports of entry. The Babylonian Noah used scraps of cedar to light the fire on an altar after the barge grounded, according to Gilgamesh XI,159.

According to Gilgamesh XI,24, the Babylonian Noah was advised to "Tear down [your] house, build a boat." Although it has been suggested that Noah was planning to recycle reeds from his house to build a reed boat, this seems unlikely, because reeds were a cheap commodity and grew wild in the marshes. Besides, reeds for boatbuilding must be specially cut[40] and hence reeds from a house would probably not be suitable for a boat. If Noah's house was made of brick, the few wood beams that could be salvaged from the ceiling and roof would not provide much wood for a boat. The Akkadian verb *u–qur* meaning to tear down, to raze, was used when a building was demolished to clear the land for a new building.

Noah probably owned or controlled land next to the Euphrates River and this property had a house on it. When he needed waterfront land on which to build the barge so that it could be launched directly into the river, Noah probably ordered the house demolished and the land cleared for a construction site. After the barge was built and launched, the land could be used for stockyards, warehouses, and a boat maintenance facility.

According to Gilgamesh XI,77–79, the barge was built next to the water so that it could be launched and used for hauling cargo. "The launching was difficult; there was shifting of load above and below, until two-thirds of the structure was submerged." If the barge had been built solely as a lifeboat, there would not have been any need to launch it into the river. The flood hero also "provided punting poles" according to Gilgamesh XI,64. Punting poles were needed by Noah's crew to keep the barge headed in the right direction[41] and away from sandbars in the river. Punting poles would be useless in deep water. If Noah provided punting poles, he was not expecting a deep deluge.

Atrahasis DT,42(w),7 mentions barley as one of the goods in the barge. Wherever barley is grown, beer is usually brewed and the flood hero supplied beer for consumption by the boatbuilders. Noah's barge probably transported thousands of sealed clay jars filled with beer for sale at Euphrates River cities and for export. Atrahasis iv,16 suggests a shortage of beer after the flood.

Noah's responsibilities

As head of the Shuruppak government and supplier of low-cost barge transportation, Noah was probably responsible for transporting cargo for the government, especially government grain being exported. Grain was a major export and Noah's barge probably transported thousands of baskets of grain to Ur for transfer to foreign sailing ships.[39] Exporting and importing were linked with foreign relations between governments. Although Noah was head of the Shuruppak government, he was probably personally responsible for the safety and honest distribution of government property that he managed.

In addition to transporting government cargo, Noah also may have transported private cargo for other merchants and/or for temples as their agent, perhaps to pay off the debts he acquired when building the barge. Since a large river barge would have economy of scale, Noah probably commissioned building of the largest barge that existing technology would permit, and financed it with loans from other merchants. These merchants would invest in Noah's venture only if their own commodities were transported on the finished barge. Except for government grain, most of the animals and other cargo on the barge during the flood may have been owned by other merchants and temples.

During the Old Babylonian Period, more than a thousand years after Noah, temples acted like banks and loaned capital in the form of commodities such as wool and barley to merchants[42] to exchange in distant places for other commodities such as copper. These merchants were acting as agents for the temple and were under state control. A similar arrangement may have been used during Noah's time to finance trade of commodities transported on Noah's barge. Debts to temples and merchants would be paid in kind with imported commodities upon the return trip.

According to Genesis 6:20 "of the animals...two of every kind shall come to you." Seekers of the supernatural assume that the animals came to the ark on their own volition. A more likely explanation is that the animals came to the barge because their owner's herdsmen brought the animals to the barge from nearby ranches to be transported as cargo.

The barge may also have carried hay as cargo for sale. The amount of hay was probably many times more than needed to feed the animals during the few days they were being transported to market. The hay would be sold to the same people who bought the animals, because the animals would have to be fed until they were ready for slaughter, perhaps months later.

Conclusions

The Euphrates River flood of 2900 BC was the flood most likely to have inspired the story about Noah and his cattle barge. Before the river flood, Noah was chief executive of the Shuruppak government and probably a wealthy land owner during the Jemdet Nasr period which ended with the river flood of 2900 BC. The ark was a commercial river barge for transporting animals, grain and beer on the Euphrates River. Although the barge was not intended as a lifeboat and Noah was not expecting a deluge, the barge happened to be loaded with cargo when a thunderstorm began.

References

1.   Alan Dundes (editor), *The Flood Myth* (CA: University of California Press, 1988).

2.   Quotations from the Epic of Ziusudra are a combination of the most clearly expressed phrases from three translations:

Samuel Noah Kramer, "Sumerian Myths and Epic Tales" in *Ancient Near Eastern Texts,* James B. Pritchard (ed), (NJ: Princeton University Press, 1950), pp. 42–44.

Thorkild Jacobsen, "The Eridu Genesis," *Journal of Biblical Literature,* 100/4 (1981), pp. 513–529.

M. Civil, "The Sumerian Flood Story" in *Atrahasis: The Babylonian Story of the Flood,* W. G. Lambert and A. R. Millard, (Oxford: Clarendon Press, 1969), pp. 138–145.

3.   W. G. Lambert and A. R. Millard, *Atrahasis: The Babylonian Story of the Flood* (Oxford: Clarendon Press, 1969).

4.   Ibid., p. 14.

5.   Text from the Epic of Gilgamesh (tablet XI) is adapted from the most clearly expressed phrases in five translations:

Maureen Gallery Kovacs, *The Epic of Gilgamesh,* (Stanford, California: Stanford University Press, 1985), pp. 97–103.

J. V. Kinnier Wilson, "The Story of the Flood in the Epic of Gilgamesh," in *Documents from Old Testament Times*, D. Winton Thomas (ed), (London: Thomas Nelson and Sons, 1958), pp. 17–26.

N. K. Sandars, *The Epic of Gilgamesh* (Baltimore, MD: Penguin Books, 1964), pp. 105–110.

E. A. Speiser, "Akkadian Myths and Epics" in *Ancient Near Eastern Texts,* James B. Pritchard (ed), (NJ: Princeton Univ. Press, 1950), pp. 93–95.

Alexander Heidel, *The Gilgamesh Epic and Old Testament Parallels* (Chicago: University of Chicago Press, 1949/1970).

6.   Berossus quoted by Syncellus, 53–56 and Josephus, *Antiquities of the Jews* I, 3, 6; also in *A Hebrew Deluge Story in Cuneiform*, Albert T. Clay (New Haven, CT: Yale University Press, 1922), pp. 82–83.

7.   Moses of Khoren, *History of the Armenians*, translation by Robert W. Thomson, vol. 4 of Harvard Armenian Texts and Studies, (Harvard University Press, 1978) pp. 79–80 (near end of section 6). Another translation is quoted in Bailey,[15] p. 194.

8.   The use of CE (common era) instead of AD is a personal preference of the author. However, BC is used herein and not BCE (before common era) to conform to popular usage.

9.   M. E. L. Mallowan, "Noah's Flood Reconsidered," *Iraq*, 26 (1964), pp. 62–82.

10.   G. R. Driver discussed in Bailey[15] pages 166 and 228 note 17.

11.   Samuel Noah Kramer, "Reflections on the Mesopotamian Flood," *Expedition*, 9, 4 (summer 1967), pp. 12–18.

12.   Thorkild Jacobsen, *The Sumerian King List* (Chicago: University of Chicago Press, 1939), p. 77.

13.   S. Langdon, "The Chaldean Kings Before the Flood," *Journal of the Royal Asiatic Society* (1923), pp. 251–259.

14.   R. L. Raikes, "The Physical Evidence for Noah's Flood," *Iraq*, 28 (1966), pp. 52–63.

15.   Lloyd R. Bailey, *Noah: The Person and the Story in History and Tradition, Studies on Personalities of the Old Testament* (Columbia, SC: University of South Carolina Press, 1989), pp. 28–37.

16.   Harriet Crawford, *Sumer and the Sumerians*, (London: Cambridge University Press, 1991), p. 19.

17.   Julius Jordan, *Zweiter vorläufiger Bericht*, Abhandlungen der Preußischen Akademie der Wissenschaften, 1929, p.20, cited by André Parrot, *The Flood and Noah's Ark*, (London: SCM Press, 1955), p. 50.

18.   Leonard Woolley, "The Flood" in *Myth or Legend*, G. E. Daniel (NY: Capricorn Books, 1955), pp. 39–47.

19.   L. Watelin and S. Landon, *Excavations at Kish*, (Oxford University, 1934), vol 4, pp. 43, 53, Plate I; see also Mallowan, op. cit., p. 79.

20.   I. E. S. Edwards and others (editors), *The Cambridge Ancient History*, third edition, Vol I, part 2, (England: Cambridge University Press, 1971), pp. 243–244, 273, 277.

21.   Edwards, op. cit., p. 244.

22.   H. P. Martin, "The Early Dynastic Cemetery at al-'Ubaid: A Re-Evaluation," *Iraq*, XLIV (1982), pp. 145–185, esp. 151, 166.

23.   Erik Schmidt, "Excavations at Fara, 1931," University of Pennsylvania's *Museum Journal*, 22 (1931), pp. 193–217.

24.   Some king lists omit the disgraced Ziusudra. See Chapter 5.

25.   H. W. F. Saggs, *Babylonians*, (Norman, Oklahoma: University of Oklahoma Press, 1995), p. 54.

26.   Langdon, op. cit., p. 258, note 5.

27.   See Chapter 9 for a fuller discussion of Lamech.

28.   Marvin A. Powell, "Ancient Mesopotamian Weight Metrology" in *Studies in Honor of Tom B. Jones*, M. A. Powell & Ronald H. Sack, (Neukirchen–Vluyn: Butzon & Bercker Kevelaer, 1979), p. 86.

29.   Hans J. Nissen, Peter Damerow, Robert K. Englund, *Archaic Bookkeeping* (Chicago: University of Chicago Press, 1993) 28, 140.

30.   Robert K. Englund, "Hard Work...Labor Management in Ur III Mesopotamia," *Journal of Near Eastern Studies,* 50 (1991), pp. 255–280, especially 257.

31.   Marie-Christine De Graeve, *The Ships of the Ancient Near East* (Leuven, Belgium: 1981), p. 152.

32.   A. Falkenstein, "Die Eridu–Hymne," *Sumer*, 7 (1951), p. 121, line 13.

33.   Thorkild Jacobsen, "The Waters of Ur," *Iraq*, 22 (1960), pp. 174–185, especially 184.

34.   C. E. Larsen, "The Mesopotamian Delta Region: A Reconstruction of Lees and Falcon," *Journal of the American Oriental Society*, 95 (1975), pp. 43–57.

35.   Margaret Whitney Green, *Eridu in Sumerian Literature*, PhD dissertation, (University of Chicago, 1975), pp. 164–165.

36.   Heidel, op. cit., p. 81, note 168.

37.   Ronald A. Veenker, "Gilgamesh and the Magic Plant," *Biblical Archeologist,* 44 (Fall 1981), pp. 199–205, esp. 202c.

38.   A. R. George, *House Most High*, (Eisenbrauns, 1993), p. 65, #30.

39.   A. L. Oppenheim, "The Seafaring Merchants of Ur," *Journal of the American Oriental Society*, 74 (1954), pp. 6–17.

40.   Thor Heyerdahl, *The Tigris Expedition*, (NY: Doubleday, 1980), pp. 15–16.

41.   De Graeve, op. cit., p. 151.

42.   Saggs, op. cit., pp. 95–96.

3

Mountain or Mound ?

"Too much amplifying things that be but
small, making mountains of molehills."
John Fox, Book of Martyrs (1570)

Stories about the near destruction of humanity by a great flood can be found all over the world. Many of these stories differ greatly in their details, but some stories, especially from the Ancient Near East, are similar to the story of Noah. One of the peculiar elements in these Noachian stories is the grounding of the hero's boat on the top of a mountain.

There has been much discussion about the possible identity and location of this mountain. In recent years it has become customary to identify as "Mount Ararat" the mountain in eastern Turkey called *Aghri Dagh* by the Turks, and *Masis* by the Armenians. This mountain has been linked to the flood story only since the eleventh century CE,[1] the result of a misreading of "the mountains of Ararat" in Genesis 8:4. Frequent references to "Mount Ararat" has led many people to assume that the general area where the boat grounded was already established, but the grounding place is far from certain. And as we shall see, Noah's barge did not ground on a mountain.

According to the conventional interpretation of the Genesis version of Noah's story,[2] the sea level rose for 150 days until it covered the tops of the mountains and then subsided for another 150 days. It is easy to prove that this is physically impossible. The local sea level can rise several feet for a few hours during a hurricane, but if the sea level rose to the 16,946 foot peak of "Mount Ararat" for 150 days, the sea would have had to rise approximately 16,946 feet all over the planet earth. That would require about 630 million cubic miles of additional water weighing 3,000,000,000,000,000,000 tons or three quintillion tons. That is an enormous volume of water. The oceans would have to triple in volume in only 150 days[3] and then quickly shrink back to normal. Where would 630 million cubic miles of water go during the second 150 days? There is nowhere an ocean can drain to, because the oceans already fill the low places. There is no geological evidence that the ocean basins that now exist formed in only 150 days. The excess water could not evaporate into the air because it would still be there and it is not.

It has long been known that rain clouds cannot possibly hold even a tenth of one percent of the water required by the conventional interpretation of the flood story. Soroka and Nelson[3] calculated that three quintillion tons of water vapor would make the earth's atmospheric pressure about 840 times higher than it is now and sunlight would not reach the surface of the ground. Such an atmosphere would be incompatible with life as we know it.

If a smaller mountain were selected, say one third the height of "Mount Ararat," one quintillion tons of water would still have to appear and disappear. If the oceans rose 8,600 feet to cover the mountain Pir Omar Gudrun[4] that is often identified as the Mount Niṣir (sometimes spelled Nimush), of Gilgamesh XI,140, then 1.5 quintillion tons of water would have to appear and disappear in 300 days. A mountain-covering deluge lasting 300 days implies a worldwide deluge, but a worldwide mountain-covering deluge is impossible.

Attempts to find physical evidence to link the Genesis flood to floods in other parts of the world have completely failed in spite of efforts by the most capable and optimistic minds in the search. In their search for evidence of a global flood "Woodward failed. Buckland failed. Prestwich failed. Wright failed. It is clear now that the evidence they were searching for simply does not exist."[5]

Apart from several physics problems of disposing of three quintillion tons of water, and the improbability of the animals surviving subfreezing temperatures on a high mountain, there are numerous impossibilities, improbabilities and practical difficulties implied by grounding on a mountain. These are discussed further in chapter 13 and by several authors who have proved that grounding on a mountain would be impossible.[3,6,7]

The high mountains nearest to Shuruppak where Noah lived are the Zagros mountains east of the Tigris–Euphrates valley. The highest peak and smaller mountains in the Zagros range are not visible more than 155 miles from an observer 16 feet above the ground because of the curvature of the earth.[8] Looking east from the Euphrates River, the Zagros mountains are beyond the horizon and Noah could not have seen them before the flood unless he traveled east of the river. The Armenian (Ararat) mountains to the north are also beyond the horizon.

Ancient mistranslations

It is commonly assumed that Noah could see mountains being flooded because the ark reportedly landed on one. But what is the evidence that the ark landed on a mountain? The Hebrew word $h\bar{a}r$ (plural $h\bar{a}r\hat{i}m$, plural possessive $h\bar{a}r\hat{e}$) translated as "mountains" in Genesis 7:20 and 8:4 can also mean "hills" and is so translated in many other places in the Old Testament including Genesis 7:19b (King James Version): "and all the high hills that were under the whole heaven were covered." There are no mountains in the southern Tigris–Euphrates valley where Noah lived, only higher or lower hills on a flat alluvial plain. Noah could have seen hills being flooded in the Euphrates valley but not mountains. Gilgamesh XI,135 reads "the tideway lay flat as a rooftop." Tidal flats are not found in mountains.

Hār is traditionally translated as mountain because there was a mountainous region known as Ararat that has long been identified with the Armenian mountains in what is now eastern Turkey, a region called Uruatri or Urartu by the Assyrians. This Ararat region was also mentioned in 2 Kings 19:37, Isaiah 37:38, Jeremiah 51:27, and by various Assyrian and Urartian kings. But if the land where Noah's barge grounded was not in a mountainous region, then it could not have been in Ararat/Urartu. Ancient scribes who wrote that the barge grounded in the mountains of Ararat made a mistake of identification because they confused two different journeys made by Noah's sons, one on water and one on foot. As discussed in Chapter 5, after the barge grounded, Noah's sons traveled on foot up the Tigris River to the base of Mount Judi, a 7,000 foot peak seventeen miles northeast of the Tigris River and within the greater Ararat/Urartu region that surrounded Lake Van. Ancient story tellers mistakenly assumed that the ark had grounded on Mount Judi in the mountains of Ararat.

The ambiguous Akkadian word for hill/mountain was *shadû* (plural *shadanû*) and is so used in the Gilgamesh Epic. If the flood story was translated from Akkadian into Hebrew, *shadû* (hill/mountain) was probably translated as *hār* (hill/mountain), thus preserving the ambiguity. *Shadû* could mean a low hill only ten feet high.[9] Since the Akkadian and Hebrew versions use a word for mountain that could also mean hill and the Zagros and Armenian mountains were beyond the horizon, it is doubtful that Noah had ever seen a real mountain.

Mount Niṣir or Niṣir Country?

The word for hill/mountain may have been even more ambiguous if the original flood story was written in Sumerian. The cuneiform sign for hill was the same in both Sumerian and Akkadian. In Sumerian the sign was pronounced KUR. In Akkadian the same sign was pronounced *shadû*.

KUR in Sumerian = hill, country, foreign land
shadû in Akkadian = hill, mountain

But *shadû* did not have the same semantic range as KUR and the sign was ambiguous in both languages. The Sumerian word KUR could mean hill but could also mean foreign land or country[9,10] and is so used in the Sumerian text of the Ziusudra Epic. In Sumerian, KUR seldom meant mountain.[9] HURSAG was the preferred word for mountain in Sumerian. In Akkadian, the KUR sign read as *shadû* could mean hill, but it could also mean mountain in Akkadian, the language in which the epics of Atrahasis and Gilgamesh were written. In Sumerian "the boat grounded in a KUR" meaning the boat grounded in a foreign land or country, could be read in Akkadian as "the boat grounded on a mountain".

When the Sumerian flood story was translated into Akkadian (see chapter 8), the KUR sign was probably copied without change because it meant hill in both Sumerian and Akkadian. Hill may have been the word sense assumed by the translator, and hence there was no need to change the cuneiform sign during translation. However, the KUR sign read as *shadû* in Akkadian could also mean mountain which would open the door to mistaken interpretation.

The section of the Ziusudra Epic about the grounding of the boat is missing from the fragmentary Sumerian tablet and therefore we cannot be certain that the Sumerian text used the word KUR for hill. But the KUR/ *shadû* sign is used repeatedly in the Akkadian text of Gilgamesh XI,140–144 in connection with the boat grounding, and therefore the KUR sign was probably also used in the Sumerian version. This is one more possible source of error if the flood story was originally written in Sumerian (about a Sumerian king) and later translated into Akkadian and still later into Hebrew.

The grounding place given in Gilgamesh XI,140 is normally translated as a proper name Mount Niṣir which is often identified as the mountain Pir Omar Gudrun in the Zagros range.[4] This 8,600 foot mountain was mentioned in the annals of Ashur-nasir-pal II (883–859 BC) of Assyria. But since it would have been physically impossible for the ocean to rise 8,600 feet all over the earth in 150 days, this mountain cannot be the place where the barge grounded. We should therefore look for an alternative reading of line 140 that would have been physically possible. This is readily done by interpreting KUR as a Sumerian, rather than Akkadian word, i.e. land, country, or hill, but not mountain. As discussed in Appendix A, the place of grounding should probably be translated Niṣir Land or Niṣir Country. This may have referred to a general land area rather than a specific spot.

The literal meaning of *niṣir* in this context is not certain.[9] *Niṣir* may have acquired its name from the root *niṣirtu*. With reference to localities, *niṣirtu* had the "connotation of hidden, inaccessible, secluded" as in a fortified place.[11] Hence, *Niṣir* could have got its name from a secluded or restricted land area that was generally inaccessible. In the original story, the barge may have grounded on a sand bar or mud mound in an estuary that was inaccessible to shipping. This may explain why Noah was not rescued by sailboat when his barge sat for several weeks after it grounded.

Ancient story tellers wanted a place-name for a specific grounding spot. Since there was no name for this spot in their received legend, the story tellers treated *Niṣir* as a specific spot, rather than the name of a broader land area, just as today people mistakenly write about "Mount Ararat" instead of the "mountains of Ararat." Trying to find a specific grounding place in "Mount Niṣir" is just as futile as trying to find the correct grounding place in the "mountains of Ararat." Even if a specific mountain were clearly identified in a surviving version of the flood story, it would still not be the grounding place, because the barge could not have landed on a mountain – any mountain. However, there are other clues that suggest where the barge grounded and these are discussed in chapter 4.

According to Genesis 7:19 "all the high hills that were under the whole sky were covered [by] the waters." The word "all" is overly general, because Noah would have no way of knowing what was happening to all of the hills. Noah would have personal knowledge only of the hills that he could see. As several Biblical commentaries have pointed out,[12] universal terms such as "all" are used in a limited sense elsewhere in the Hebrew Bible and the hills mentioned would be those within the range of Noah's visible horizon.

The word "high" is also an ambiguous word. A mountain is high, but the roof of a house is also high on a different scale. The people living in a river valley that has annual inundations would want to clearly distinguish land that was flooded every year from high ground that normally escaped flooding. By definition, some of this high ground would be flooded whenever the river rose above the normal high-water marks. The "high hills/mountains" of Genesis 7:19 may have been the high ground in the Euphrates valley that usually remained dry during annual inundations, but could have been flooded by unusually high water that overflowed the levees. Noah could have seen some of this high ground being flooded, but most of the high ground in the valley could have remained above the flood water without Noah being aware of it, especially high ground that was too far away to see.

Fifteen cubits is a local flood

According to Genesis 7:20, "Fifteen cubits upward rose the waters and covered the mountains/hills." Fifteen cubits is not very much compared with a flood tens of thousands of feet deep imagined in modern rewrites of the flood story that have the oceans rising to cover high mountain peaks. The flood stories do not mention thousands of cubits and Noah would have had no way of measuring such huge depths during the flood. Even if all he could see was sky, clouds and water from horizon to horizon and it looked like his whole world was flooded, he would have had no way of knowing how large a region was flooded or the depth of the water on the land distant from his boat or beyond the horizon. If, after the barge grounded, Noah surveyed the flood damage and concluded that the flood was more than ten thousand cubits deep, why would he and the story tellers forget to mention such an impressive number while remembering to mention an insignificant number like 15 cubits? Fifteen cubits defines the magnitude of the flood.

It was not a deluge, but it was deep enough to breach the levees and cover the lowlands and some hills with water for many miles in all directions. The average depth in the flooded region may have been only a few feet. Some cities in the valley could escape the flood entirely while others may have had shallow water in their houses[13] as happens whenever the water level in a river gets unusually high.

There is no word meaning "deep" or "depth" or "draft" in the Hebrew text or the Greek text of Genesis 7:20. A literal translation from Hebrew is "Five ten cubits up-from-there rose the waters and they covered the hills." In plain English: "The waters rose fifteen cubits higher[14] and covered the hills." The fifteen cubits refers to how much the water rose, not how deep the water was. Depths would be different at different locations. As a modern news reporter might say, the water rose 22 feet above flood stage.

Why the top of a mountain?

Josephus wrote "After the ark rested on the top of a certain mountain…". Why the top? Because if it landed farther down, Noah would have seen the top of the mountain before the ark grounded which would conflict with Genesis 8:4–5: "in the seventh month…the ark came to rest…in the tenth month…the tops of the mountains were seen." But it is extremely unlikely that a boat would settle on the exact peak of the highest mountain. If the ark missed the exact peak by only a short distance, Noah would have seen the mountain before grounding and the receding water would have washed the ark some distance down the side of the mountain before it grounded. The conventional interpretation does not permit the ark to ground in the foothills of a mountain or in the lowlands. But since the conventional interpretation is physically impossible, we should look for another explanation that makes more sense and we can do that only if we abandon the mistaken notion that Noah's ark grounded on a mountain top.

But alternative explanations do not seem plausible either. Suppose a boat grounded on a flat valley that was temporarily flooded and where the nearest mountains were too far away to see. Such a boat could easily ground before the mountains were seen, as in Genesis 8:4. However, after the boat grounded, the mountains would not get any closer and hence Noah would not have been able to see the mountains mentioned in Genesis 8:5. The implausibility of such an alternative scenario has led commentators to accept the conventional notion that the ark defied probability and just happened to settle on the exact peak of the highest mountain.

Some get around this problem by having the ark ground near a high mountain when Noah was too busy to look outside or by assuming that Noah could not look out of the ark until months after it grounded or that thick clouds prevented him from seeing nearby mountains. It does not seem likely that the ark was so poorly designed that it had only one window (mentioned in Genesis 8:6) that by chance happened to be facing away from the supposed mountain on which the ark grounded. Nor is it possible to imagine a king sitting contentedly inside a sealed barge for months after it grounded and making no effort to go outside. Such *ad hoc* explanations are not plausible and result from attempts to explain how the ark could have grounded before the mountain tops were seen.

There is another possibility discussed below that is consistent with a river barge grounding in lowlands before the tops of hills were seen.

Annual inundations

Each spring the Euphrates river flow increases several fold from melting snow in the Armenian mountains. The river crests in May.[15] Farmers welcomed this annual inundation because they needed the water to irrigate their fields. Transportation of cargo on the river was busiest during the inundation when the river channels were deep enough for large boats. In the winter, the water depth is often less than four feet. Noah probably scheduled an annual sales trip each June after the spring inundation had crested and a fresh crop of barley and hay had been harvested. Livestock, hay, wool, baskets of barley, and jars of beer, dates and vegetable oil were transported down the river in June. The return trip would take place a few weeks later in late June or early July while the river was still deep enough for large boats. It took about ten days to tow a barge up the river from Ur to Shuruppak.[16] During the return trip the barge would carry imported and sea products such as salt, fish, lumber, stone, and metals brought in sailing ships to Ur and products from Uruk.

According to Berossus,[17] the flood of Xisuthros (Noah) occurred on the fifteenth day of Daisios, the eighth Macedonian month corresponding approximately to our month of June.[18] Daisios also corresponded to Iyyar, the second month in the Babylonian calendar[19] which agrees with the second month mentioned in Genesis 7:11. Seven days before the storm began, on the tenth day of the second month, Noah's workers began loading cargo into the barge for another June voyage on the Euphrates River. Normally there is no rain in June and Noah could not have known that a storm was coming. Seven days later (Genesis 7:10), on the seventeenth day,[20] most of the cargo had been loaded. The barge was not sitting on a hill awaiting a deluge. The barge was in the Euphrates River at a Shuruppak wharf and loaded with cargo, ready for another routine voyage down the river.

Unexpected thunderstorm in June

Gilgamesh XI,92–102 clearly describes the conditions that immediately preceded the flood. First there was a thunderstorm and then a river flood:

"...the weather was fearful to behold... A black cloud arose from the horizon. Adad [the storm god] thundered within it...going as heralds over hill and plain... Erragal tore out the dam posts, Ninurta made the dikes overflow". Atrahasis III,ii,48–49 reads: "The appearance of the weather changed. Adad thundered in the clouds." This was clearly a thunderstorm.

According to Atrahasis III,ii,40–43 this storm interrupted a family banquet on board the boat: "He invited his people to a banquet. He sent his family on board. They ate and they drank." He noticed a "black cloud from the horizon" and "thundering within it." He "looked up at the appearance of the weather; it was fearful to behold" according to Gilgamesh XI,92,97–98. Why would Noah be fearful of a thunderstorm? Thunderstorms occur almost every year in the Tigris–Euphrates valley and a few inches of rain often falls during the winter when the river level is low. But this thunderstorm was coming in June when the average rainfall is zero during dry years. Noah was greatly alarmed because with the river level still at crest stage from the annual spring inundation, heavy rain meant further rising of the river and imminent failure of the levees.

Atrahasis III,ii,41–47 continues: "He sent his family on board. They ate and they drank. But he was in and out. He could not sit, could not crouch, for his composure was broken and he was vomiting gall." Noah and his servants were working frantically to get the remaining cargo on board before the rising river overflowed the levees. His warehouses and stockyards next to the wharf probably still contained goods and livestock he had not planned to transport on the barge, perhaps goods he had just received for sale in Shuruppak. These goods would be destroyed when the river overflowed the levees. When Noah realized that a flood was imminent, he probably ordered his family members to remain on the barge while his workers loaded the remaining cargo into the barge. If his family remained on shore they might get trapped in rapidly rising water. When the water level in the river rose to the tops of the levees, Noah boarded the barge because it was too late to evacuate to high hills that would remain above the water.

According to Genesis 7:12–13 Noah entered the ark on the very same day that abnormally heavy rain (geshem) began to fall. His family and most of his cargo were already on board. Although his commercial barge was never intended as a life boat, it served that function well. Noah was not expecting the storm and the flood; otherwise, he would not have left behind the library of clay tablets in Sippar which had to be dug out of the mud after the flood.[17] Noah "provided punting poles" that would be useless in deep water. The barge was built next to the river so that it could be launched and used for hauling cargo. If the barge had been built solely as a lifeboat, there would not have been any need to launch it into the river. Noah was not expecting a deep flood.

Conclusions

It would be physically impossible for the ocean to rise several thousands of feet in only 150 days and then fall back to normal in another 150 days. Noah's ark, if it existed, did not land on a mountain. The words for hill and country were mistranslated as mountain. "Mount Ararat" played no roll in Noah's flood story. Noah's flood was a river flood caused by a thunderstorm in June when the river was at crest stage. Noah did not know a flood was coming until he saw storm clouds approaching. The Euphrates River rose more than 15 cubits, breached the levees, and flooded the lowlands.

Noah did not have supernatural knowledge of the future. He was a smart leader who acted decisively in an unexpected crisis. He had commissioned building of a commercial river barge because it would increase his personal wealth and would benefit the city where he was chief executive. At the usual time in June, Noah ordered his workers to load cattle, grain and other cargo into the barge for another routine voyage down the Euphrates River. Then a freak storm changed his life.

References

1.   Lloyd R. Bailey, *Noah: The Person and the Story in History and Tradition, Studies on Personalities of the Old Testament* (Columbia, SC: University of South Carolina Press, 1989), p. 114.

2.   Lloyd M. Barre, "The Riddle of the Flood Chronology", *Journal for the Study of the Old Testament,* 41 (1988), pp. 3–20.

3.   Leonard G. Soroka and Charles L. Nelson, "Physical Constraints on the Noachian Deluge", *Journal of Geological Education,* 31 (1983), pp. 135–139.

4.   Alexander Heidel, *The Gilgamesh Epic and Old Testament Parallels* (Chicago, University of Chicago Press, 1949/1970), p. 250.

5.   Davis A. Young, *The Biblical Flood* (Grand Rapids, MI: William B. Eerdmans Publishing Co., 1995), p. 225.

6.   Robert A. Moore, "The Impossible Voyage of Noah's Ark", *Creation/Evolution,* 4, 1, issue XI (winter 1983), PO Box 146, Amherst Branch, Buffalo, NY 14226.

7.   Chris McGowan, *In the Beginning,* (Buffalo, NY: Prometheus Books, 1984), pp. 54–67.

8.   Here is the formula for calculating the distance to the horizon: Multiply 1.23 times the square root of your altitude in feet which gives the distance to the horizon in miles. The same formula is used to calculate the distance in miles to a mountain peak as it disappears over the horizon when viewed from sea level. The sum of both distances is the distance from an elevated observer to the peak of a mountain that is just beyond the horizon.

9.   Prof. Åke Sjöberg, University of Pennsylvania Museum, personal communication.

10.   Samuel Noah Kramer, "Dilmun, The Land of the Living", *Bulletin of the American Schools of Oriental Research,* 96, (Dec 1944), pp. 18–28.

11.   John A. Brinkman and others (editors), *The Assyrian Dictionary* (Chicago, Oriental Institute, 1980), Vol. N2, p. 276.

12.   Young, op. cit., pp. 162–163.

13.   M. E. L. Mallowan, "Noah's Flood Reconsidered", *Iraq,* 26 (1964), pp. 62–82.

14.   The Hebrew *mi-la-ma'al-ah* literally translates 'up from there' meaning above some reference level. The word *mi-la-ma'al-ah* modifies 'rose' in the 15 cubits clause and is not in the same clause as hills/mountains. A literal translation from the Septuagint Greek Genesis 7:20 is: "Ten five cubits on-up was raised the water and it covered all the high mountains." The word επανω (*epano*) literally meaning 'on-up' is used in a comparative sense of 'above normal' or 'higher.' *Epano* modifies υψωθη (*hypsothe*) meaning 'raised,' and is not in the same clause as mountains. In both the Hebrew and Greek versions, "The water(s) was-raised/rose 15 cubits up-from [some reference level] and covered the hills/mountains." Mountains/hills are not mentioned until the second clause. This sentence does *not* say the water rose 15 cubits above the mountains. To translate Genesis 7:20 as "The waters rose and covered the mountains to a depth of 15 cubits" is a mistranslation. The water rising 15 cubits was relative to some prior water level, i.e. the normal water level or the highest water level during annual inundations.

The same word *mi-la-ma'al-ah* is used in Genesis 6:16b "... finish it to a cubit above [the standard level for a roof]" or "... finish it to a cubit above [the heads of workers]." In both uses of *mi-la-ma'al-ah,* one or fifteen "cubits above" was measured up from a lower level. An interpretive translation of Genesis 7:20 can therefore be: "The waters rose fifteen cubits above [the highest water level previously recorded], and the waters covered the hills."

15.   Marie–Christine De Graeve, *The Ships of the Ancient Near East* (Leuven, Belgium: 1981), p. 11.

16.   ibid., De Graeve, p. 152.

17.   Berossus quoted by Syncellus, translated by Gerald P. Verbrugghe and John M. Wickersham, *Berossos and Manetho,* (MI: University of Michigan Press, 1996), pp. 49–50.

18.   Henry Fynes Clinton, *Fasti Hellenici,* Vol III, *The Civil and Literary Chronology of Greece,* monograph 119 in Burt Franklin Research and Source Works Series (1965), pp. 349, 358.

19.   W. G. Lambert and A. R. Millard, *Atrahasis: The Babylonian Story of the Flood* (Oxford: Clarendon Press, 1969), p. 137.

20.   The Septuagint has "twenty seventh of the month".

4

Months of Deep Water

"Things are not always what they seem."
Phaedrus, Fables (25 BC)

The storm came from the south, from the Arabian Sea, and lasted six days. Gilgamesh XI,108–131 describes it: "For one whole day the south wind blew, gathering speed as it passed over the land like a battle. One person could not see another... For six days and seven nights the wind blew; the storm flood overwhelmed the land. When the seventh day arrived, the storm subsided... The sea grew calm; the wind abated; the flood ceased." The six-day storm and flood ended. The Epic of Ziusudra v,203 and the Epic of Atrahasis III,iv,24 also have the storm lasting "seven days and seven nights." Hence, it is possible that the "forty days" of Genesis 7:4 and 7:12 was a memory error for the Sumerian seven days during oral transmission. Six or seven days of rain is more plausible than forty, because after forty days of rain and high humidity, the hay and grain would have become rotten and infested with fungus. Regardless of whether the rain continued for a full forty days or not, it is clear that Noah's flood was caused by a thunderstorm and the flood lasted less than seven days.

According to Atrahasis III,iv,6–9 the storm caused a river flood: "They [dead bodies] have filled the river like dragon flies. Like a raft they have moved to the edge [of the barge]. Like a raft they have moved into the riverbank." Noah's flood was a river flood.

According to Gilgamesh XI,131 "the flood ceased" after six days. But according to Genesis 8:13 the water was on the earth for more than a year. Commentators usually note the apparent conflict between the flood lasting a year in Genesis and seven days in Gilgamesh. Is there a conflict or did the deep water occur in two phases? In Genesis 6–9 there is a subtle change in the words used to describe the flood. Between Genesis 6:17 and 7:17, the word *flood* is used five times to describe the early phase. But after 7:17 and before 9:11, the word *flood* is not mentioned. Genesis 8 does not use the word *flood* at all. Instead the expression *the waters* is used. As we shall see, there is no conflict between deep water lasting a year and the river flood ending after six days. The word *flood* was not used between Genesis 7:17 and 9:11 because the deep water phase was not really a flood.

The cause of the river flood was clearly an unseasonable thunderstorm as described in Gilgamesh XI,97–111. Some commentators have used the word hurricane to describe this storm. Hurricanes, called cyclones in this region, seldom if ever enter the Persian (Arabian) Gulf or the arid Tigris–Euphrates valley.[1] However, tropical storms and the edges of cyclones in the Arabian Sea from April to December sometimes affect the Gulf region.

Brookes[2] described such a storm and the resulting flood that occurred about 1000 CE in the Qara Su basin in the nearby Zagros mountains. Brookes compared this flood to the Colorado Big Thompson River flood of July 1976 which was associated with a deep low pressure area that stalled for 24 hours and was assigned a minimum recurrence interval of 1000 years.

Another storm-related flood that was similar in some ways to Noah's flood occurred in the Mississippi valley states of Iowa, Illinois, Missouri and adjacent regions during July 1993. The river rose 49.6 feet at St. Louis. Frequent thunderstorms are welcomed by farmers during the spring when the Mississippi River is relatively low. But if heavy rains continue into the summer months, flooding may result. In this instance, the polar jet stream, which is usually weak during the summer, strengthened during late spring and early summer 1993 and moved farther south than usual.[3] Meanwhile, a high pressure area from the Atlantic Ocean moved farther west than is usual during the summer. Furthermore, these massive systems became semi-fixed in close proximity, resulting in unusually heavy rainfall for several weeks and the largest United States flood since May 1927.

According to the present theory, Noah's flood occurred in June as a result of several days of unusually heavy rain that came when the rivers were already at crest stage from the annual spring inundation. As with the Mississippi River flood of 1993, Noah's river flood of 2900 BC was unusual, but was not a catastrophic deluge, except for people who lived in the lowlands.

Hurricanes (cyclones) occur frequently in Bangladesh and the nearby Bay of Bengal.[4] A hurricane that flooded Bangladesh[5] in April 1991 raised the local level of the sea 18 feet with waves 30 feet higher, and with winds of 145 miles per hour, killed 139,000 people and left 10 million homeless. In this region of heavy rainfall, monsoonal rains occur every year from June to September. In 1993, a monsoonal storm flooded almost half of Bangladesh after six days of steady rain. Monsoonal rains do not occur in the arid Tigris–Euphrates valley because the prevailing wind from the northwest[6] is dry, but a six-day thunder storm from the south and several days of heavy rainfall are possible if the wind changed direction.

The wind during Noah's storm probably did not reach hurricane velocity. A hurricane would have smashed Noah's cattle barge against docks and pilings, blown away the awnings and subjected the wood and reed barge to destructive stresses. The wind may have been unusually brisk and the intensity and duration of the storm was clearly unusual for the Tigris–Euphrates valley, but a steady, heavy thunderstorm would be consistent with the record. The Mississippi valley storm of 1993 seems a better model for Noah's storm than the hurricanes of Bangladesh.

According to Atrahasis III,ii,55, the Babylonian Noah cut the mooring lines during the storm. He had to do this to prevent the lines from holding the barge down in the rising water and submerging the barge. The swollen river carried the runaway barge down toward the Persian Gulf and it lost contact with potential rescuers. Raikes[7] noted that the ark "would have been completely at the mercy of the current" and "would have been swept into the Persian Gulf." Did the barge enter the Gulf? The barge grounded five months after the beginning of the flood according to Genesis 8:4. The six-day storm did not cause the river to be deep for five months; the river current moved the barge down the river and out into deep water, in the Gulf (see Figure 1).

Deep water of the Persian (Arabian) Gulf

According to Gilgamesh XI,131–132 after the storm and flood ended, "the sea grew calm... I looked upon the sea." Yes, the sea – what the Sumerians and Assyrians called the Lower Sea – the Persian Gulf.[8]

The water current carried the barge down the river in a southeast direction past the cities of Uruk, Ur, and Eridu and several miles out into the deep water of the Gulf without Noah or Puzur fully understanding what was happening. Being an experienced river barge operator, Puzur would repeatedly measure the water depth with a sounding line. Noah and Puzur knew they were in water that was deeper than anything in their experience, although the water was not too deep to measure. They may have assumed that deeper water meant rising water, because earlier they had seen the river rising as the water became deeper near the wharf at Shuruppak. But the water was not rising in the Gulf. The water continued to get deeper simply because water currents and wind moved the barge into deeper water.

Noah and Puzur may have had little or no experience with the deep water of the Gulf. The river barge was not designed for sailing and normally it was not allowed to cross the bar into the Gulf. Noah was not able to see the barge entering the Gulf during the six-day storm when "one person could not see another." Flotsam moving downstream near the barge would create an illusion that the barge was standing still, when actually the runaway barge was being carried down the river for about 70 miles to the Gulf. After the barge was in the Gulf, the river current would be slight and the barge would drift slowly from the tide and currents in the Gulf and from the wind.

When the six-day storm ended, the local level of the sea and the river quickly returned to normal. But Noah would not have seen this, because the barge had already entered the Gulf before the end of the six days, and

The whole world looked flooded,

from Noah's point of view, the horizon to horizon water in the Gulf was indistinguishable from horizon to horizon water in the Euphrates valley. Noah was not able to determine where he was, because no land was visible. This was not because all land was flooded, but because the nearest dry land was more than ten miles away and therefore beyond the horizon.

Dry land beyond the horizon

The curvature of the earth greatly affects what a person can see when standing on a boat several miles from shore. If the top of a hill near shore is more than ten miles away and less than 16 feet above the water, a person whose eyes are less than 16 feet above the water will not see the hill, because the hill is beyond the horizon.[9] The phrase of Genesis 7:19 "under the whole sky" means horizon to horizon in all directions from Noah's viewpoint. Noah reported only what he could see and he could not see any land as far as the horizon. The barge drifted about the Gulf for five months beyond sight of land and could have easily drifted there for many more months.

Fortunately for Noah and his family, the wind mentioned in Genesis 8:1 blew the barge back toward shore where the water was shallow. According to Genesis 8:1b "God made a wind blow over the earth and the waters subsided." Noah knew that the water was becoming shallow because he or Puzur measured the depth. But without visible landmarks they could not have known why it was becoming shallow. Story tellers apparently assumed that the wind caused the water to subside (sink down) because the water reportedly became shallow after the wind blew. But the wind did not blow the water away or make the water shallow. The wind blew the barge into shallow water.

Wind blew the barge into an estuary

It has been suggested[10] that the words of Genesis 7:11b "all the fountains of the great deep burst forth" refer to ejecting of subterranean waters as a result of an earthquake or a tsunami. These would necessarily be events of short duration. But the "fountains of the great deep" were "open" for five months, because they were not "closed" until Genesis 8:2. We should ask because all dry land was beyond the horizon.

what facts Noah would know from firsthand observation that were different than his normal experience, instead of giving a mythical interpretation to the story teller's obscure words. Noah knew that the water next to his barge was salty, unlike the fresh water in the Euphrates River. The surface salinity of the north end of the Persian Gulf (30 parts salt per thousand) is nearly as great as that of the open sea (36 parts per thousand). Therefore, he or a story teller probably reasoned that the water near the barge must have come from the great deep, the ocean. Hence, the fountains of the great deep, i.e. the sources of salt water, must be open. Five months later the fountains were closed. Why would Noah believe that the sources of salt water were closed? Because the water was no longer salty.

The water near Noah's barge was salty for five months, because the barge was in the Gulf. After five months the barge was surrounded by fresh water. This implies that the barge was at the mouth of the river again where wind and eddy currents near the river mouth had moved the barge. This location is confirmed in Gilgamesh XI,195 (line 203 in recent translations) that places the Babylonian Noah and his wife "at the mouth of the rivers" after the barge grounded.

Noah and his wife were "at the mouth of the rivers" after the barge grounded.

The barge grounded in the 7th month and we are told that the waters continued to recede, so why did it take 6½ more months before Noah could leave the barge? When the barge grounded, the water was only several feet deep. If the water had continued to subside after the barge grounded, there soon would have been plenty of dry land around the barge. The inference should be clear, that the water depth remained about the same for months after the barge grounded, although story tellers assumed that the water was still subsiding. Recall that the barge grounded five months (Genesis 7:24) after the beginning of the flood. The flood began in June. Five months later was November when the river was near its lowest level. But Noah was still surrounded by water. His barge had grounded several miles from shore in the muddy bottom of a shallow estuary that was always under water, even at low tide when the river was low.

Water remained at the same depth

A clear distinction should be made between water depth and water level. The average water level of the deep part of the Gulf remained at about the same level, i.e. sea level. The average water level in the Gulf near the river mouth was slightly above sea level during the annual inundation when the river current was high. When the barge was drifting in the Gulf, the water depth near the barge changed as the barge drifted sometimes into deeper water, sometimes into shallow water. The water was deep for months because the barge was in a deep part of the Gulf for months. In the 7th month the water depth became shallow, because the barge drifted into shallow water in the 7th month.

After the barge grounded in a shallow estuary several miles from shore, the depth of the water and the water level remained the same for months, except for tidal ebbing and flooding (see Appendix C), because the barge was not moving. The grounding spot was not in the intertidal zone of the estuary and therefore the barge continued to be surrounded by water even at low tide. If the barge had remained grounded there, Noah would not have been able to leave the barge and we never would have heard his story.

Islands and birds

The barge grounded in November, Noah's seventh month. Two months later in January, Noah's ninth month, the river was rising again as it normally does in January[11] from winter rain in the valley. Noah's barge refloated on this rising water and drifted close to some islands which later story tellers assumed were tops of mountains/hills (*hārîm*) which Noah saw on the first day of the tenth month (Genesis 8:5). Gilgamesh XI,138–139 reads "I looked for coastlines in the expanse of the sea. Twelve times[12] an island emerged." Noah saw islands, but not because the water was subsiding. He saw the islands because the barge had refloated at high tide on increased river current and had drifted near enough to the islands that he could see them.

There were legends about the ark grounding and then refloating and then grounding again: "It was said that the ark, floating north, temporarily came to rest on a peak, then journeyed on to its final resting place." [13]

More than a month passed (Genesis 8:6) and Noah could still see only horizon to horizon water. His supplies of fodder, food, and beer were getting smaller every day. Soon he would have to begin slaughtering the animals. He sent some birds on a reconnaissance mission in hopes that they might see land. Birds were often used for navigation in antiquity, but Noah's first birds did not see any land. If the water was still subsiding from the islands (or the tops of hills) that Noah had seen 40 days earlier, the islands should still be visible. Why did Noah need the birds to find land that he could see with his own eyes? Why didn't the birds simply fly over to the islands?

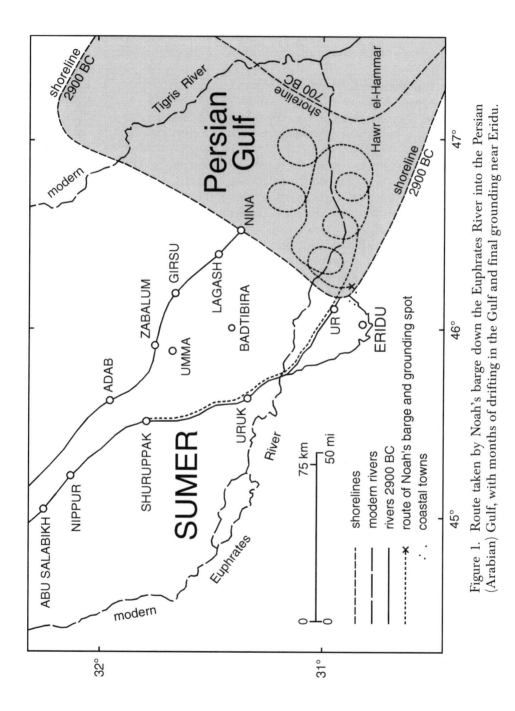

Figure 1. Route taken by Noah's barge down the Euphrates River into the Persian (Arabian) Gulf, with months of drifting in the Gulf and final grounding near Eridu.

Because the islands could no longer be seen, not even by the birds. This should be a clear indication that the barge was still drifting and had drifted too far away from these islands for Noah or the birds to see them.

Second grounding in an estuary

During high tide in May, the wind blew the barge closer to shore where the estuary was normally dry at low tide during much of the year, but was temporarily under water because there was a higher "spring tide" and the river current was at its maximum. Again the barge grounded in the mud of the estuary in the first month (May) of the second year near low hills of the delta. Noah could see this dry land (Genesis 8:13) at a distance, but the barge was still in several feet of water where it grounded. Noah had to wait nearly two months for the river current to subside, accompanied by a neap tide (when high tide is lower than normal), so that the part of the estuary where the barge grounded was no longer under water at high tide. He also had to wait for the surface of the mud flat to bake dry in the hot summer sun.

After the spring inundation subsided, the estuary where the barge grounded "lay flat as a rooftop" according to Gilgamesh XI,135 and was dry enough to walk on. This second grounding spot in the intertidal zone of the estuary at the mouth of the Euphrates River was probably several miles southeast of Ur and several miles east of Eridu (see Figure 1). Noah and his family took the animals and other cargo to the nearby hills at the shore of the estuary.

The hilltop altar

After his family and the cargo were safely on high ground, Noah offered a sacrifice on an altar (Genesis 8:20). He did this at the top of a hill (*shadû*) according to Gilgamesh XI,156. The barge was not at the top of a hill; the altar was at the top of a hill.

Here we can see how story tellers got the mistaken notion that the barge grounded on the top of a mountain. By interpreting *shadû* as mountain instead of hill, when they read that Noah offered a sacrifice on an altar at the top of a mountain, the story tellers assumed that the barge, being nearby, must also have been at the top of the mountain. But the barge was actually at sea level in an estuary several miles from the base of the hill and the altar was at the top of the hill only a few dozen feet above sea level.

After Noah's barge grounded on the shore of the Persian Gulf in an estuary in part of the intertidal zone that was temporarily dry, the barge could have floated away with the next spring tide. Or Noah may have sold it or transferred it to his creditors. If the barge was abandoned, its wood was probably recycled as building material. Construction timber, especially cedar, was very valuable in a land with few trees. The only way that portions of the barge could have survived to the present is by being quickly buried in dry sand and forgotten. But the chances of this having happened are practically zero, because estuaries at the mouth of the Euphrates River near Ur and Eridu remained marshy for many years. Wood buried there, even wood covered with pitch, would eventually rot. It is very unlikely that Noah's barge has survived to the present. A more likely although slim possibility is that legal or commercial records dating from the third millennium may be found on clay tablets that mention the river barge described here.

Conclusions

During the Euphrates River flood of 2900 BC, the swollen river carried Noah's runaway barge down river into the deep water of the Persian Gulf. The barge drifted for several months in the Gulf, beyond sight of land. After months of drifting, the barge was blown by a south wind into shallow water and grounded several miles from shore in the muddy bottom of an estuary at the mouth of the Euphrates River. Later, the barge refloated and grounded a second time near the shore, southeast of Ur and several miles east of the city of Eridu. Noah offered a sacrifice at the top of a hill which story tellers misinterpreted as mountain. This led to the mistaken idea that the barge grounded near the top of a mountain. Noah's barge will never be found because the wood was either recycled as building material or rotted away millennia ago in the marshes at the mouth of the Euphrates River.

References

1.   Bendt Alster, "Dilmun, Bahrain, and the Alleged Paradise in Sumerian Myth and Literature" in Daniel T. Potts, *Dilmun: New Studies in the Archaeology and Early History of Bahrain* (see Bibliography), p. 47.

2.   Ian A. Brookes, "A Medieval Catastrophic Flood in Central West Iran" in *Catastrophic Flooding*, L. Mayer and D. Nash (eds), (Boston, MA: Allen & Unwin, 1987), pp. 225–246.

3.   Bob Scott, "What's Causing All the Floods?" in *Storm, the World Weather Magazine* (September 1993), pp. 22–24.

4.   Mosharaff Hossain, *Floods in Bangladesh* (Dhaka, Bangladesh: Universities Research Centre, 1987), pp. 6–20.

5.   *Science News* (May 11, 1991), p. 295.

6.   Lionel Casson, *Ships and Seamanship in the Ancient World*, (NJ: Princeton Univ, 1971), pp. 17, 23.

7.   R. L. Raikes, "The Physical Evidence for Noah's Flood", *Iraq*, 28 (1966), pp. 52–63.

8.   J. Nicholas Postgate, *Early Mesopotamia* (London: Routledge, 1992), p. 35.

9.   See note 8 in Chapter 3 herein for the distance to the horizon.

10.   Eduard Suess, *The Face of the Earth*, Vol. I, English translation (Oxford: Clarendon Press, 1904), pp. 17–72.

11.   Marie–Christine De Graeve, *The Ships of the Ancient Near East* (Leuven, Belgium: 1981), p. 11.

12.   See discussion in Appendix A.

13.   Lloyd R. Bailey, *Noah: The Person and the Story in History and Tradition*, Studies on Personalities of the Old Testament (Columbia, SC: University of South Carolina Press, 1989), pp. 78–79.

5

After the Barge Grounded

*"Wherever you find a God you'll find
somebody waiting to take charge of
the burnt offerings."*

O. Henry, *He Also Serves*

In most versions of the Noachian flood stories, the flood hero and his family
are said to be the only people who survived the flood. Everyone else drowned
according to Genesis 7:21–23: "All flesh died that moved upon the earth…and
every man… Only Noah was left and those that were with him in the ark."
Gilgamesh XI,133 reads: "All of humanity had turned to clay." This element
of the flood story is clearly mythical, because it presents incredible facts,
without evidence, about which neither Noah nor his story tellers could have
knowledge. Noah could not possibly have searched all of the cities of the
earth after the flood looking for survivors or even all of the cities of the
ancient Near East.

Genesis 7:13 mentions only eight people surviving the flood, but
according to Berossus at least two more people, the flood hero's daughter
and his boatman, were also on board during the flood. If some story tellers
neglected to mention the daughter and boatman, how many other people
did the story tellers neglect to mention? How many survivors did Noah find
in the cities he visited after the ark grounded? The received texts are silent
on these questions, because it is not the job of a story teller to discuss people
who are beyond the scope of the story. The overly broad words "all" and
"every" are a story teller's generalizations based on the fact that his received
text did not mention other survivors.

The Tigris–Euphrates river flood of 2900 BC occurred at the end of the
Jemdet Nasr period in ancient Sumer, but the Early Dynastic I period that
immediately followed the flood did not have a population shortage. Many
people probably died in the six-day river flood, but many, many more
survived, especially in cities that had little or no flood damage. According to
archaeologist Max Mallowan,[1] "no flood was ever of sufficient magnitude to
interrupt the continuity of Mesopotamian civilization."

According to Genesis 7:19 "all the high hills that were under the whole
sky were covered [by] the waters." This also is mythical, because the general

word "all" asserts as fact something Noah would have no way of knowing. Noah and the others could accurately report only what they could see. As the storm began they would see the river rising next to the barge. During the storm they would not have been able to see much of anything when "one person could not see another person." After the storm Noah looked out over the water and saw no land. He may have concluded that the nearby hills were flooded, but he would have no knowledge about hills that were too far away to see. If there were hills near the cities on the Euphrates River that were not submerged, there were other survivors in the valley in addition to people living in distant lands that were not affected by the storm.

Josephus quoted a legend about survivors of the flood:[2] "Nicholas of Damascus in his ninety-sixth book relates the story as follows: 'There is above Minyas in Armenia a great mountain called Baris, upon which it is reported, many refugees found safety at the time of the flood, and one man who was carried in an ark came on shore'..." This quotation reflects ancient flood legends in which references to other survivors had not been expurgated by story tellers.

Berossus alluded to other survivors when he wrote that Noah's relatives were to "recover the writings at Sippar and publish them to men." To publish writings implies that potential readers were not all dead. In the cities in the Euphrates valley that escaped the flood or suffered only minor flooding, there were many survivors and Noah probably met some of them after the barge grounded. In the original version of the flood story some of these other survivors were probably mentioned. But with retelling of the story, references to these survivors were deleted or disguised because they conflicted with the story teller's objective of portraying Noah as a super hero who accomplished what nobody else had accomplished. We should therefore look in the surviving texts for disguised references to other survivors.

The Temple of Enki at Eridu

Five versions of the flood story have the flood hero offering a sacrifice to a god after the boat grounded. The hill on which this offering was made was not an ordinary hill. It is identified in Gilgamesh XI,156 as a "hill-like ziggurat" *(ziq-qur-rat šad-i)*.[3] A ziggurat was an artificial hill or elevated platform and several Sumerian cities had temples with such elevated platforms. In 2900 BC, one of the cities with a ziggurat was Eridu located west of an arm of the Persian Gulf known as the *apsû*.[4] The only ziggurat at Eridu was at the temple of the god Ea/Enki known as the *apsû*-house.[5] In Gilgamesh XI,42 the flood hero said "I will go down [the river] to the *apsû* to live with Ea, my Lord." In Atrahasis fragment RS 22.421,7 the flood hero says "I lived in the temple of Ea, my lord." Noah "placed an offering on top of the hill-like ziggurat" at the temple of the god Ea/Enki in the city of Eridu.

The ruins of this man-made hill have been excavated at Eridu (see Figure 13).[6] The altar was at the top of the ziggurat and was a fireplace for cooking meat donated to the temple of Enki. Since a sacrifice at a temple was really a donation of food to support the priests, and since there were real priests working at the Eridu temple of Enki during the periods before and after the flood of 2900 BC, priests were probably present at Noah's sacrifice and were probably mentioned in the archetype flood story. But when we look in the epics of Atrahasis and Gilgamesh, wherever we would expect to find some mention of the priests, instead we find references to "gods."

When the editor of the Epic of Gilgamesh tablet XI adapted the flood story from the Epic of Atrahasis, he copied many phrases verbatim. He even left unchanged the name of the flood hero Atrahasis at line 187. But the Gilgamesh author selectively omitted certain lines from Atrahasis. According to Tigay,[7] the editor of Gilgamesh XI "incorporated the story largely as he found it in one or more versions [of Atrahasis] that were available to him." However, "…the dropping of individual lines right in between others which are preserved…appears to be a more deliberate editorial act [than simple lack of interest.] The surgery is too delicate to be accidental. These [omitted] lines share a common theme, the hunger and thirst of the gods during the flood… [and] the immediate aftermath of the flood."

The Gilgamesh editor omitted or changed the meaning of these phrases from Atrahasis:

Atrahasis III		Gilgamesh XI	
7	Like dragonflies they have filled the river.	123	Like the spawn of fishes they fill the sea.
17	[Nintu] thirsted for beer.		[omitted]
21	Their lips were athirst with fever.	126	Their lips burn, they have contracted fever.
22	From hunger they		[omitted]
23	were suffering cramp.		[omitted]
30	To the [four] directions	155	…to the four directions
31	he offered [a sacrifice]		[I] offered a sacrifice.
32	providing food.	156	I poured out a libation…
35	They were gathered [like flies] about the sacrifice.	161	The gods gathered like flies about the one who offered the sacrifice.
36	[After] they had eaten the sacrifice…	162	When at length… [omitted]

Tigay concludes: "These omissions and modifications add up to a systematic elimination of implications that the gods starved and thirsted during the flood."

In the earliest versions of the flood story, after the barge grounded, the characters who "thirsted for beer" and "had eaten the sacrifice" may have been identified as priests rather than gods. Although mythical references to gods and the names of gods can often be found in ancient literature, historical kings and other people often adopted the names of gods. Some kings claimed divinity during their lifetime by placing the divine determinative (DINGIR) before their names.[8] It is therefore not always possible to clearly distinguish gods from people in the received texts, especially when story tellers or priests intentionally blurred that distinction. Sacrifices to the temple and the priests were said to be sacrifices to the gods. Decisions made by priests were said to be a god's decisions. Advice from an oracle and letters signed "from God" by anonymous priests[9] were said to be counsel from a god.

The tendency of ancient story tellers to obscure the distinction between gods and priests was very apparent when food sacrifices to a god were being described. Sacrificial food was usually eaten by the priests according to Deut 18:1: "The Levitical priests... they shall eat the offerings by fire to the Lord". Sacrificial food also supported the priests and temple workers in Mesopotamia.[10,11] In the words of Oppenheim: "...immense herds of cattle, sheep, and goats, were sent to the temple, to be used...as income or rations for the administrators and workers who supervised and prepared the food for the god's table...".

Temples, like any other human institution, must have income and its workers and management must be fed. But this was a sensitive matter and a poet might get into trouble with temple officials if the poet made it too obvious that sacrifices were used for food by describing the gods as being hungry. Story tellers and poets downplayed thirst and hunger when mentioning sacrifices and pretended that the food was burned up during the cooking ritual. That is why the Gilgamesh editor deliberately removed references to hunger and thirst of the gods during the flood.

Whenever a storm or other natural event is said to be caused by a god or the proper name of a deity is used, the mythical nature of the sentence is clear. But when ordinary human needs, actions or feelings are described and a character is vaguely referred to as a god, the sentence is not necessarily fiction or anthropomorphic metaphor. It may refer to real people. The tendency of later story tellers to mythologize ordinary people, places, and things was so widespread that one can assume this process was also at work in earlier versions of the flood story. References to generic gods with human needs in the Epic of Atrahasis may have been oblique references to priests whose actions and very human needs were described in the original version of the archetype story.

Noah's "burnt offerings on the altar" in Genesis 8:20b would be useless if the offerings were made at the top of a desolate mountain. The cooked

Figure 2. Noah's sacrifice on an altar at the top of the temple ziggurat of Enki at Eridu was the occasion for a banquet, with Noah supplying the roast beef and beer. The highpriestess gave permission to the priests to eat the sacrifice.[12]

food would be wasted. But if we keep in mind that sacrifices were eaten by the priests, then Noah's offering on the altar at the top of an artificial hill at a temple makes sense, because priests were present to eat the offering.

The lines of the Epic of Atrahasis III,17–36 may include a partly mythical description of the actions of priests from the temple of the god Enki. When Noah's barge grounded near Eridu and Noah offered a sacrifice on an altar at the top of the temple ziggurat, the priests of Enki were probably present at the sacrifice. The gods (priests) "smelled the sweet savor [and] gathered like flies about the sacrifice."[13]

After the meat was cooked, "the great goddess arrived" at the altar and told the gods (priests) they could "approach the offering", and eat the sacrifice, according the Gilgamesh XI,162–166.[13] This "great/noble/high goddess" (DINGIR–MAH) was probably a highpriestess of Enki in the original story. The DINGIR sign was usually a determinative meaning a deity, but it did not always mean a god or goddess. For example, a NIN–DINGIR was a human priestess who received foodstuffs donated to the temple.[14]

Before the flood, according to Ziusudra,148, the flood hero had visited the temple of Enki every day. He knew exactly what his obligations were to the temple. Enki was the local god of Eridu.[15] After arriving safely at Eridu, ship captains and kings were expected to make a donation in gratitude to the gods. One unrelated tablet reads: "He performed numerous sacrifices on the seashore, as was his duty as king."[16] The phrase "sweet savor" or "soothing odor" in Genesis 8:21a, Atrahasis III,v,34, and Gilgamesh XI,160 appears frequently as a technical term for acceptance of a priestly offering.[17] Noah's arrival at the temple of Enki was the occasion for a banquet with Noah supplying the roast beef and beer. By the end of the banquet, the gods (priests) "had eaten the sacrifice" (Atrahasis III,v,36).

After the flood a year earlier, the temple may have fallen on hard times because the local farmers, ranchers and fruit growers, who used to enrich the temple with their offerings, saw their crops and stock destroyed by the flood. Trade routes had also been disrupted because roads were washed out, canals silted up, pack animals drowned, and storage facilities destroyed. At least 53 villages in southern Sumer were abandoned and not resettled at the end of the Jemdet Nasr period.[18] Fresh meat and beer were probably very scarce in southern Sumer during the year after the flood. Hence the references in the Epic of Atrahasis to thirst and hunger of the gods (priests).

Noah's barge did not ground next to the main temple of Enki at Eridu. At the end of the Jemdet Nasr period, Eridu was several miles west of the Persian Gulf coast and the estuary at the mouth of the Euphrates River southeast of Ur.[19] After the barge was carried into shallow water by eddy currents at the mouth of the river, the barge probably grounded in the intertidal zone near coastal towns that provided ports for Eridu. After Noah and his family moved the animals and other cargo across the dry mud flat to one of the coastal towns for storage, Noah then probably took some of the animals several miles west to Eridu to offer on the temple altar.

Noah's animals did not restock the entire world or even the entire valley. Only Noah's sons, the temple, and local ranchers near Eridu benefitted. Noah had no trouble making deals for the sale of the cargo to the temple of Enki and other buyers. But as we shall see, it was important that he do this quickly.

Noah's legal problems

Noah did not return to Shuruppak. He could not tow the barge back up the river because it would take years to rebuild all the damaged levees along the river with towpaths on top for barge-towing oxen or human towing teams. The spot in the estuary where the barge grounded may have been many miles from the nearest navigable channel. Moreover, the water level was low. It was the wrong time of year for heavy river traffic. Even if Noah were willing to abandon his barge and move the animals overland to Shuruppak, there were other reasons why Noah did not return to Shuruppak or to his job as chief executive.

If Noah returned to Shuruppak, he would have to face debts he owed to Shuruppak creditors, perhaps to a temple, debts that were probably in default and which he probably could not repay. Noah was responsible for government grain in his custody, much of which he and his family and the animals had eaten. And Noah had not paid any taxes for more than a year. Sumerian kings were trustees, not autocrats and were not exempt from the law.[20] People who failed to pay their debts or taxes were forced into slavery.[21]

More than a year had passed since the flood and Noah had been presumed dead. Noah had been king of Shuruppak before the flood, but another king would be ruling there now and Noah would be viewed as a rival. Ziusudra,160 mentions "the overthrowing of the kingship" in connection with the flood. Atrahasis III,i,44 mentions that the flood hero was "expelled." Gilgamesh XI,39–41 has the flood hero saying that a god "hates me. I dare no longer walk in his land nor live in his city."

Noah was a deposed, disgraced, ex-king. This may explain why the flood hero is not identified as a king in the epics of Atrahasis or Gilgamesh XI and why his name Ziusudra does not appear on some of the king lists.

As mentioned in Chapter 2, temples sometimes acted like banks and loaned commodities to merchants[22] to exchange in distant ports for other commodities. A temple may have financed some of the commodities transported on Noah's barge. The god who hated the flood hero was Enlil according to Gilgamesh XI,39–41. The temple of Enlil was at Nippur (see Ziusudra,151) about 28 miles up the river from Shuruppak. The temple of Enlil may have invested heavily in Noah's venture, but after the flood they

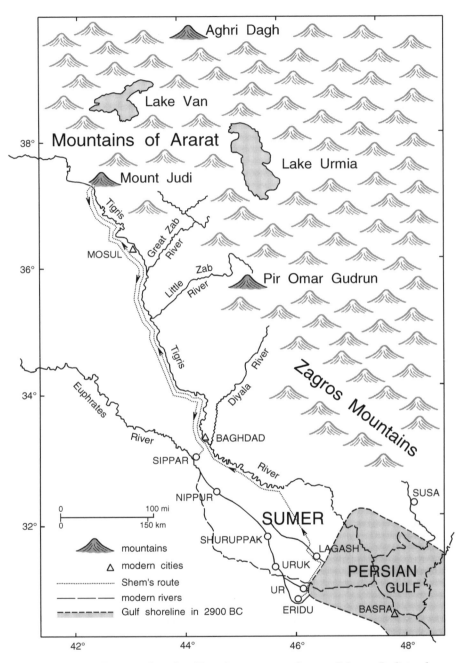

Figure 3. Route taken by Shem's group on foot to Mount Judi in the
Ararat mountains and the "roundabout way" they traveled to Sippar.

were left with uncollectible loans. When news reached the priests of Enlil that Noah was still alive but the temple's cargo had disappeared, the priests would be angry with Noah and seek his capture and punishment.

Since temples acted as forums for various judicial proceedings,[23] especially in disputes involving other temples, the temple of Enki could decide whether Noah could be prosecuted for unpaid debts. Since some of these debts may have been owed to the temple of Enlil, the priests of Enlil would be very unhappy if the temple of Enki entered a judgement in favor of Noah, especially if the temple of Enki acquired some of the disputed cargo. According to Atrahasis III,i,43 "Enki and [Enlil] are angry with one another." It is possible that this reflects a dispute between the priests of Enki and the priests of Enlil involving the flood hero. Although the nature of this dispute is not explained, it is possible that the dispute concerned disposition of the cargo and Noah's debts to the temple of Enlil. Interurban conflicts were sometimes described as conflicts between the gods.[24]

Wealthy stockbreeders, farmers, temple officials and the government of Shuruppak also may have entrusted part of their annual crop production, cattle, and revenue to Noah who then disappeared with the cargo for more than a year. This would look suspicious if Noah did not normally ride on the barge. What would investors do today if their broker disappeared with their investments? The Shuruppak police would be watching for Noah and would jail him for fraud, unpaid debts and unpaid taxes if he entered Shuruppak.

Noah's family separates

The Genesis narrative does not tell us what Noah did next, but Berossus[25] does. The people from the barge divided into two groups that went in different directions. According to Berossus, the flood hero "disembarked with his wife, daughter and the boatman...Those who had remained in the boat... were requested to return to Babylonia and told to recover the tablets from Sippar." They never saw the flood hero again. Sippar was about 190 miles up the Euphrates river from Eridu and had not been destroyed by the flood, only damaged. Many years later, Babylonians were still aware that Sippar had escaped destruction and mentioned it in the myth Erra and Ishum:[26] "Even Sippar, the eternal city, which the Lord of Lands did not allow the flood to overwhelm..." Noah's sons, their wives and other unnamed people went up the river to Sippar, perhaps to live with friends or relatives.

Noah probably sold most of the animals, grain and the remaining cargo to Eridu merchants or to the temple of Enki soon after the barge grounded, because news of his arrival would quickly reach his creditors who would then come to repossess all of the remaining cargo and Noah's assets. Noah would be taken into custody and transported to Shuruppak or Nippur to stand trial for fraud, tax evasion, and failure to pay his debts. Under Sumer law, Noah's wife and their sons would also be liable for Noah's taxes and debts[27] and they too would be arrested and taken to Shuruppak or Nippur for trial. To avoid arrest, Noah's sons went to Sippar.

Noah may have given some of the animals to his sons so that they would not have to work as common laborers. If Noah's sons took these animals to their friends or relatives who owned land at Sippar, this would provide the sons with a family to live with and access to land to work on, something Noah could no longer provide. The "two of every kind" mentioned in Genesis 6:19 may have been the clean animals that Noah gave to his sons to take to Sippar.

To travel from Eridu to Sippar, one would normally pass through Shuruppak and Nippur. But Noah's sons could not travel through Shuruppak, because as members of Noah's family, they would be recognized and arrested by Shuruppak border guards. According to Berossus,[25] the people "went by a roundabout way" to Sippar. They knew they would be in danger if they traveled through Shuruppak or Nippur.

Mount Judi and the mountains of Ararat

A legend was preserved by Moses of Khoren[28] that "There was a book about Khsisuthros [Ziusudra, the Sumerian Noah] and his sons, which has not survived to the present." After Khsisuthros' boat landed, "one of his sons, named Sim [Shem] moved northwest to explore the land. He arrived at a small plain at the foot of an extensive mountain through which rivers flowed to the region of Assyria, lived by the river for two months, and named the mountain 'Sim' after himself. Then he returned to the southeast in the direction from which he had come..." If Shem and his brothers and their wives traveled on foot northwest of Eridu to the region later named Assyria, they would be traveling up the Tigris River. Later they could travel on foot back down the Tigris River in a southeast direction to about where Baghdad is today and cross overland to Sippar on the Euphrates River. This describes how Noah's sons "went by a roundabout way" to Sippar.

The "plain at the foot of an extensive mountain" would have been between the mountain and the Tigris River. The Tigris does pass within several miles of the foothills of a mountain that was referred to by ancient writers as the place where the ark landed.[30] This mountain in Kurdistan is now called Cudi Dagh (Judi Mountain) by the Turks. Eutychius of Alexandria wrote "the ark rested on the mountains of Ararat, that is Jabal Judi near Mosul." Mosul is a town about 80 miles south of Judi Mountain and across the Tigris from the ruins of Nineveh, a major city in ancient Assyria. Al Masudi said "The ark came to rest on Jabal Judi...eight parasangs from the Tigris." The Quran (Hud 11:44) says "The ark rested on the Judi." The Nestorian (Syriac-speaking) Christians built several monasteries on Mount Judi, including one on the summit called the Cloister of the Ark. Benjamin of Tudela, a twelfth century author, said that 'Omar Ben al-Khatab removed the ark [replica] from the summit of the two mountains near Jezireh Ben 'Omar, an island in the Tigris, and made a mosque of it.[30] This island is near Mount Judi.

Mount Judi is in a region now called Kurdistan that is split into parts of Turkey, Syria, Iraq, and Iran. Three Targums (Aramaic translations of the Hebrew Bible) render the "mountains of Ararat" in Genesis 8:4 as the "mountains of Qardu" as does the Peshitta (the Syriac Bible).[30] Berossus located the grounding place of the boat in "the mountains of the Gordyaeans". Epiphanius says "the remains of Noah's ark are still shown in the land of the Gordians." Faustus of Byzantium placed the ark in the canton of Gordukh. Isidore of Seville wrote that the ark landed in the Gordyaean mountains.

The name of this 7,000 foot peak was spelled variously as Judi, Guti, Cudi, Kutu, etc. The province in which it is located was spelled Cardu, Qardu, Karduch, Gordukh, Gordyene, Gordyaea, Gordian, Gordhaik, or Korcaik, etc. The peak of Mount Judi is located at 37°22'N, 42°37'E in southern Turkey (Kurdistan) 17.4 miles northeast of the Tigris River near the Syrian and Iraq borders. The peak is about 75 miles south of Lake Van and was in the Ararat/Urartu region that surrounded Lake Van. Mount Judi is about 580 miles walking distance northwest from Eridu, the city next to the Persian Gulf estuary where Noah's barge grounded. The return trip from Mount Judi to Sippar was about 380 miles walking distance. This journey, totaling 960 miles, would have taken more than a few months on foot in addition to the two months stay at Mount Judi.

It is likely that the myth of the ark landing on Mount Judi in the mountains of Ararat was a garbled version of the story that Shem told his listeners at Sippar. His journey to Mount Judi was on foot after the barge grounded, not a voyage on the water during the flood, a distinction later story tellers may have misunderstood. After arriving at the base of Mount Judi, Shem and his brothers may have climbed part way up the mountain, because it was probably the highest mountain, perhaps the only mountain, they had ever seen. Later, Shem told the people of Sippar about his adventures, including floating in his father's barge for a year and descending from the heights of Mount Judi. Story tellers reported these events, but later story tellers falsely assumed that the ark had grounded on Mount Judi in the mountains of Ararat.

It might be objected that the mountain Shem climbed was probably Mount Niṣir (sometimes spelled Nimush), because Mount Niṣir was mentioned in Gilgamesh XI,140–144 as the grounding place. Mount Niṣir is sometimes identified as Pir Omar Gudrun,[31] an 8,445 foot peak located at 35°45'N, 45°15'E near the Little Zab River, east of the Tigris. However, since Shem's ultimate destination was Sippar, which was on the Euphrates west of the Tigris, it does not seem likely that Shem would leave the Tigris and travel east up the Little Zab River to Pir Omar Gudrun.

Since Eridu and Ur are west of the Tigris River, Shem and his brothers and their wives probably traveled up the west side of the Tigris from Eridu. When they reached the plain at the foot of Mount Judi, the water level of the Tigris was probably low because they arrived late in the year. Some of the family may have forded the river to explore Mount Judi, leaving the animals with the remaining family members on the west side of the river.

According to Mallowan[32] the city of Ur lay on the east bank of the Euphrates at the time of the flood of 2900 BC. At Eridu, Noah may have arranged for small boats to ferry his sons, their wives, their animals and supplies across the Euphrates River to Ur.

Before reaching the Tigris River by traveling east along the (then) shore of the Persian Gulf, Shem and his group would encounter another branch of the Euphrates River that passed through Lagash. Shem may have traveled northwest on the west bank of this river through Lagash, forded the river north of Girsu, and continued northwest along the west bank of the Tigris, which then included the Shatt al–Gharraf, west of the present Tigris.[33]

According to Berossus,[25] "a voice from the air" (an oracle) told the flood hero's relatives to "dig up the tablets buried at Sippar." A library of baked tablets of inscribed clay was buried in mud by the heavy rain and overflowing rivers at Sippar in a place, probably in a low area, where Noah's sons could find the library in spite of the flood damage. The tablets buried at Sippar included "the beginning, middle, and end of all things." The oracle priest at Eridu may have needed someone to send to Sippar to make sure that the tablets in a flooded library at Sippar were recovered from the debris.

Noah and his wife in exile

After the barge grounded, according to Gilgamesh XI,195 (new line numbers 203), the Babylonian Noah "and his wife...shall live far away at the mouth of the rivers" which was then near Eridu and Ur. According to Atrahasis fragment RS 22.421 line 7, the Babylonian Noah said "I lived in the temple of Ea, my lord." Ea was known in Sumerian as Enki. Hence, Noah probably lived at Eridu in the temple of Enki at the mouth of the rivers. Prior to the Early Dynastic III period, a king's residence was part of a temple.[34] But Noah probably stayed there only long enough to dispose of the barge, the animals, the remaining barley and other cargo. Noah no longer needed the barge, because he could no longer travel up the river to Shuruppak, Uruk, or Nippur. He may have sold the barge to an agent of the company that supplied the timber for building the barge. Thus Noah's debts to the company would be satisfied and ownership of the barge would be transferred beyond the reach of Noah's other creditors.

Even if the temple of Enki entered a judgement in favor of Noah, he could still be declared a common thief by a judge at the temple of Enlil and any country that Noah fled to might send him back to Sumer for trial. The priests of Enki apparently solved Noah's problem by making Noah a priest. Noah had already developed a special relationship with the priests of Enki prior to the flood. According to Ziusudra,148, "Every day he stood constantly present at [the reed wall]" where he received advice from an omen diviner, an oracle. Each such visit probably involved a payment to the temple. According to Gilgamesh XI,19 the advice came from the god Ea (Enki), and therefore the oracle probably involved a priest of Enki/Ea at Eridu.

It has been suggested[35] that the flood hero was a priest before the flood. According to Ziusudra,145 the flood hero was both a $GUDU_4$ and a lugal (king). A $GUDU_4$ was a priest responsible for certain bloodless offerings, oaths, judicial proceedings, and temple administration.[36] If Noah had been a priest–king before the flood, it is not likely that he would receive advice from an oracle. It is more likely that Noah became a $GUDU_4$ priest after the barge grounded. A religious ceremony which made the flood hero a priest is actually recorded in mythical language in Gilgamesh XI.

During this ceremony shortly after the sacrifice, the flood hero and his wife were apparently given the status of honorary gods (priests) according to Gilgamesh XI,189–195 (new line numbers 196–201). This ceremony was performed by Ea,[37] i.e. the highpriest of Ea. Although most translations of XI,189 (new line numbers 196 or 197) say "Then Enlil went into the boat," Enlil is not mentioned by name in this line[38] which literally reads "Then ^{d}IDIM went into the boat." ^{d}IDIM was a generic sign for Lord referring to the gods Enlil or Ea.[39] Since the flood hero refers to Ea as his Lord at line 32 and Ea is the speaker at lines 100–187 (new line numbers 178–195), ^{d}IDIM refers to Ea, i.e. the highpriest of Ea/Enki.

"Then Ea went into the boat. Holding me [the flood hero] by the hand, he took me aboard. He took my wife aboard and had her kneel by my side. Standing between us, he touched our foreheads to bless us." The priest of Ea said "…now [the flood hero] and his wife are associates; they shall be like gods to us." According to Berossus, the flood hero "was gone to live with the gods [priests] and his wife, his daughter, and the boatman shared in the same honor." As we shall see, this new status as honorary gods (priests) would prove very important to these four people.

Since the act of blessing Noah and his wife was attributed to a god, which normally should be treated as pure myth, interpreting "he touched our foreheads to bless us" as an actual act by a highpriest is conjecture. Although it may be fiction, this ceremony fits the reconstructed legend and is therefore included here to flesh out the story. One need not euhemerize the god Enki to allow that sometimes story tellers misidentified priests as gods.

Although we are left with the impression that this ceremony was aboard Noah's barge, this seems unlikely because the highpriest would have no reason to board Noah's abandoned barge. It is more likely that the ceremony was held on board the sailboat that would soon take Noah and his wife and daughter far from Eridu after he sold the cargo and the barge. The barge remained grounded in the estuary, awaiting salvage by its new owners.

People search for Noah

Meanwhile, news of Noah's barge grounding near Eridu reached officials at Shuruppak and Nippur. Before the barge grounded, the officials probably assumed that Noah was dead and the barge and its cargo were destroyed during the storm. When news reached them that the barge was still intact and grounded near Eridu and Noah was still alive, but the cargo had disappeared, they would naturally suspect fraud and would be angry with Noah. Noah's political rivals would accuse Noah of taking advantage of the confusion during the flood to conceal theft of government property. The officials may have sent a squad of soldiers to the place where the barge grounded with an order for Noah's arrest. If they found Noah and/or his family, the soldiers would take them into custody and transport them back to Shuruppak and/or Nippur to stand trial for fraud, tax evasion, and unpaid debts.

By the time the soldiers arrived at Eridu, Noah's sons and their wives were safely on their way up the Tigris River, and the flood hero, his wife, their daughter, and the boatman had left for a place "far away." A priest of Enki spoke as an oracle through a reed wall to people who were searching for Noah, possibly the soldiers. According to Berossus, "a voice came from the air, telling them that they must respect the gods." They must follow the advice given them by the oracle.

The oracle reportedly said that the flood hero "was gone to live with the gods [priests], and his wife, his daughter and the boatman shared in the same honor." This told the soldiers that Noah was exempt from prosecution because he was a god. He was also beyond the reach of the law because he had gone to live with the gods. By asking a few more questions at the waterfront, the soldiers would quickly discover that Noah and his family had left on a sailboat bound for a foreign country that was called the home of the gods. The soldiers were satisfied. Nothing would be gained by pursuing Noah further.

Noah was safe. But having lost his job as chief executive, and with his merchanting business ruined, Noah probably wanted only to retire in comfort in a land where his creditors and the governments of Shuruppak and Nippur would not bother him, i.e. in a foreign country where he had no debts. So where did Noah and his wife go?

According to Ziusudra vi,260, the Sumerian Noah went to live in the land of Dilmun. Dilmun (also spelled Tilmun) was a port city on an island in the Persian Gulf and is identified by scholars as the island of Bahrain.[40,41] Dilmun was a major trading port and Noah had probably been a merchant or trade official before becoming chief executive of Shuruppak. Therefore Noah probably had friends in Dilmun with whom he had previously developed business relationships. If he had to live in exile, Noah would probably find Dilmun an attractive place in which to retire.

The island of Dilmun

According to Cornwall,[42] some inscriptions of Sargon of Assyria state that Uperi King of Dilmun lived "30 *bēru* away in the midst of the sea of the rising sun" and another inscription of Assurbanipal declares that Dilmun "is in the midst of the Lower Sea." The Assyrian expressions "sea of the rising sun" and "Lower Sea" referred to the Persian (Arabian) Gulf.[42] The expression "in the midst of the sea" was a frequent term for an island. The distance "30 *bēru*" was more than 300 miles according to Cornwall, but close to 200 miles if one *bēru* = 10.8km.[43] Bahrain Island is on the west side of the Persian Gulf about 300 miles southeast of the present mouth of the Tigris-Euphrates rivers. Dilmun had "sweet water" and Bahrain today still has fresh water springs. It therefore offered a natural watering place for international shipping. According to Cornwall, Dilmun included both Bahrain island and part of the nearby Arabian mainland.

Identifying Dilmun with Bahrain island was strengthened by archaeological work done by Glob[44] and Bibby[41] who discovered remains of an ancient port on the north shore of Bahrain where they found soapstone stamp seals that resembled seals found during excavations at Ur. A cuneiform inscription found on Bahrain mentions the god Enzak the local god of Dilmun. Dilmun is often mentioned in ancient documents in connection with Makan a country famous for its copper mines which have been found east of Bahrain in the interior of the Oman peninsula. Bibby found bits of copper near the abandoned port at Bahrain. Business records have been found in Ur referring to copper from Makan being transported through Dilmun to Ur. There is no doubt that trade was transacted between Ur and Bahrain and that Bahrain was called Dilmun at one time. But was this Bahrain/Dilmun the same Dilmun referred to in the Ziusudra epic?

Kramer[45] argued that the Ziusudra Dilmun was on the east side of the Persian Gulf, because Dilmun was near Elam and Elam was ancient Persia on the east side of the Persian Gulf. Ziusudra,261 describes Dilmun[46] as "the place where the sun rises" which clearly suggests that the Ziusudra Dilmun was east of Sumer, except, as Alster commented, the sun rises in the southeast during half of the year. Bahrain Island was south of Sumer. Kramer placed Dilmun in southwest Iran south of Anshan, south of Elam which was east of Sumer. Dilmun was noted for it cedars, a tree native to Dilmun, and Dilmun was described as "Cedar Land".[47] Cedar grew in the Zagros mountains east of Sumer, but not on Bahrain island.

Commercial references to Dilmun[48] are attested as early as the Uruk period (before 3000 BC) hundreds of years before Noah. But the name Dilmun may have had a different toponymic meaning after the Akkad dynasty. According to Saggs,[49] "Although after 2200 BC this name [Tilmun] denoted Bahrain and Failaka and perhaps nearby parts of the Arabian side of the Persian Gulf, in the early third millennium it seems to have meant somewhere in south Iran." Perhaps there were two ports named Dilmun, which flourished at different times. Resolving this issue is beyond the scope of this book.

Failaka island was then and is now closer to the mouth of the rivers than Bahrain island. Since the flood hero and his wife settled "at the mouth of the rivers," according to Gilgamesh XI,196, their retirement home may have been on Failaka which would still qualify as Dilmun because Failaka was controlled by Dilmun.

Although Dilmun was a commercial seaport, it was also described as a paradise:[50] "The land Dilmun is pure; the land Dilmun is clean... The sick-eyed says not 'I am sick-eyed'... Its old man says not 'I am an old man'... Her sweet water flows from the earth... its houses are good houses," etc. This almost sounds like an ancient advertisement for a retirement community. The sentence "Its old man says not 'I am an old man'..." does not mean that Dilmun was a place of eternal youth and old men cannot be found there. It says that old men are welcome there and need not say apologetically "I am an old man." The next line reads "The young girl places not water for her bath in the city." It is not uncommon for retirement communities to exclude young children except as visitors. A young girl who placed water for her bath would be a resident and that apparently was not allowed in the exclusive Dilmun retirement community.

Bahrain island has more than 170,000 tombs,[51] built over the centuries with expensive imported stone, which indicates that wealthy people were buried there. Since Dilmun was a prosperous trade center, the wealthy residents of the retirement community probably included retired merchants. Since Enzak, the god of Dilmun, was said to be a son of the god Enki, there was probably a close relationship between the temple at Dilmun and the temple of Enki at Eridu. Hence, retired priests of Enki may also have lived on Dilmun and were buried there. Noah had been made an honorary priest of Enki at Eridu. Dilmun was where Noah and his wife and daughter (apparently no longer a young girl) lived in retirement and in exile after the barge grounded near Eridu.

The second Ararat and mistakes of identification

Ancient story tellers who told their listeners that Noah's boat had grounded in the mountains of Ararat misunderstood their received story, partly because of Shem's trip on foot from Eridu to Sippar via Mount Judi in the Ararat mountains, and partly as a result of mistranslating *shadû* as mountain instead of a ziggurat hill at Eridu where Noah sacrificed animals on an altar at the temple of Enki. A third reason they misunderstood the flood story may have been confusion of Ararat with Aratta, two names associated with Noah that sound enough alike to cause misunderstanding.

Aratta was a god of Shuruppak,[52] the city where Noah was chief executive. The spouse of Aratta was the goddess Sud of Shuruppak. The cuneiform signs representing the name of the Shuruppak king who reigned before Noah (SU.KUR.LAM in Sumerian) could be read in Akkadian as Aratta.[52] Even though there was no etymological connection between Aratta and Ararat, Noah was indirectly connected to both names.

There was also a city named Aratta in a mountainous region. The location of this Aratta is not certain, but Kramer[45] placed it adjacent to Anshan, south of Elam in southwest Iran. The six-day storm that caused massive flooding in the Tigris–Euphrates valley would also have caused flooding in nearby Aratta. An Aratta flood was mentioned in the epic poem[53] "Enmerkar and the Lord of Aratta" at lines 572–577: "After the violence of the flood had raged, Inanna, the queen of all the lands… the water of life for them."

The name Aratta may have become attached to Noah's story when Aratta story tellers heard that Noah had escaped a flood and left his river barge where it grounded. The story tellers may have merged Noah's story with a local Aratta story about an Aratta flood that occurred at the same time as the Euphrates River flood. The story tellers may have assumed that Noah's barge grounded in a river in the nearby mountains of Aratta. Meanwhile at Sippar, Shem was talking about his journey to Mount Judi in the mountains of Ararat. Thus began the myth of a universal deluge that involved the mountains of Ararat.

Conclusions

The river flood of 2900 BC drowned many people but did not interrupt civilization in the Tigris–Euphrates valley. There were many survivors of the flood and many more who were not affected by the flood. Noah was greeted by some of them when his barge grounded near the mouth of the Euphrates River on the shore of the Persian Gulf. When Noah offered a sacrifice on an altar at the top of a hill at Eridu, he was offering cooked food at the top of a ziggurat at the temple of Enki. Noah could not return to Shuruppak because he would be faced with criminal prosecution for fraud and tax evasion. Noah, his wife, daughter and his boatman sailed from Eridu to the island of Dilmun where they lived in exile.

Meanwhile, Noah's sons and their wives traveled on foot up the Tigris River to avoid passing through Shuruppak and Nippur. After staying for two months at Mount Judi in the mountains of Ararat, they traveled on foot back down the Tigris River and crossed overland to Sippar on the Euphrates River. They dug into the flood debris at Sippar to recover a library of clay tablets. Story tellers misunderstood Shem's story and thought the barge had grounded on Mount Judi in the mountains of Ararat.

References

1.   M. E. L. Mallowan, "Noah's Flood Reconsidered", *Iraq*, 26 (1964), pp. 62–82, especially p. 81.

2.   Josephus, Complete Works, *Antiquities of the Jews* I, 3, 6, (Grand Rapids, MI: Kregel Publications, 1974), p. 29.

3.   Steven W. Holloway, "What Ship Goes There: The Flood Narratives in the Gilgamesh Epic…" *Zeitschrift für die alttestamentliche Wissenschaft*, 103 (1991), 328–355, especially p. 343–344 where Holloway translates *ziq-qur-rat šadi* as "mountain ziggurat." "Hill-like ziggurat" would also be accurate.

4.   Margaret Whitney Green, *Eridu in Sumerian Literature*, PhD dissertation, (University of Chicago, 1975), pp. 180–181.

5.   A. R. George, *House Most High: The Temples of Ancient Mesopotamia*, (Winona Lake, Indiana: Eisenbrauns, 1993), p. 65, temple # 30.

6.   See Figure 13 for a drawing of the temple (reconstructed) at Eridu ca. 3000 BC. The Eridu ziggurat was enlarged into a step-pyramid during the Ur III period by Ur–Nammu (about 2112–2095 BC). The word *ziggurat* comes from the verb *zaqaru* which means "to build high".

7.   Jeffrey H. Tigay, *The Evolution of the Gilgamesh Epic*, (Philadelphia, PA: University of Pennsylvania Press, 1982), p. 225–228, 237.

8.   H. W. F. Saggs, *Babylonians,* (Norman, Oklahoma: University of Oklahoma Press, 1995), p. 89.

9.   A. Leo Oppenheim, *Ancient Mesopotamia,* (Chicago: University of Chicago Press, 1977), p. 280.

10.   J. Nicholas Postgate, *Early Mesopotamia,* (London: Routledge, 1992), pp. 124–128.

11.   Oppenheim, op. cit., pp. 187–192.

12.   According to Gilgamesh XI,163 (Kovacs translation) "She lifted up the large flies… this lapis lazuli around my neck…" Such an amulet in the form of a fly carved from the blue stone lapis lazuli (see front cover) has been found and was mentioned for the Jemdet Nasr period by Lissie von Rosen, *Lapis Lazuli in Archaeological Contexts*, Studies in Mediterranean Archaeology and Literature 93, (Jonsered, Sweden: Paul Åströms Förlag, 1990), p. 26. The tablet of destinies, a lapis lazuli object, was used as "a sort of emblem of legitimate office" according to Green,[4] p.175.

13.   In Gilgamesh XI,160–166, 189–195 and Atrahasis III,v,34–36, "gods" are assumed to be a euphemism for priests.

14.   Green, op. cit., p. 224.

15.   Postgate, 1992, op. cit., p. 299.

16.   John A. Brinkman and others (editors), *The Assyrian Dictionary,* (Chicago, Oriental Institute, 1980), Vol. Ṣ, p. 49 top left.

17.   James R. Davila, "The Flood Hero as King and Priest," *Journal of Near Eastern Studies,* 54, 3 (July 1995), pp. 199–214, especially p. 208.

18.   J. N. Postgate, "The transition from Uruk to Early Dynastic: continuities and discontinuities in the record of settlement" in *Gamdat Nasr,* Uwe Finkbeiner and Wolfgang Röllig (ed), (Wiesbaden: 1986), pp. 93, 105.

19.   See the map (Figure 1) in Chapter 4. The Ur and Eridu area on the map is after Postgate, 1986, op. cit., p. 103, Fig. 8. In Postgate's Fig. 8, note the blank area east of Ur and the end of the river. There are no settlements shown which suggests the blank area may have been an estuary or marsh during the Jemdet Nasr and ED I periods. According to Green[4] p. 169, "Eridu is located on the edge of a large depression to the southeast." Gulf coast ports of Eridu, not the city of Eridu, were then "on the shore of the sea." See also A. Falkenstein, "Die Eridu-Hymne", *Sumer,* 7 (1951), p. 121.

20.   E. A. Speiser, "Authority and Law in Mesopotamia", *Supplement to the Journal of the American Oriental Society,* 17 (July–Sept 1954), pp. 8–15.

21.   Debt-slaves are discussed by Postgate, 1992, op. cit., pp. 107, 194–196, 215.

22.   Saggs, op. cit., pp. 95–96.

23.   Postgate, 1992, op. cit., p. 136.

24.   Green, op. cit., p. 378.

25.   Berossus quoted in *The Gilgamesh Epic and Old Testament Parallels,* Alexander Heidel (Chicago: University of Chicago Press, 1963), pp. 116–119. The Greek version of Berossus has "by a roundabout way."

26.   Stephanie Dalley, *Myths from Mesopotamia* (New York: Oxford University Press, 1991), p. 305, third line.

27.   Robert K. Englund, "Hard Work – Where Will It Get You? – Labor Management in Ur III Mesopotamia," *Journal of Near Eastern Studies,* 50 (1991), pp. 255–280, esp. 267–268.

28.   Moses of Khoren, *History of the Armenians,* translation by Robert W. Thomson, vol. 4 of Harvard Armenian Texts and Studies, (Harvard University Press, 1978) pp. 79–80 (near end of section 6). A different translation is quoted in Bailey.[29]

29.   Lloyd R. Bailey, *Noah: The Person and the Story in History and Tradition,* (Columbia, SC: University of South Carolina Press, 1989), p. 194.

30.   Bailey, op. cit., pp. 65–67.

31.   Bailey, op. cit., p. 65. This mountain is now known as Bira Mukron.

32.   Mallowan, op. cit., p. 76, note 42.

33.   Green, op. cit., p. 7.

34. I. E. S. Edwards and others (editors), *The Cambridge Ancient History,* third edition, Vol I, part 2, (Cambridge University Press, 1971), p. 276.

35. Davila, op. cit., p. 213.

36. Davila, op. cit., p. 203.

37. Albert T. Clay, *A Hebrew Deluge Story in Cuneiform* (New Haven: Yale University Press, 1922), p. 81.

38. Simo Parpola, *The Standard Babylonian Epic of Gilgamesh* (Helsinki, Finland: University of Helsinki, 1997), page 61, line 197.

39. Rene Labat, *Manuel D'Épigraphie Akkadienne,* (Winona Lake, Indiana: Eisenbrauns, 1988), p. 67, sign 69.

40. Bendt Alster, "Dilmun, Bahrain, and the Alleged Paradise in Sumerian Myth and Literature" in Daniel T. Potts (editor) *Dilmun: New Studies in the Archaeology and Early History of Bahrain* (Berlin: Berliner Beiträge zum Vorderen Orient 2, 1983), pp. 39–74.

41. Geoffrey Bibby, *Looking for Dilmun,* (New York: Knopf, 1969), p. 381.

42. P. B. Cornwall, "On the Location of Dilmun," *Bulletin of the American Schools of Oriental Research,* 103 (Oct 1946), pp. 3–10.

43. Marvin A. Powell, "Masse und Gewiechte," *Reallexikon der Assyriologie,* 7 (1990), pp. 457–517, especially p. 459 (1 *bēru* = about 10.8km).

44. Peter V. Glob and T. G. Bibby, "A Forgotten Civilization of the Persian Gulf," *Scientific American,* 203 (1960), pp. 62–71.

45. Samuel Noah Kramer, "Dilmun, The Land of the Living," *Bulletin of the American Schools of Oriental Research,* 96, (Dec 1944), pp. 18–28.

46. Samuel Noah Kramer, "Sumerian Myths and Epic Tales," *Ancient Near Eastern Texts,* James B. Pritchard (editor), (NJ: Princeton University Press, 1950), p. 44 line 261.

47. Samuel Noah Kramer, *The Sumerians,* (Chicago: University of Chicago Press, 1963), pp. 281–282.

48. Robert Englund, "Dilmun in the Archaic Uruk Corpus" in Potts, *Dilmun,* op.cit. pp. 35–37.

49. Saggs, op. cit., p. 32.

50. Samuel Noah Kramer, "Enki and Ninhursag," *Ancient Near Eastern Texts,* James B. Pritchard (editor), (NJ: Princeton Univ. Press, 1950), p. 38.

51. C. C. Lamberg–Karlovsky, "Dilmun: Gateway to Immortality," *Journal of Near Eastern Studies,* 41, 1 (January 1982), pp. 45–50, especially p. 49. Most of the tombs on Bahrain were built between the Ur III and Isin–Larsa periods, ca. 2100–1800 BC.

52. S. Langdon, "The Chaldean Kings Before the Flood," *Journal of the Royal Asiatic Society* (1923), pp. 255, 258 (note 5).

53. Samuel Noah Kramer, *Enmerkar and the Lord of Aratta,* Museum Monograph (PA: University of Pennsylvania, 1952).

6

Construction of Noah's Barge

*"The idea of a boat made up of planks
sewn together seems strange. Actually,
it is a type that has been in wide use"*
Lionel Casson
Ships and Seafaring in Ancient Times

The familiar image of Noah standing on the deck of his boat surrounded by elephants, giraffes and other zoo animals is popular with modern artists. Their cartoon drawings and paintings have established the mythical image of Noah and his ark that appears often in newspapers, magazines, Bible illustrations, and children's books. This image conflicts in several particulars with the Genesis, Gilgamesh and Atrahasis versions of the story.

Modern artists traditionally draw Noah's ark as a rounded-hull seagoing ship with a projecting keel. But deep keels and rounded hulls are required only on sailboats. Noah's barge had no sails because the prevailing wind in the Tigris–Euphrates valley is toward the southeast,[1] the same general direction as the river current, thus making tacking upriver against both the wind and current impractical. Noah's barge was a flatboat, not a keelboat.

Ancient barges had a nearly rectangular cross section to maximize clear space for the cargo.[2] Noah's barge was designed to transport cargo in the calm, slowly moving water of the lower Euphrates river. Whatever the construction method used (shell-first, log raft, reed raft, quffa, etc.) Noah's barge used the technology of 2900 BC and was probably constructed in the same manner as river boats built hundreds of years later in Mesopotamia and Egypt.

Construction described

Genesis 6:14–16 describes construction of Noah's barge as follows:

14 Make for yourself an ark of gopher wood. Make rooms in the ark and cover it inside and outside with pitch.

15 And this is how you shall build it: the length of the ark three hundred cubits, its breadth fifty cubits and its height thirty cubits.

16   Make a tsohar for the ark and finish it to a cubit above and
       set the door of the ark in its side. Make it with lower, second,
       and third [decks].

Atrahasis fragment CBS 13532 specifies one of the building materials:[3]
7   Let its structure be of good reeds.

Atrahasis III,i,29–31 adds extra details about an awning:
29   As [usual in] the *apsû*, likewise roof-over it [with an awning]
30   so that the sun will not see inside it.
31   Let it be roofed above and below.

Atrahasis DT 42(W) mentions the design phase:
14   Draw the design on the ground
15   That I may see [the design] and [build] the boat.

Gilgamesh XI describes construction of the barge:
28   The wooden boat that you shall build
29   Let its dimensions be measured.
30   Let equal-size [be] its width and its length.
31   As [usual in] the *apsû*, likewise roof-over it. [with an awning]
56   On the fifth day I laid-out its plan.
57   One acre its extent,[4]
       120 cubits [length] each I raised its walls.
58   120 cubits [length] each equal-size [were] edges [of] its upperpart.[4]
59   I erected its body [frame] to it. I marked it.
60   I provided an upper deck with six [rooms?]
61   I divided [its width] into seven [sections].
62   Its interior I divided into nine [subsections].
63   Wooden water[–resistant] pegs I surely hammered into its
       interior.
64   I provided punting poles and laid in supplies.
65   Six shars of crude-pitch I poured into the kiln [for caulking].
66   Three shars refined-pitch [I poured] into the inside.
67   Three shars of oil the carriers brought.
68   Besides [one] shar of oil consumed by "dust",
69   two shars of oil were stowed by the boatman.

Some of the Akkadian words and phrases are ambiguous and each
translator puts a different interpretation on their probable meaning. For
example, in line 59 the word *la-an*,[5] translated here as "body" (which probably
refers to the framing) has also been translated as figure, size, shape,
configuration, height, form, hull, structure, outside, and contours.

Barge smaller than expected

In the conventional interpretation of the Genesis story the ark is incredibly large. The dimensions given in Genesis 6:15 are 300 cubits long, 50 cubits wide, and 30 cubits high. How long is a cubit? Or more to the point, how long was the unit of length that was later translated into the Hebrew word *ammah* for cubit? It has long been assumed that this unit was the length of a man's forearm or about one and a half feet. A barge 300 cubits long would have had a length of about 450 feet, or more than half the length of the Titanic. That would be longer than any modern ocean vessel built before 1858 and more than twice as long as the longest barges used in Egypt to transport obelisks.[6] Wood boats much longer than 200 feet leak excessively. It is therefore very unlikely that Noah's barge was 450 feet long.

If the meaning of cubit changed or was mistranslated or if cubits was an editorial gloss, the size of Noah's barge could have been much smaller. Noah's barge was 30 "cubits" high and had 3 decks according to Genesis 6:15–16b, suggesting 10 "cubits" or 15 feet from deck to deck. Doesn't 15 feet seem excessive? If you were building a barge to transport animals would you make the stalls 15 feet high? Of course not. To minimize your construction costs you would build the stalls just high enough to clear the height of standing animals and adult workers. Wooden barges used on the Mississippi River in the early 19th century had an inside clearance of about 6 feet.[7]

Assuming 6 feet for each of the three decks in Noah's barge plus another 2 feet for decking, bottom planking, and dunnage, the estimated total height would be about 20 feet. Hence, the unit of measurement would be about 8 to 9 inches (20 to 23 cm). This is the span of a man's hand, i.e. the distance between the tips of thumb and little finger when the fingers are spread apart. The Genesis 6:15 unit of measurement probably should have been hand span (*zereth* in Hebrew) in this instance or less than half a cubit (*ammah*). The source text used by an editor of Genesis 6:15 may have omitted the unit of measurement, just as we omit inches in the expression "two by four." A story teller or editor may have added *cubits* to the story. Alternatively, an archaic sign or pictograph for hand spans may have been used that was unfamiliar to an ancient translator who assumed it meant cubits. A barge measuring 300 hand spans in length would be about 200 feet (61 m) long.

Gilgamesh and Genesis agree on length

In Gilgamesh XI,58 the length of the barge is given as ten ninda and a ninda was a dozen cubits. Hence the barge was 120 cubits long. The Sumerian cubit *(kùš)* was about 20 inches,[8] which again yields a calculated length of 200 feet. This confirms that the Genesis 6:15 dimensions were in hand spans rather than cubits.

Use of the word "equal-size" at Gilgamesh XI,30 regarding the width and length and the word "equal-size" at line 58 regarding the edges of the upper part of the boat has led scholars to conclude that the boat had square decks (see discussion in Appendix A). But in the archetype flood story, use of the word "equal-size" probably meant that the barge had equal widths and also had equal lengths, i.e. the sides were straight and parallel. Unlike sailboats and marsh boats, the barge did not have a variable width and curved sides that converged to a pointed bow and stern. Although the dimensions of the barge were explicitly given in the archetype story and survived in Genesis 6:15, when the flood story was added to the Gilgamesh epic, perhaps the poet's abridged source did not include the exact width and height and therefore the poet may have misunderstood the "equal-size" sentence.

The beginning phrase in line 57 is usually translated "One *iku* (acre) in its extent/circumference." However, one of the Akkadian signs in this phrase can be translated "field".[4] This field may have been next to the Euphrates River, so the barge could be launched into the river. The field may have had a house on it (the house mentioned at Gilgamesh XI,24) that Noah ordered demolished to provide a construction site on which to build the barge.

The second part of line 57 does not give the height of the walls. It literally reads "120 cubits each I raised its walls".[4] There is no additional indication of whether the 120 cubits was height or length and therefore the text is ambiguous. The 120 cubits was probably a measurement of wall length rather than wall height, because a boat as high as its length would roll over in the water, if anyone were foolish enough to build such a boat. Other texts that specify wall measurements often omit an indication of whether the number means length or height, but length is implied.[4]

Likewise, line 58 literally reads "120 cubits each equal-size [were the] edges [of] its-upper-part". This may be saying that the left edge and the right edge of the upper part of the hull or the superstructure had equal lengths of 120 cubits. In other words, the upper part was symmetrical and ran the full length of the barge.

Repeating the length but not giving dimensions for the width or height is not how an architect or carpenter would describe a boat. But the author of Gilgamesh XI was a poet not a carpenter. We should be happy that at least he remembered to mention the length. The width and height are not given in Gilgamesh, but are given in Genesis.

The dimensions of a barge measuring 300 x 50 x 30 spans would be about 200 feet long, 33 feet wide, and 20 feet high, a large vessel by ancient standards but quite within the limits imposed by a wood structure. Barges with a length of 150–200 feet were used in the Old Kingdom of Egypt.[6] It is not unreasonable to imagine that Sumerian merchants in 2900 BC might transport a few hundred animals and other cargo on a 200 foot barge.

Fewer than 280 animals

Does a few hundred animals seem too few? The popular myth of an ark containing tens of thousands, or hundreds of thousands, or millions of species is not supported by Genesis 7:2–3 which describes the herd as seven pairs (fourteen) of each clean animal (i.e. animals used for temple offerings and food), one pair of each unclean animal and bird and seven pairs of clean birds.[9] Deuteronomy 14:4–5 lists 10 species of clean animals, which implies 140 clean animals in Noah's barge. Assuming a minimum average of 12 square feet per animal (cramped but adequate), 1680 square feet of deck area would be needed, which is little more than one quarter of a 200 x 33 foot deck.

In a text from the Ur III period[10] the following clean animals were offered to the gods Enlil, Ninlil and Nanna. This text is dated day 21, month 2, year 7 of Amar–Suen:

> 1 calf, unweaned
> 4 oxen, grain-fed
> 6 oxen, grain-fed
> 1 cow, unweaned
> 1 calf
> 4 sheep
> 20 goats
> 1 fleeced sheep, grain-fed
> 2 sheep, grain-fed, second-rate
> 2 adult goats, grain-fed, second-rate
> 1 nanny goat, grain-fed, second-rate
> 1 ox, grain-fed

This list includes only four species: cattle, oxen, sheep and goats. Seven pairs of four species is a total of 56 animals. At 12 square feet per animal, 672 square feet of deck area would be needed which is only about ten percent of a 200 x 33 foot deck. If Noah's workers loaded only the animals that happened to be in Noah's stockyard when the river started rising, the barge may have contained only 56 or so clean animals. Clean animals are also mentioned at Atrahasis III,ii,32.

How much deck area was needed for the unclean animals and birds? Leviticus 11:4–19 and Deuteronomy 14:7–18 list about 30 species of unclean animals and birds. Thirty pairs would be 60 animals. These small animals would fit in 2 feet by 2 feet cages. In addition, seven pairs of each of the five species of clean birds is a total of 70 clean birds. Assuming 4 square feet for each caged small animal and bird, only 520 square feet were needed. Thus the total deck area required for the estimated 270 animals was 2200 square feet or about one third of the 6600 square foot deck, leaving the other two thirds for walkways and baskets of grain piled several deep.

Genesis 7:2a literally reads: "Of all the clean animals take with you seven seven male and his female." The Hebrew idiom "seven seven" normally means "seven each".[11] Repeating a number to mean each is also used in Numbers 3:47, Numbers 7:86, I Chronicles 26:17, and Ezekiel 10:21. Seven each modifies "male and his female" which apparently means mated pair. Hence Genesis 7:2a means "Take with you seven of each mated pair of clean animals." Or simply, seven pairs of clean animals. Two is not repeated in Genesis 7:2b for the unclean animals and therefore only one pair of each kind of unclean animal is specified.

The broad words of Genesis 6:19: "And of every living thing of all flesh, you shall bring two of every kind into the ark" and a similar phrase in Genesis 7:15 are clearly inconsistent with the sacrifices of Genesis 8:20 and the seven pairs mentioned in Genesis 7:2–3. Since the phrase "two of every kind" is an overgeneralization, the preceding phrase "every living thing" can also be treated as an overgeneralization and be interpreted narrowly to mean every living thing of importance that Noah owned or had custody of. If Noah was asked years later how many animals he took on the barge, Noah may have replied, "Every one; I took them all." In such a remark, the words "every" and "all" would mean only that he did not leave any of his animals behind, not that he took every species on the planet. As with the proverbial fish story, the scope of "every" grew with the retelling.

No giraffes, no elephants, no kangaroos

Noah's clean animals included cattle, sheep and goats. His unclean animals included raven, swine and eagles. They were his inventory, his stock in trade. But most of the world's animals were not included. Exotic zoo animals such as elephants, giraffes, hippos, lions, apes and kangaroos are not mentioned in Genesis or Deuteronomy and were not included in Noah's inventory. Since it would be impossible for Noah to attract millions of animals from all over the planet, he did not do so. According to Gilgamesh XI,82 "All the living beings I had, I loaded aboard." Yes, all he had, and only those he had.

Would it be practical for 9 people (Noah, his 3 sons and their wives plus the boatman Puzur-Amurri) to feed and water 270 animals and haul out the manure each day? Assuming 10 hour work days (not including rest and dinner breaks) each person would have 20 minutes per animal each day. Entirely practical. Gilgamesh XI,84 reads "I sent all my family and relatives into the boat." There may have been additional relatives who were not mentioned in Genesis 7:7 and who could have helped with the animals.

Atrahasis DT 42(W),9 mentions "all the wild creatures of the steppe that eat grass." Noah would have transported hay to sell to his customers to feed the animals they bought from Noah until the animals were ready for slaughter. Noah also carried additional hay on his barge to feed the hay-eating animals during the few days they were being transported to market.

"All the living beings I had, I loaded aboard."
[And only those he had.]

Concentrated grain feed such as provender[12] used for pack animals in caravans would be less likely than hay as cargo on the barge, because Noah's customers would want the lowest-priced fodder. On the barge, some of the animals could be fed barley, rather than hay. After the hay was used up, Noah's family would feed barley to the sheep, goats and cattle.

The hay, being light, was probably piled on the upper deck which served as a hay loft. Heavy cargo would not be stored on the upper deck, because that would make the barge top heavy. The heavy clay jars of beer, wine, dates and vegetable oil were stored on the lower deck just above the dunnage. The middle deck was where the animals were kept. Baskets of grain were probably also stored on the middle deck.

If Noah stored thousands of gallons of beer and wine in his barge and thousands of cubic feet of hay and thousands of baskets of grain, he must have had a good reason for it. The animals, beer, wine, grain, and hay were part of his inventory that he expected to sell at the ports the barge visited. Noah transported to market as much cargo as the barge could carry, because it was profitable to do so. He did not transport rats or lions or spiders, because no one would want to buy them. He transported thousands of jars of beer and wine because there was a market for beer and wine. Wine was produced in the nearby Zagros mountains[13] prior to 5000 BC. Wine was mentioned at Gilgamesh XI,72 and beer was mentioned at Atrahasis III,iv,16.

The door of the barge (Genesis 6:16) was in its side and opened onto the middle deck, probably a few feet above the water line when the barge was fully loaded. This would be a ridiculous place for a door in a lifeboat intended for a stormy sea, but it is the usual place for a door in large river boats designed for calm water. Such a door allowed the animals to be loaded and unloaded onto wharves from the middle deck using a short horizontal gangplank.

There was enough space

Would there be enough deck area for the hay, beer, and wine for the 382 days the barge was occupied? Assuming each clean animal consumed half of a cubic foot of hay per day, 140 animals would consume 70 cubic feet per day or 26,700 cubic feet in 382 days. In a hayloft 6 feet high about 4460 square feet of deck area would be required for the hay, which would easily fit on a 6600 square foot deck, leaving enough space on the upper deck for walkways.

Assuming each person and large animal consumed three quarts of water (as beer or wine) per day, 152 large animals and people would consume about 44,000 gallons in 382 days. Four gallons in a clay jar occupy about one square foot. If the jars were stacked two deep, about 5500 square feet of deck area would be required to store the beer and wine, leaving enough deck area for structural members, walkways, and jars of other commodities. This is assuming three quarts of water/beer/wine per day. Small animals would require less than half of that amount. The adult people may have consumed eight quarts of beer per day. Only a small amount of well water would have been stowed in the barge for the animals during the expected few days of travel. Water would not have been hauled as cargo because nobody would want to buy well water, but jars of beer and wine would have provided the necessary drinking water on the barge. After the barge grounded in an estuary, Noah could have used brackish river water.

Since Noah loaded only the animals that he had, if he had fewer than ten species of clean animals, the total number of animals may have been much smaller than estimated here. This means the amount of beer, hay, and grain that were used to keep those animals alive would also have been smaller than estimated.

Bill of materials

According to Greenhill, "Not only in Egypt but throughout the world methods of shipbuilding are notoriously unchanging".[14] If we assume that boat builders in Noah's time used the same materials and technology as in the Ur III period 800 years after Noah, then the following bill of materials[15] for boatbuilding during the Ur III period suggests what Noah's workmen would have used.

     178 big date-palms
     1400 big pines
     36 big tamarisks
     32 big she-hi trees
     10 tamarisks of 3 cubits each
     276 talents palm-fiber ropes
     34 talents palm-leaf ropes
     418 talents of rushes
     1695 liters of fish-oil
     300 ...
     4260 bundles of ... reeds
     12,384 bundles of dried reeds
     951,000 liters of purified bitumen

Shell-first construction

The three-deck design mentioned in Genesis 6:16b implies that Noah's barge had a hollow hull and the lower deck was below the water line. The barge was caulked with pitch according to Genesis 6:14b: "Cover it inside and out with pitch."

Some translators erroneously assume that the skeleton or frame of the ark was built before the hull planking was attached. Heidel[16] stated "Utnapishtim [Noah] now attached the planking to the framework." But this frame-first construction technique for boat building was not invented until after the seventh century CE when it was first used in the Mediterranean.[17] If Noah's barge had a hull or hulls, then shell-first construction was used.

When ancient boat builders built a hull, they started with the planking. The planks were laid side by side and their edges and ends were joined together with thin wood tenons or round dowels which were inserted into mortise holes cut along the edges and ends of the planks. Dovetail fasteners, hook scarfs, and ropes prevented these joints from pulling apart. The planks were sewn together with palm fiber ropes through V-shaped lashing holes drilled through the inner surfaces of the planks.[14] The sides of the hull were constructed using the same techniques. The Egyptian funeral boat of Khufu built of cedar planks (about 2650 BC) is the earliest known example of this type of shell-first construction and is 145 feet long.[18]

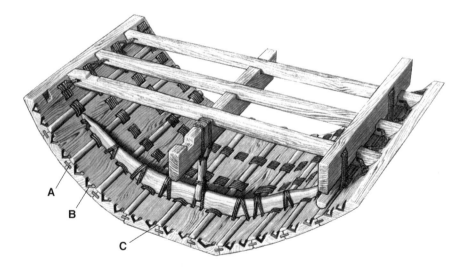

Figure 4. The Egyptian Khufu boat was built shell-first and was held together with dowels (A) and ropes in V-shaped lashing holes (B). Battens (C) held pitch caulking in the seams.[19]

Frames, consisting of ribs, stringers, braces, stanchions and deck beams, were then cut to fit the inside of this shell of planks and stiffened with rope trusses. The boat's "body" that was erected at Gilgamesh XI,59, may have been the frames that were built into the barge after the hull was raised at lines 57–58 and before the upper deck was built at line 60 (see discussion in Appendix A). In barges, the bows and sterns were rectangular and were fitted with bow planks and stern planks.[20]

The most difficult problem with building a hull is preventing leaks and the larger the hull, the more difficult this problem. Regardless of how expertly caulked, a modern 200 foot hull will leak as the planking flexes slightly from stresses exerted by water currents, wind, and cargo loading. Seams open slightly between the planks. Large wood hulls must be frequently pumped or bailed when not in dry dock. Under the hot sun, the planks dry out and shrink. This is under the best of conditions with a modern frame-first hull.

But with shell-first construction using split and hewn planks, the frames would not snugly fit the shell of planks and hull deformation and opened seams under stress would be very likely. A conventional shell-first hull 200 feet long would have been very leaky and would have required frequent bailing. Some method of reducing leaks was probably used so that additional crew members would not be required for bailing. How this problem may have been solved using the technology of 2900 BC, is considered below.

Although shell-first construction seems to us like a strange way of building a boat compared to modern shipbuilding in which the frame is built first, the ancient boatbuilders would have had great difficulty using frame-first construction to build a large flat-bottom barge. This is because the frame of a large barge is heavy and could not be easily raised to attach bottom planking to the frame or to apply hot pitch or caulking to the bottom planking. Although the frame could have been suspended a few feet above the ground as it was being built so that workmen could attach planking underneath to the flat-bottom frame, this would probably seem to ancient boatbuilders as impractical as building a house from the roof down. It would be much easier for them to build the hull from the ground up, which implies shell-first construction. Although they could have built the hull bottom first, then the frame, then the hull sides, this still would have made it very difficult to apply pitch on the outside of the hull during construction and during annual maintenance.

Genesis, Gilgamesh and Berossus agree that pitch was used to waterproof the barge. This pitch would have covered the entire hull, not just the seams, to protect the wood from shipworms. In addition, the hull may have been covered with layers of sheathing consisting of pitch-filled woven-reed matting that would reduce leakage. The problem of how the boatbuilders were able to apply hot pitch and sheathing to the bottom of the barge is discussed below in the next section.

Early drawings and seals of Sumerian boats show parallel lines on the hull like ropes used to tie reeds into bundles.[21] Such ropes could also hold sheathing against hulls. Tarred fabrics[22] were used in the first century BC to cover wood hulls of sail boats. A similar method may have been used to waterproof Noah's barge.

According to Gilgamesh XI,65 the pitch was applied hot and this process may have been similar to the hot tar process used by modern roofers. Oil was mixed with the pitch according to Gilgamesh XI,65–68 in a ratio of one part oil to six parts pitch. The oil was a plasticizer, making the pitch flexible and less likely to crack.[23]

Genesis 6:14b says the ark was covered inside and outside with pitch. Covering the inside of a conventional hull with pitch can reduce rot, but does not prevent leaking because water pressure forces the pitch away from the inside of the seams.[24] The "inside" may therefore refer not to the inner surface of the planking, but to the inner surface of the sheathing. When woven reed matting is covered inside and outside with pitch, the two layers of pitch fuse together through the tiny holes between the reed fibers, just as in modern fiberglass the outer and inner layers of resin bond through spaces between the glass fibers.

If the hull had to be covered with hot pitch or if layers of pitch-filled sheathing had to be applied hot to the outside of the hull after the hull was built, how would the workers get access to the flat bottom of the hull without lifting the entire barge or suspending it as it was being built?

Barge built in sections

There is a much simpler way of coating and sheathing a hull after the wood shell and the internal frames have been built. The boatbuilders could build the hull in small sections, each section being a rectangular box-shaped boat and light enough for several workmen to carry and turn upside down so the sheathing and hot pitch could be applied to the outside of each hull section. After all the layers of hot pitch and sheathing were applied and cooled, each finished hull section would be turned over to its upright position, carried to the water, and roped to other hull sections like pontoons in a floating bridge.

The double walls where each sheathed pontoon touched the next pontoon would resemble bulkheads. Major leakage in one pontoon would not spill over into the other pontoons. Noah's barge may have consisted of dozens of such small, shell-first pontoons roped together, each covered with layers of pitch and perhaps woven-reed sheathing.

Gilgamesh XI,61–62 indicates that the interior of the barge was divided into seven [sections] and nine [subsections], which suggests that there were 63 separate pontoons. Instead of a conventional hull divided by bulkheads, the barge may have consisted of 63 pontoons roped together in a horizontal rectangular array of 7 columns abeam and 9 rows from bow to stern. Nine rows of pontoons from bow to stern could support walls for three rooms on each side, a total of six rooms on the middle deck (called the upper deck in Gilgamesh XI,60). The wall frames of each room on the middle deck would be supported by a double wall of pontoons. The middle deck wall frames would support the top deck (the roof).

The width of Noah's barge was 33 feet (50 hand spans) and the length 200 feet (300 spans). Each pontoon would be about 4.7 feet wide, about 22 feet long and about 7.5 feet deep. Multiplied by 63 pontoons, this would provide a lower cargo area of about 5400 square feet and a volume of about 38,000 cubic feet after allowing for a few inches of planking and internal framing in each pontoon. When fully loaded, the upper third of each pontoon hull would be freeboard above the water line.

Planks laid on top of deck beams supported by the pontoon frames would form the middle deck on which the animals and baskets of grain were stored, a few feet above the water line. A superstructure of wood poles or reed bundles would be built on top of the middle deck and would support the upper deck. Walls of the superstructure would be made of woven reed matting. Palm or acacia wood could have been used for the deck and cane poles for the superstructure. If imported building material was used, cedar would be the preferred material for the hull and decks, and bamboo for the superstructure.

The barge design suggested here with 63 pontoons lashed together is simply small boat technology multiplied 63 times. No new technology would be needed. Such a design is consistent with the primitive construction techniques that were probably used on Euphrates River boats during the third millennium BC, although there is no known archaeological evidence for this design.

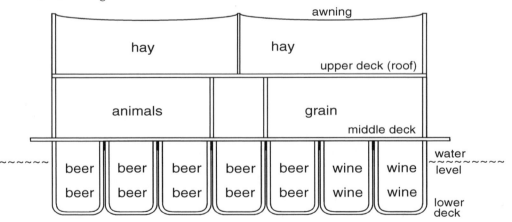

Figure 5. End view of hypothetical 3-deck barge

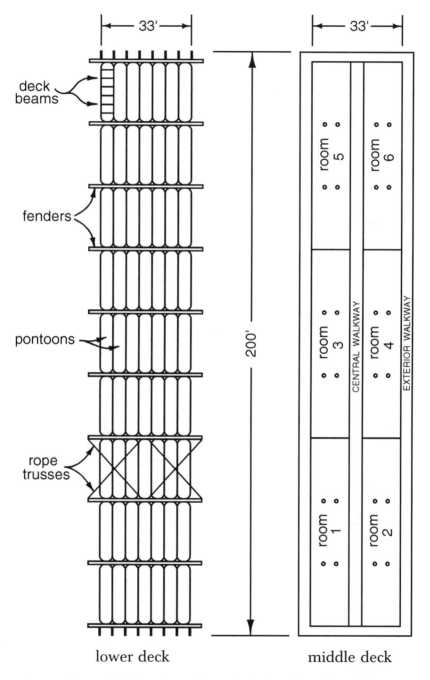

Figure 6. Plan views of two decks in a hypothetical barge

Shell-first construction techniques, that were used to build the round-bottom Egyptian Khufu boat illustrated above in Figure 4, could have been used with only minor changes for building flat-bottom pontoons such as illustrated in Figure 7 below. Battens (to hold pitch caulking in the seams) and bracing, trusses, and decking are not shown in Figure 7.

To retrieve a jar of beer or wine from a pontoon, a crew member would remove a few of the deck planks, hook a pole under a rope attached to a jar and then use the rope to lift the jar up onto the middle deck. Bilge water and animal waste in the pontoons would be removed daily with weighted buckets on the ends of ropes.

Cargo that could be damaged by water would not be carried in the pontoons because of leakage and dripping animal waste from the middle deck. Only sealed jars, stone, metals, and other heavy cargo not damaged

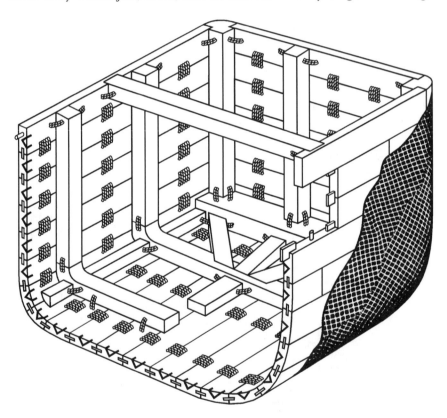

Figure 7. Hypothetical pontoon hull with framing and tar-filled sheathing using the same shell-first technology that was used to build the Egyptian Khufu boat shown in Figure 4.

Figure 8. Pontoons for a barge being built as separate units

by water or animal waste would be carried in the pontoons. It would not matter if some of the clay jars of beer, wine and oil were temporarily submerged in partly flooded pontoons, because the jars were sealed.

> And Noah he often said to his wife
> When he sat down to dine,
> "I don't care where the water goes
> if it doesn't get into the wine."
>> *Wine and Water*
>> G. K. Chesterton

The best wood for hull planking is cedar[25] because cedar resists waterlogging and rot, is easy to work, is lightweight, grows to huge dimensions, floats well for at least thirty or forty years, and was quite plentiful in the Zagros mountains east of the Tigris–Euphrates valley.[26] Noah had scraps of cedarwood that he used to light the fire on the altar after the barge grounded according to Gilgamesh XI,158. But as the Ur III bill of materials shows, boatbuilders also used pine, tamarisk, and date palm wood.

In Egypt, according to Casson[6] "From early in the third millennium BC on, Egypt imported excellent ship timber... they now turned out vessels running up to 150 feet in length... A thousand years later they were able to build some of the largest vessels known from the ancient world, the brobdingnagian barges that hauled obelisks downriver from the quarries at Aswan, vessels that must have measured well over 200 feet long and 70 wide..." Snefru of Egypt (about 2600 BC) listed among his accomplishments: "Bringing forty ships filled with cedar logs." If Egypt could import large quantities of cedar during the early third millennium, Sumer may also have imported cedar for boat building about the same time.

Reeds, wood, or both?

The surviving versions of Noah's flood story do not describe the construction method used for building the barge and do not clearly specify the overall design. Also the text does not indicate which parts of the barge were made of reeds and which were made of wood.

There was both wood and reed construction in the barge according to Atrahasis III,ii,11–12 and the corresponding lines in Gilgamesh XI,50–51: "The carpenter carried his axe, the reed worker carried his stone." Atrahasis fragment CBS 13532,7 reads: "Let its structure be of good reeds".[3] An alternative translation[27] is "Let its structure be entirely of reeds." A large raft can be built of reed bundles as was the reed sailing ship *Tigris* built by Thor Heyerdahl.[28] But a reed raft barge, using bundles of reeds for floatation, would not have had a deck below the water line and would not have an "inside" that required pitch caulking. If Noah had a barge built entirely of reeds, it may have been an earlier model that was later replaced by multiple shell-first wood hulls that required pitch caulking. The superstructure probably consisted of woven reed matting on wood poles. The wood hulls were probably sheathed with pitch-filled reed matting. Both carpenters and reed workers were needed to build the barge.

The Hebrew word in Genesis 6:14b for rooms in the ark is *q–n–m* which translators assume means rooms or stalls from the context. Since Hebrew script did not have vowels when Genesis was first written, *q–n–m* can be vocalized as *qinnîm* or *qānîm*. The traditional vocalization *qinnîm* literally means "nests" as in bird nests. Since pontoon hulls would be accessible only from the top, the word "nests" seems appropriate. The alternative vocalization *qānîm* means "reeds".[29] "Of reeds you shall make the ark." Reeds fits the context even better, especially if reed matting was used for partitions between middle-deck rooms and as sheathing on the outside of multiple hulls.

The expression "gopher wood" of Genesis 6:14 may refer to a tree known in Sumerian as GISH.GI.PAR.[30] *Gish* means wood or things made of wood and *gipar* means pasture or meadow. *Gish gipar* may have meant literally meadow wood, i.e. wood from a species of tree that grew in moist lowlands and was used as building material. This tree was also known as *liparu* and its leaves were used as an ingredient in poultices.[31]

The Septuagint translates *gipar* as "four angled" i.e. trimmed lumber. Gopher may also be related to *kopher* 'pitch' or *kuparissos* 'cypress'.

It has also been suggested that gopher wood was a reed[32] material. Some reeds grow to large dimensions and were used for building material. Houses near the marshes in ancient Sumer were built with bundles of reeds[33] and were still being built prior to 1978 when cement block houses became cheaper to build than reed houses.[34,35] Gopher wood or *gish gipar*, may have meant a wood or reed material of the kind used for building houses.

Gipar also meant a residence of a priest.[36] When a Hebrew translator was collecting material for Genesis and found *gipar* in his source document, he would not have wanted to translate it as priest-house. Not knowing what else it could mean, he transliterated *gipar* into Hebrew as *g–p–r*, later vocalized as gopher.

The Hebrew word *tebah*, translated in Genesis as ark, is also used in Exodus 2:3–5 where it refers to a small reed basket into which the baby Moses was placed. This basket was coated with pitch to make it waterproof according to Exodus 2:3b. Since pitch was also specified for Noah's ark in Genesis 6:14b, some commentators[37] have suggested that Noah's ark may have been constructed of reeds like the ark of baby Moses.

Hence, there are four clues supporting a theory that Noah's barge was made partly of reeds:

> the ark was built "of good reeds" in Atrahasis CBS 13532;
>
> *qānîm* can mean reeds in Genesis 6:14;
>
> *gopher* wood in Genesis 6:14 could mean reeds; and
>
> *tebah* (ark) means a reed basket in Exodus 2:3.

Reed rafts do not provide any deck or cargo space below the water line and are less buoyant than hollow hulls. Heavy cargo loaded on top of a raft places the center of gravity above the loaded water line which limits the amount of cargo that a raft can carry without becoming top heavy. Cargo on an upper deck would make the raft unstable. If heavy cargo can be stowed below the water line, the center of gravity is lowered and increases the amount of cargo that can be carried on upper decks. Moreover, a hollow hull greatly increases buoyancy which increases the amount of heavy cargo a barge can carry. The design most likely for a three-deck river barge built with 2900 BC technology would be multiple pontoon hulls, but there are alternative designs that should also be considered.

Woven reed quffas

As mentioned above, the Hebrew word for ark in Genesis is *tebah* and this word is also used in Exodus 2:3–5 where it refers to a small reed basket boat coated with pitch.

Large reed basket boats coated with pitch are now called quffas[38] and were being used on the Euphrates River before 3400 BC and are still being used there. The whole quffa is coated inside and out with bituminous pitch mixed with oil. The ribs of these reed basket boats are now made from palm or willow branches and prevent the quffa from being crushed by water pressure. Some modern quffas are 20 feet in diameter and can carry sixty people or tons of cargo.[32] Quffas are still being used in the Euphrates River marshes because reeds are still in plentiful supply near the river mouth. The quffa was to Baghdad what the gondola is to Venice.

Figure 9. Quffa-like coracles were used to haul heavy cargo.[39]

Although a single 200 foot long quffa would not be practical, dozens of smaller quffas could be roped together in chains or arrays like a pontoon bridge. Even if some of the quffas leaked and partly filled with water, the remaining quffas would continue to support the flooded quffas. The barge and its cargo would be in no danger of sinking.

When large quffas are launched independently, each quffa is normally punted or rowed by two to four oarsmen. To reduce the number of oarsmen that had to be fed, the quffa owners would want to lash several quffas together, so that one small towing team could tow a chain of quffas with ropes from the river bank or from a towpath on top of the levees. Early combinations of quffas in large chains or arrays probably had only one deck, i.e. the bottoms of the quffas:

Figure 10.   Round quffas tied together in a chain.

So that cargo handlers could walk between the quffas during loading and unloading of cargo, a few deck planks would be laid on top of the internal frames. The remaining deck planks would be laid down only after loading of the quffas was complete. This arrangement would provide two decks.

Inside each quffa on the bottom and sides there would be the usual open frame of wood ribs to resist water pressure and protect the inner surface of the quffas from damage. The inner bottom would be covered with a few inches of sand ballast and dunnage to support and protect the clay jars. The tops of the quffas and the wood frames would be roped together at the level of the second deck. The weight of the cargo on the second deck would be supported by the internal frames in the quffas. A barge of quffas would be disassembled each year to recoat the outside of the quffas with pitch.[40]

Convergence of technologies

As economy of scale dictated multiple decks and increasingly deeper quffas, stronger frames would be required inside each quffa to resist the increased water pressure and to support the weight of the superstructure. Narrow frames that were practical in small quffas would, under this higher pressure, damage the fragile reed matting in large quffas. To protect the reed matting, a wood lining would be built between the frame and the matting to distribute the pressure evenly over the interior surface of the matting, especially on the bottoms of the quffas where water pressure was greatest. The result would resemble a shell-first hull covered with a pitch-filled quffa basket similar to the wood pontoon hull covered with pitch-filled sheathing proposed above. Boat builders with experience building small shell-first hulls would know how to build similar linings inside quffas. The shell-first hull technology and the quffa technology would converge and the combined technology would be used for building large barges of multiple quffa-like pontoons.

Apparently, this convergence occurred before 2900 BC, thus making Noah's large three-deck barge practical. However, there is no archaeological evidence that barges were built this way.

Rooms, awnings and hatches

According to Gilgamesh XI,77–79: "there was shifting of load above and below, until two-thirds of the structure was submerged." A draft of two-thirds of the hull would leave one-third of freeboard, i.e. the part of the hull above the water line. Since the top of the freeboard was no higher than the bottom of the door at the level of the middle deck, the height of the hull (assuming no gunwales) was about 7.5 feet, i.e. the distance between the bottom planking and the middle deck. Freeboard was therefore one third of 7.5 feet or about 2.5 feet, the distance between the middle deck and the water line when the barge was fully loaded. During the voyage, the crew stood on narrow extensions of the middle deck 2.5 feet above the water.

Gilgamesh XI,60 reads "I provided an upper deck/story sixfold." The verb *ur-tag-gi-ib-ši* means to provide with an upper story or upper floor and is based on the root *rugbu* meaning attic, roof, story.[41] This was done sixfold according to Gilgamesh XI,60. Translators usually translate this as six decks, because each deck could be "upper" relative to a lower deck. But just as building a house with six roofs implies that the roofs are arranged horizontally and not stacked vertically, building an upper deck six times implies one upper deck built in six horizontal sections. Six decks would conflict with the three decks of Genesis 6:16b and a barge with six decks stacked vertically would have been impractical in 2900 BC. This upper deck may have been what we would think of as the middle deck, i.e. it was not the bottom deck and it was not the roof (top deck). Providing an upper (middle) deck six times could mean it was constructed as six separate rooms separated by walls made of poles and reed matting. If there was a central walkway from bow to stern with three rooms on each side, the walls of these six rooms would separate the animals from the grain and other cargo.

Genesis 6:16 tells us that the barge had a *tsohar* finished "to a cubit above." *Tsohar* is often translated as roof and the ark is usually pictured with a long superstructure with a sloping gable roof. But a wood roof above a wood superstructure would have made the barge top heavy and would have been excessively expensive in a land with few trees. A sloping roof would not be needed because annual rainfall was only a few inches. Instead, the roof was probably flat and was the same as the top deck. If the *tsohar* was not a roof, what was it?

Tsohar or *tsohoraim* is the generic word for noon or midday.[42] A *tsohar* cannot be a window because Atrahasis III,i,29–30 clearly precludes this: "As [in] the *apsû*, likewise roof/cover-over it [the boat], so that the sun will not see inside it." The word "roof" suggests to us a solid wood fixture permanently attached to the walls. However, roofs in ancient Sumer were often made of removable woven-reed matting spread over a frame made of bundles of reeds. Such roofing techniques are still in use today.[34] The Akkadian verb *ṣullulu* meaning to roof-over, can also mean to put on top and can refer to clouds covering the sky. It can also mean to provide shade.[43] It would be consistent with the semantic range of *ṣullulu* to refer to the woven reed covering as an awning rather than a roof. A *tsohar* was probably a horizontal awning or canopy to shield the deck and hatches from the midday sun, so the barge would not overheat.

The *apsû* mentioned in Atrahasis III,i,29 and the corresponding line in Gilgamesh XI,31 refer to marsh land next to the Persian Gulf in the vicinity of Eridu.[44,45] Hence, Atrahasis III,i,29–30 seems to be saying: "Cover the top of the barge with an awning similar to those used on marsh boats so that direct sunlight will not shine through open hatches."

This woven reed awning would be secured on a wood or bamboo frame a cubit above the heads of the crew members and a cubit above the top of the hay to allow air to circulate under the awning. Such an awning would not obstruct removal of hay by the crew.

After mentioning the awning, Atrahasis III,i,31 adds this detail: "Let it be roofed/covered above and below." This could be a reference to two levels of awnings: an upper awning above the hay loft to cover the top deck, and a small lower awning to cover the narrow exterior middle deck where the boatman and his officers stood or sat in the shade while the barge was in use.

During the storm, these awnings were securely tied down to prevent the hay and the awnings from blowing away. The upper awning would not keep rain off the deck or hay, because the awning was designed for use only during the summer voyage when normally no rain falls and would be porous for air circulation. Unlike a roof, the awning was removable and Noah removed it (Genesis 8:13b) after the rain stopped, perhaps to allow the rain-soaked hay to dry out so it would not become moldy.

The barge had hatches or windows (*challon*) mentioned in Genesis 8:6. These hatches would normally be open during most of the year to provide air circulation and indirect light, but not direct sunlight. Genesis 8:6 mentions that Noah opened a window, but this does not imply he opened a window or a hatch only once. Every day when it was not raining, Noah probably left these hatches open and he and his family climbed onto the upper deck to look for land and lower bundles of hay to the middle deck.

Conclusions

Noah's commercial barge had a flat bottom and no keel. The barge was about 200 feet long, 33 feet wide and 20 feet high. The Genesis 6:15 dimensions were originally in hand-spans rather than cubits. There were fewer than 280 animals on Noah's barge and they occupied less than one third of the middle deck. Walkways and thousands of baskets of grain piled several deep filled the remainder of the middle deck. The animals included cattle, sheep, goats, and poultry. Exotic zoo animals such as elephants, giraffes, hippos, lions, apes and kangaroos were not carried in Noah's barge.

Thousands of clay jars of beer, wine, and vegetable oil were stored on the lower deck. Well water or river water was not hauled as cargo, but jars of beer and wine provided the necessary drinking water during the several months the barge was adrift in the Persian Gulf. The roof was flat and served as an upper deck on which hay was transported. An awning above the roof shielded the deck and hay from the sun. The animals, grain, beer, wine, and hay were part of Noah's inventory that he expected to sell at the ports the barge visited.

The barge consisted of 63 boxlike hulls roped together like a pontoon bridge arranged in a horizontal, rectangular array of 7 columns and 9 rows. Shell-first construction was used to build each of the cedar hulls, similar to that used in constructing the Egyptian funeral boat of Khufu. Each hull was covered with pitch and may also have been covered with layers of sheathing consisting of pitch-filled woven-reed matting. The pitch was mixed with oil and was applied hot like the hot tar process used by modern roofers.

The sheathing may have been built first like a quffa and coated inside and outside with hot pitch before a shell of planks was constructed inside each quffa pontoon. An internal frame of ribs, stringers, braces, and deck beams were then cut to fit inside each pontoon shell.

There is no evidence that Noah's river barge was constructed in the manner suggested above, but the technology used on the barge must have been the technology known at the time the barge was constructed. Several variations on the above designs would have been physically possible, practical to build and operate in 2900 BC, consistent with the vague language in Atrahasis, Gilgamesh, and Genesis, and consistent with the primative technology used in 2900 BC.

References

1. Marie–Christine De Graeve, *The Ships of the Ancient Near East* (Leuven, Belgium: 1981), pp. 13, 151.

2. De Graeve, op. cit., p. 120–122.

3. John A. Brinkman and others (eds), *The Assyrian Dictionary* [CAD], (Chicago, Oriental Institute, 1980), Vol. Q, p. 87 bottom left.

4. See discussion in Appendix A.

5. CAD, op. cit., vol. L, p. 80, left middle.

6. Lionel Casson, *Ships and Seamanship in the Ancient World*, (NJ: Princeton University Press, 1971), p. 17.

7. Erik F. Haites, James Mak and Gary M. Walton, *Western River Transportation* (Baltimore, Maryland: Johns Hopkins University Press, 1975), p. 15.

8. Samuel Noah Kramer, *The Sumerians*, (Chicago: University of Chicago Press, 1963), p. 107.

9. The *Septuagint* has "clean birds".

10. Postgate, op. cit., p. 162.

11. Francis Brown, S. R. Driver and C. A. Briggs, *Hebrew and English Lexicon of the Old Testament*, p. 988a, section 1.b.

12. A. K. Short, *Ancient and Modern Agriculture*, (San Antonio, Texas: Naylor Company, 1938) p. 29.

13. Patrick E. McGovern, et al, "Neolithic Resinated Wine," *Nature*, 381 (6 June 1996), pp. 480–481.

14. Basil Greenhill, *Archaeology of the Boat* (Middletown, CT: Wesleyan University Press, 1976), pp. 161–162.

15. J. N. Postgate, *Early Mesopotamia*, (London: Routledge, 1994), p. 218.

16. Alexander Heidel, *The Gilgamesh Epic and Old Testament Parallels* (Chicago: University of Chicago Press, 1949/1970), p. 82, note 174.

17. Lionel Casson, *Ships and Seafaring in Ancient Times* (Austin, Texas: University of Texas Press, 1994), pp. 106–107.

18. Cheryl Ward Haldane, "Boat Construction in Ancient Egypt" in *The Pharaoh's Boat at The Carnegie* by Diana Craig Patch, (Pittsburgh: Carnegie Museum of Natural History, 1990), p. 25.

19. Björn Landström, *Ships of the Pharaohs*, (New York: Doubleday, 1970), p. 29, Fig. 86.

20. Casson 1971, op. cit., p. 28.

21. Casson 1971, op. cit., pp. 22–23, Fig. 21.

22. Casson 1994, op. cit., p. 34, Fig. 29.

23. Thor Heyerdahl, *The Tigris Expedition* (Doubleday, 1981), p. 263.

24. The problem of pitch caulking being squeezed from the seams by water pressure was reduced in the Egyptian Khufu boat by covering the

seams with narrow wooden strips that were held against the planking by ropes. These battens can be seen in Figure 4.

25. Larry Pardey, *Details of Classic Boat Construction* (NY: Norton, 1991), pp. 281–284.

26. The cedars of Asia and the Middle East were true cedar (*cedrus*). American cedars used for cedar chests are actually juniper or cypress.

27. W. G. Lambert and A. R. Millard, *Atrahasis: The Babylonian Story of the Flood* (Oxford: Clarendon Press, 1969), pp. 126–127. A photograph of the CBS 13532 Nippur tablet from the University of Pennsylvania museum, shows *ṭa-bi* (good) and not *gáb-bi* (entirely).

28. Heyerdahl, op. cit., plate 8 prior to page 40.

29. Edward Ullendorf, "The Construction of Noah's Ark," *Vetus Testamentum*, 4 (1954), pp. 95–96.

30. CAD, op. cit., vol. G, p. 84.

31. CAD, op. cit., vol. L, p. 198, lower right.

32. C. C. R. Murphy, "What is Gopher Wood?", *Asiatic Review*, N.S., 42 (January 1946), pp. 79–81.

33. Samuel Noah Kramer, *Cradle of Civilization*, (NY: Time–Life Books, 1967), p. 91 (interpolated page number).

34. Gavin Young, *Return to the Marshes, Life with the Marsh Arabs of Iraq* (London: Collins, 1977).

35. Edward Ochsenschlager, "Ethnographic Evidence for Wood, Boat, Bitumen and Reeds in Southern Iraq", in *Trees and Timber in Mesopotamia* by J. N. Postgate (editor), Bulletin on Sumerian Agriculture, Vol. VI, (Cambridge, UK: University of Cambridge, 1992), p. 69.

36. Postgate, op. cit., p. 129–131.

37. Derek Kidner, *Genesis* (Chicago, InterVarsity Press, 1967), p. 88; and Harold Stigers, *A Commentary on Genesis* (Grand Rapids: Zondervan, 1975), p. 104.

38. De Graeve, op. cit., p. 86–89, Figs. 110–112.

39. Kramer, *Cradle of Civilization*, op. cit., p. 84, redrawn from an Assyrian relief, southwest palace, Kuyunjik.

40. De Graeve, op. cit., p. 106.

41. Wolfram Von Soden, *Akkadisches Handwörterbuch* (Wiesbaden, Germany: Otto Harrassowitz, 1965), p. 993 under *rugbu*.

42. Robert Young, *Young's Analytical Concordance to the Bible*, (Nashville: Thomas Nelson, 1981), pp. 658, 699.

43. CAD, op. cit., Vol. Ṣ, pp. 239–240.

44. Ronald A. Veenker, "Gilgamesh and the Magic Plant," *Biblical Archeologist*, 44 (Fall 1981), pp. 199–205, especially 202c.

45. Margaret Whitney Green, *Eridu in Sumerian Literature*, Ph.D. dissertation, (University of Chicago, 1975), p. 160–169.

7

How Old Was Noah ?

"An old error is an error."

Benjamin Franklin
Poor Richard's Almanac

One of the peculiarities of Genesis that gives it a mythical quality is the impossibly large ages attributed to the characters, especially those who lived before the flood. The oldest of the antediluvians listed in Genesis 5 was Methuselah who has become the epitome of longevity because he was reported to have lived 969 years. Noah was given an equally incredible age of 950 in Genesis 9:29. The Genesis genealogy numbers have been analyzed by many Biblical commentators, both ancient and modern. Those who have not rejected the text as mythical,[1] have usually taken the numbers at face[2] value. Commentators have constructed precise but impossible chronologies with these numbers[3] and others who attempted to rationalize the numbers have encountered difficulties. For example, changing the word *years* to *months* will not produce credible results, because then Mahalalel and Enoch would have been only five years old when they fathered sons.

Nearly all modern translations of Genesis are derived from the Masoretic (Hebrew) Text, because it is generally the most reliable. But there are also two other versions of Genesis: the Samaritan (in an early Hebrew script) and the Septuagint (a Greek translation of an early Hebrew text). Although, scholars are aware that these three versions of Genesis 5 have different numbers, people who have seen only the commonly available translations are often unaware that other versions exist. Even among scholars, it is customary to see every difference outside of the Masoretic Text (MT) as an error or a correction, an emendation, because the Masoretic Text is the standard with which other texts are compared. But this preference, as one scholar[4] commented, "is a mere convention for the scholarly world" and "it should not be postulated in advance that MT reflects the original text of the biblical books better than the other texts." Equal weight will be given here to the three versions, at least initially.

The numbers[5] in the Masoretic, Samaritan, and Lucianic Septuagint versions of Genesis 5 are shown in Table I.

	Masoretic			Samaritan			Septuagint		
	son		total	son		total	son		total
	born	remain		born	remain		born	remain	
Adam	130	800	930	130	800	930	230	700	930
Seth	105	807	912	105	807	912	205	707	912
Enosh	90	815	905	90	815	905	190	715	905
Kenan	70	840	910	70	840	910	170	740	910
Mahalalel	65	830	895	65	830	895	165	730	895
Jared	162	800	962	62	785	847	162	800	962
Enoch	65	300	365	65	300	365	165	200	365
Methuselah	187	782	969	67	653	720	167	802	969
Lamech	182	595	777	53	600	653	188	565	753
Noah	500	–	–	500	–	–	500	–	–
Until flood	100	350	950	100	350	950	100	350	950

Table I

A comparison of the numbers in Table I shows that each version is internally consistent. The ages when the sons were born plus the remainders equal the totals given in each version, but each version uses different numbers to arrive at these totals. This implies that the differences between the three versions were not accidental or the result of scribal errors. The differences are due to carefully constructed systems of chronology. By comparing the three versions it may be possible to determine which chronology is closest to the original Priestly chronology.

The three versions agree on some of the total ages at death, but many of the other numbers differ by exactly 100. The Septuagint numbers for the ages of the fathers at the birth of their sons, are in many instances 100 greater than the corresponding numbers in the other two versions. It is therefore tempting to suspect, as some commentators have,[6,7] that the Septuagint translators added 100 to the original numbers. But in the case of Jared, the Septuagint and Masoretic versions agree; the Samaritan version is the non-conformer. Hence, it is just as possible that the Samaritan editor subtracted 100 from the ages at son's birth, as did the Masoretic editor, except that the latter left Jared's numbers unchanged. The Samaritan editor also reduced the ages at death of Jared and Methuselah so they would not live after the flood.

This problem of the antediluvians living after the flood was important to the editors of the Masoretic and Samaritan versions. Because the story in Genesis 7 failed to mention anyone surviving the flood besides Noah, his sons and their wives, the Samaritan editor apparently felt obliged to alter the text so that Jared, Methuselah and Lamech would die in precisely the 600th "year" of Noah, the flood year. The Masoretic Text also has Methuselah dying in Noah's 600th year, but the editor of the Masoretic Text arrived at this through a different chronology than the Samaritan.

The Septuagint translators were apparently not concerned with whether other people besides Noah and his family survived the flood. As Klein[6] noted, the Lucianic Septuagint chronology has Methuselah living through the flood and thus the differences of 100 were not an attempt by the Septuagint editors to have Jared, Methuselah or Lamech die prior to the flood. But later Septuagint manuscripts were altered by giving Methuselah an extra 20 years before his son's birth,[5] so that he would die before the flood.

Larsson[7] discussed the differences between these versions and noted "many peculiarities" in the Masoretic version of the Pentateuch that are not present in the corresponding Septuagint version. He argued that these differences can be explained as alterations designed to rationalize a primary Masoretic system of chronology to a later Septuagint system. Most of these peculiarities are found outside of Genesis 5 and are therefore beyond the scope of this chapter. But even if Larsson is correct that the Masoretic Text was primary for most of the Pentateuch, the Septuagint could still be primary for Genesis 5. Alterations from the Septuagint to the Masoretic Text, according to Larsson, make no sense. I will show that the Septuagint numbers do make sense and the Masoretic and Samaritan editors had sensible but erroneous reasons for altering their received text of Genesis 5.

The three versions of the Shemite genealogical data[5] of Genesis 11:12–22 are given in Table II. The Shemite data is further analyzed in Chapter 9. When a comparison is made of the three versions in Table II, the same discrepancy of 100 is found, but the Septuagint and the Samaritan versions agree on the ages at son's birth. The Masoretic version is the non-conformer in Genesis 11 just as the Septuagint is the non-conformer in Genesis 5.

	Masoretic		Samaritan			Septuagint	
	son		son		total	son	
	born	remain	born	remain		born	remain
Arpachshad	35	403	135	303	438	135	430
Kenan	–	–	–	–	–	130	330
Shelah	30	403	130	303	433	130	330
Eber	34	430	134	270	404	134	370
Peleg	30	209	130	109	239	130	209
Reu	32	207	132	107	239	132	207
Serug	30	200	130	100	230	130	200

Table II

Although the differences of 100 in Genesis 5 suggest the Masoretic Text is primary, similar differences of 100 in Genesis 11 suggest the Septuagint is primary. Therefore, we cannot rely on these differences to determine which version is primary. Determining which of the three versions reflects the original Priestly text is a problem that is best approached by relating the numbers to facts that are independent of the texts and by finding plausible reasons why the texts were altered.

The Septuagint numbers

It would not be surprising if the Septuagint numbers were primary because when scholars translated the Hebrew Pentateuch (which includes Genesis) into Greek at Alexandria, Egypt about 280 BC, they used a Hebrew text that was edited in the 5th and 4th centuries BC.[8] This would be centuries older than the proto–Masoretic Text selected as the official text by the Masoretes after 70 CE, "a text that was already corrupted."[9]

Starting with the Septuagint numbers in Table I, we can avoid making assumptions about what time-units the word *years* represents by calculating ratios. If each age at death is divided by the age at son's birth for each man, the resulting age ratios vary between 4 and 6 except for Enoch and Noah, regardless of what time-units are used, as shown by the following calculations:

Jared	962	÷	162	=	5.94
Methuselah	969	÷	167	=	5.80
Mahalalel	895	÷	165	=	5.42
Kenan	910	÷	170	=	5.35
Enosh	905	÷	190	=	4.76
Seth	912	÷	205	=	4.45
Adam	930	÷	230	=	4.04
Lamech	753	÷	188	=	4.01
Enoch	365	÷	165	=	2.21
Noah	950	÷	500	=	1.90

These ratios are entirely consistent with age ratios of people living today. For example, a young man might became a father at age 16 and die at age 80, which is a ratio of 5. Likewise a death age of 72 divided by a birth age of 18 is a ratio of 4. And a man who lived to be 90 could have been 15 when he fathered his first son, a ratio of 6. The close similarity of the age ratios in the text compared with people living today suggests that the life expectancy of these men was much closer to modern life expectancies than nine-hundred years. Although this does not prove that the numbers represent ages of real people, especially as the average life expectancy was less in the past[10] than it is now, at least finding ratios similar to those of real people reduces some of the mythical quality of Genesis 5. When similar calculations are made using the Masoretic and Samaritan numbers, the ratios increase to 13.00 and 13.77 which are not possible with real people. But all of the Septuagint age ratios are possible.

If the maximum credible age at death (then and now) is assumed to be 100 solar years of 365.25 days, the Septuagint ages of these men must have been represented in time-units no larger than 37.7 days, and probably less than that. It might be tempting to infer from this that the ages are given in months, not years. Genesis 7:11 and 8:3–4 imply that the calendar month used by the Priestly writer was 30 days. If years are changed to months, Jared would have been 162 months old when he fathered his son which converts to 13.3 years (12.5 years at conception), an age that is still too low. An alternative possibility is that the writer used a different notational system than we are accustomed to.

A clue to the notational system can be found by examining the units digits of the Septuagint numbers in Table I. For example, in the number 165, the units digit is a 5 which counts as one occurrence of the numeral 5 in Table I. Counting the number of times each units digit is used from Adam to Methuselah:

0 occurs   ten times
2 occurs   four times
5 occurs seven times
7 occurs   two times

It has been suggested[11] that this number pattern reflects divisibility by five with an occasional seven as a standard complement. Left unexplained is *why* the numbers are divisible by five with occasional sevens. Five years of twelve months each would be 60 months, suggestive of the Babylonian sexagesimal number system. However, as discussed below, the numbers of Genesis 5 were probably first recorded using archaic numbers before the rise of the sexagesimal system, and not in a decimal system.

Because the text has the numerals 0, 2, 5 and 7 in the units position, but not 1, 3, 4, 6, 8 or 9 prior to Methuselah, it seems more probable that the units digit represented quarters of some time unit converted to tenths. Two tenths and 7 tenths were simply single-digit approximations for 1 quarter and 3 quarters. The 5 meant one half. If these were quarters of solar years, the low-order (right) digit may have represented tenths of years, not years and the 165 "years" of Mahalalel meant 16.5 solar years, i.e. Mahalalel was sixteen and a half years old when he became the father of Jared.[12]

By assuming one decimal place in the Genesis 5 and 9:28 numbers, the Septuagint numbers yield ages in solar years as shown in Table III.

	Son Born	Total Life
Adam	23.0	93.0
Seth	20.5	91.2
Enosh	19.0	90.5
Kenan	17.0	91.0
Mahalalel	16.5	89.5
Jared	16.2	96.2
Enoch	16.5	36.5
Methuselah	16.7	96.9
Lamech	18.8	75.3
Noah	50.0	95.0

Table III

All of the ages in Table III are consistent with the ages of people living today. The numbers become much more credible once the notational system of the writer is understood. The fantastic stories about these men living over nine hundred years and not getting around to fathering their children until they had lived a century or two, are based on a misunderstanding of the number system. Except for Noah, each young man fathered his first son during his late teens or early twenties, just as young men do today.

To cling to the notion that the Genesis 5 numbers represent hundreds of solar years creates three problems: how could these men live to be over nine hundred years, how could they have fathered children when they were over a century old, and why did they wait so long to have children? All three of these problems disappear if we make two simple assumptions: the Septuagint has the original numbers and each of the numbers has one decimal place.[12]

Why the text was altered

The Masoretic and Samaritan editors were probably skeptical about men fathering children when they were more than a century old. This apparently led them to use the following procedures to alter the text (decimal points omitted). They initially subtracted 100 from all ages at son's birth, thus yielding more plausible ages such as 65 and 62. But this immediately created a problem with Jared, Methuselah, and Lamech living after the flood.

The Samaritan editor recognized that Lamech's remaining years after Noah's birth would have to be 600 if Lamech were to die in Noah's 600th year, the flood year. But Lamech's age at Noah's birth was still too large when calculated backwards from Lamech's death:

$$753 - 600 = 153.$$

The Samaritan editor eliminated this problem by subtracting 100 from Lamech's death age:

$$753 - 100 = 653$$
$$653 - 600 = 53$$

The Samaritan editor then reduced the death ages of Jared and Methuselah by exactly the amounts required for them to die in Noah's 600th year.

The Masoretic editor used a different approach to the same problem. After subtracting 100 from all ages at son's birth and finding that this created a problem with Jared, Methuselah, and Lamech, the Masoretic editor then restored the original birth ages for Jared (162), Methuselah (167), and Lamech (188). Jared and Lamech would thus die before the flood, but Methuselah would die 14 years after the flood. The editor eliminated this problem by increasing Methuselah's 167 to 187. Thus the flood would be delayed 20 years and Methuselah would die 6 years before the flood. The editor then eliminated this 6 years by subtracting 6 from Lamech's 188 so that Methuselah would die in the year of the flood. The Masoretic editor also subtracted 100 from the ages at son's birth in Genesis 11.

Except for the differences of 100, the only other differences between the three versions of Genesis 5 are for Jared, Methuselah and Lamech. These are the very people whose deaths would occur after the flood if the hundreds digit were omitted from the ages at son's birth. Moreover, the hundreds digits of the Masoretic ages at son's birth agree with the Septuagint prior to Noah only for Jared, Methuselah and Lamech. It is very improbable that these coincidences occurred by chance. They are the result of emendation procedures used by the Masoretic and Samaritan editors and provide the clues from which those procedures can be reconstructed.

Mistaking fractions for integers[12]

Use of the tenths digit to represent quarters in Table III suggests that the original data prior to Methuselah was recorded in years and quarter years (seasons) rather than years and months. For example, the birth of Jared son of Mahalalel may have been recorded like this: "When Mahalalel lived 16 years and 2 seasons his son Jared was born." Fractional years of .3, .8 and .9 began with Methuselah which suggests that some of the data was recorded in years and lunar months for events within recent memory of people still living at the time of the flood, but the best available data from old family tradition or from the temple archives was years and seasons.

The person who first calculated the numbers in Genesis 5 may have been using tenths of years rather than months simply for personal convenience, just as we sometimes calculate tenths of feet when we do not want to bother with inches. Calculating in tenths of years would have been easier than calculating lunar months and years with frequent intercalary periods. Just as the calculator of the numbers represented seasons to the nearest tenth year, he may have represented lunar months to the nearest tenth year or the next lowest tenth year. Use of tenths of years does not imply use of a ten-month calendar and may have been only the personal notation of one scribe.

As discussed in Chapter 2, Noah was a Sumerian chief executive during the Jemdet Nasr period which ended with the flood of 2900 BC.[13] The Genesis 5 numbers, representing ages of Noah and his ancestors, were probably based on records written in clay before the flood in an archaic (pre-cuneiform) Sumerian number system. Some of the numbers may have been recorded by Noah or his father from the memories of their elderly relatives. It also seems likely that most of the deaths (including Noah's) were originally recorded by temple scribes who routinely recorded deaths, especially in families of the nobility in Shuruppak.

Although the Babylonians used place-value notation[14] after 2000 BC and a sign for zero after 400 BC, these features had not yet been invented in 2900 BC. Hence, the original Genesis 5 numbers were not originally recorded using place-value notation or zero or decimal digits as they appear in Table III. But Sumerian number signs representing tenths, quarters and other fractions were already in use in 2900 BC before the invention of cuneiform numerals and the sexagesimal system.[15]

Prior to 2000 BC, the Sumerians used a round stylus for making archaic number signs in soft clay. A small diameter round stylus held perpendicular to a tablet made a small circular impression in the clay that often meant ten but could also mean six, depending on context.[16] The same small diameter stylus held obliquely and pressed into the clay tablet made a horizontal cup-shaped sign that often meant one. When held at different angles in different combinations, a round stylus could make other kinds of number signs. But the different signs that could be made by a round stylus were limited and such archaic signs were gradually replaced by cuneiform signs using a wedge shaped stylus between 2600 BC and 2000 BC.[17]

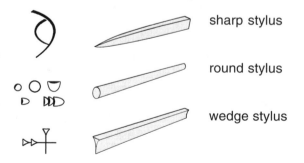

sharp stylus

round stylus

wedge stylus

Figure 11. Clay impressions and the stylus shapes that made them.[18]

In 2900 BC there was no single standard number system in Sumer. In the city of Uruk, more than a dozen different archaic number systems[19] were used for counting different things. One system was used to count discrete objects such as animals. Another system was used for counting volumes of grain and cereal products. A different system was used for volume measures in beer brewing. Another system was used for time and calendar units which seldom exceeded eleven years.[20] These number systems were as different from each other as Roman numerals are from the decimal system we commonly use. Since the same round stylus was used in each of these number systems, the round-stylus number signs had different meanings in the various systems depending on what was being counted.

When the compiler of the Genesis 5 numbers calculated the years/seasons data in years and tenths of years, he used one of several number systems then in common use. The compiler could not have written 16 years and one season as 16.2 years because the decimal point and place-value notation had not yet been invented. Instead, he probably used one or more archaic number sign for tens, a different sign for units and a different sign for tenths. This is called sign-value notation. A scribe familiar with the archaic signs might still have difficulty interpreting them correctly if he did not know in which number system they were written and the context in which they were written.

As discussed in the next section, tens of years were misunderstood as hundreds of years in the Genesis 5 numbers probably when a scribe translated the original archaic numbers into cuneiform using sexagesimal notation. The scribe incorrectly assumed that the archaic numbers were written in the Sumerian proto-sexagesimal number system designed for counting discrete objects such as animals, when actually the Genesis 5 numbers were written in a number system designed for counting volumes of grain. This error converted tens of years to hundreds, years to tens of years, tenths of years to years, and also inflated the ages at death.

Conflicting number systems

Only two simple assumptions are needed for the Genesis 5 numbers to conform to ages of people living today, i.e. that the Septuagint has the original numbers and each of the numbers has one decimal place in modern decimal notation. But men living into their 90's for seven generations is still improbable. In this section, an additional amendment is proposed that reduces by 12 most of the death ages in Table III and also explains why tens of years became hundreds of years.

To understand what probably happened during transmission of the Genesis 5 numbers, we should distinguish how the numbers were processed during four periods of time:

- when the raw birth and death data for Noah's ancestors were recorded during the two centuries before the flood (ca. 3100–2900 BC);
- when the Genesis 5 numbers were calculated from the raw data during the Early Dynastic IIIa period (ca. 2600 BC);
- when the archaic calculated numbers were mistranslated into cuneiform during the Old Babylonian period (ca. 1800 BC); and
- when the proto-Masoretic text of Genesis 5 was altered (ca. 300 BC).

Original contemporaneous records of each ancestor's death were probably created at the times of their deaths for tax reasons and dated by year name by taxation scribes. These separate records would be stored with similar death records in the temple archives in Shuruppak from before and after the flood of 2900 BC. These records included Noah's death and the Genesis numbers were calculated after Noah's death.

The flood story was first written in clay during the Early Dynastic IIIa period.[21] The scribe who compiled the flood story from various oral traditions about previous floods, was probably the same scribe who searched the archives for records of Noah and his ancestors and calculated the Genesis 5 numbers from raw birth and death records which the scribe found in the archives. The Genesis 5 numbers were probably calculated using one of the archaic (pre-cuneiform) Sumerian number systems during the Early Dynastic IIIa period (ca. 2600–2500 BC).

Among the dozen or so number systems used in Sumer, the SHE–GUR system for counting volumes of grain was widely used because grain had become the usual medium of exchange.[22] People who frequently calculated volumes of grain learned to add and subtract in this grain number system. The peculiar SHE–GUR number system used in Shuruppak during the Early Dynastic III period is of special interest to us because records of Noah and his ancestors would most likely be stored in Shuruppak where Noah had been chief executive. A Shuruppak scribe apparently calculated the Genesis 5 numbers during the Early Dynastic III period from birth and death records stored at Shuruppak, and he did his calculations in a peculiar version of the SHE–GUR number system that was used only at Shuruppak.

In the SHE–GUR system, the number of *barigs*[23] in a *gur* changed from time to time. In Shuruppak during the Early Dynastic III period, there were 8 *barigs*[24,25] in a *gur* in the SHE–GUR–MAH number system. There were 4 *barigs* in a *gur* in the later GUR–SAG–GAL number system.[24] There were 5 *barigs* in a *gur* in the still later GUR–LUGAL number system. The Shuruppak *gur* of 8 *barigs*, attested only at Shuruppak,[20] was termed GUR–MAH, meaning large *gur*, to distinguish it from the regular *gur* of 4 or 5 *barigs*.

In the Shuruppak SHE–GUR–MAH number system, ⊣ the *bán* sign represented the basic unit of capacity,[16] a volume of 8.4 to 10 liters. Various number signs represented fractions of a *bán*, especially the *sila* sign[26] which represented one tenth of a *bán*. The SHE–GUR–MAH system units are shown in the following factor diagram. The numbers over the horizontal lines represent ratios of larger units to smaller units. For example, there were six *báns* in a *barig*.

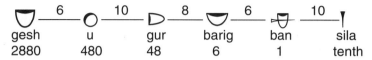

gesh	u	gur	barig	ban	sila
2880	480	48	6	1	tenth

Such volume-measure signs were also used as numerals. According to Schmandt–Besserat,[27] "It appears that the impressed signs, while retaining their primary meaning, for example as grain or land measures and as animal count, acquired a secondary meaning as numerals." This phenomenon "is particularly explicit on tablets where, in the same text, the same signs are used alternately (but according to a different ratio) to express grain measures or numerals."

The Shuruppak scribe who calculated the Genesis 5 numbers probably understood the archaic number signs used in archive records for representing years and months. But adding and subtracting in these archaic number signs used before the flood may have been as difficult for him as adding and subtracting in Roman numerals would be for us. Today, if someone wanted to subtract CCXXIX from CMXLVI, they would probably convert to decimal numbers, do the subtraction in decimals and leave the result in decimals, rather than convert the result to DCCXVII.

The Shuruppak scribe had a similar problem. He probably knew how to add and subtract integers in the animal-counting number system, but this system originally had no signs for fractions, because there was seldom any need to refer to a tenth of a sheep or a fifth of a goat. The scribe also probably knew how to add and subtract integers and fractions in the SHE–GUR grain-measuring number system which already had signs for fractions, originally used to represent fractional cups of grain. The scribe probably converted the Jemdet Nasr year and season numbers he found in the archives into grain number signs so he could more easily add and subtract years and fractional years. Rather than convert the results back into Jemdet Nasr number signs, he left the years and tenths of years in grain number signs. The original Genesis 5 numbers were probably first calculated using SHE–GUR–MAH number signs with *bán* representing year and *sila* representing a tenth of a year, because a *bán* was equal to ten *silas*.

Hundreds of years later during the Old Babylonian period (1800–1600 BC), when a different scribe, perhaps a student scribe, translated these numbers into cuneiform in the classical Sumerian sexagesimal number system, he erroneously assumed that the archaic SHE–GUR–MAH number signs were in the proto-sexagesimal system. He made this error because of similarities in the signs that can be seen in the following diagram:

SHE–GUR–MAH numbers	⟗ —8— ⌣ —6— ⊟ —10— ❙			
	gur	barig	ban	sila
original meaning	48	6	1	tenth
erroneously assumed to be proto-sexagesimal	⟗ —10— ⌣ —6— ○ —10— ⌣			
	geshu	gesh	u	dish
erroneous translation in cuneiform	𐎗	𐏑	⟨	𐏑
meaning in decimals	600	60	10	1

The Babylonian scribe was misled by five similarities between the SHE–GUR–MAH number signs in his received tablet and number signs in the proto-sexagesimal and classical Sumerian sexagesimal systems:

1. In his received tablet the low order *sila* sign resembled the vertical wedge meaning **one** in cuneiform.

2. The *barig* sign in his received tablet resembled the cup-shaped *gesh* sign in proto-sexagesimal.

3. The high-order *gur* sign in his received tablet resembled the cup-shaped *geshu* sign in proto-sexagesimal, but without the small round punch mark.

4. A *bán* was equal to ten *silas*, just as in proto-sexagesimal where *u* meant ten *dish*.

5. A *barig* was equal to six *báns*, just as in proto-sexagesimal where a *gesh* was equal to six *u*.

The presence of the *bán* sign with the distinctive cross stroke alerted the scribe to the fact that the signs were in the SHE–GUR number system which continued to be used in modified form until the final phase of the Old Akkadian period (about 2250 BC).[26] In this number system, a *gur* was equal to 4 *barig*. But in the scribe's received tablet, the number of *barig* in a *gur* was greater than 6 because the tablet showed numbers with up to 6 *barig*. This was not the SHE–GUR system the scribe was familiar with. He probably studied the tablet to determine what other number system may have been used.

Since the low-order *sila* sign was a vertical wedge like the cuneiform sign for **one**, the scribe would assume that *sila* meant units, although it actually meant tenths. He would then reason that if the low-order sign was one, the next higher *bán* sign should mean ten (although it actually meant one) and that agreed with his tablet which had nine *silas* for Methuselah. He would expect the next higher *barig* sign to be 6 *báns* and that also agreed with his tablet which never had more than 5 *báns*. The next larger *gur* sign would be a number greater than 6 *barig* because the tablet sometimes had 6 *barigs* (e.g. for Jared and Methuselah). The scribe would probably assume a *gur* was 10 *barigs*, similar to the number system used during the Jemdet Nasr period,[28] because in his received tablet a *gur* was more than 6 *barigs*. The true value of a Shuruppak *gur* was 8 *barig*, but the scribe apparently did not know that. By assuming a *gur* equal to 10 *barigs*, a *barig* equal to 6 *bán*, and a *bán* equal to 10 *sila*, the ratios alternated 10 then 6 then 10, just like the sexagesimal system. The scribe probably concluded that the numbers were in proto-sexagesimal notation and translated them as such. But he was mistaken, not only about the number system, but also about which number signs represented integers and which were fractions.

When the Genesis 5 numbers were first calculated in the SHE–GUR–MAH number system, a few tens of years could be recorded using the *bán* and *barig* signs. If the number of *báns* exceeded 48, the larger *gur* sign would be used, just as we often count years if the number of months exceeds 12. But suppose the flood occurred when a Shuruppak man was 48 years old and his age was calculated as one *gur* using Shuruppak number signs. Later, when these archaic numbers were translated into classical Sumerian sexagesimal notation, the scribe might easily mistranslate *gur* (meaning 48 in Shuruppak) as the corresponding *geshu* meaning 600. Similarly, the other numbers greater than 48 would be inflated by 12 and then effectively multiplied by ten by mistaking tenths for units. Something like this probably happened to the Genesis 5 numbers when an ancient scribe translated them from archaic numerals into cuneiform.

To use Methuselah as an example, his age 16.7 when his son Lamech was born may have been calculated during the Early Dynastic III period in Shuruppak SHE–GUR–MAH number signs as:

> 2 barig, 4 ban, 7 sila
> $2 \times 6 + 4 \times 1 + .7 = 16.7$

and Methuselah's age at death as:

> 1 gur, 6 barig, 9 sila
> $1 \times 48 + 6 \times 6 + .9 = 84.9$

Later if *gur* was mistranslated as 600, *barig* mistranslated as 60, and *sila* mistranslated as 1, Methuselah's age at death would be translated:

> $1 \times 600 + 6 \times 60 + 9 = 969$

but should have been translated as 84.9.

The above example for Methuselah's age at death (Genesis 5:27) was probably written in archaic and cuneiform numerals as follows (where d indicates the place between integers and fractions):

value:	48	36	.9 =	84.9

original Shuruppak numerals:

value:	600	360	9 =	969.

mistranslation in archaic
proto-sexagesimal:

value:	600	360	9 =	969.

mistranslation in cuneiform
sexagesimal:

The fraction of .9 years in Methuselah's age at death may have resulted from a truncation error by adding Methuselah's age at his son's birth 16.7 to the 68.2 remaining years of his life. Since .2 meant one quarter and .7 meant three quarters, Methuselah's death age would be more accurately calculated 16.75 + 68.25 = 85.0.

If the Genesis 5 numbers were calculated using Shuruppak number signs that were mistranslated as described above, all numbers in Genesis 5 greater than or equal to 48 would be inflated by 12 to numbers greater than or equal to 60. Hence, all numbers 60 or greater in Table III should be reduced by 12 yielding the numbers shown in Table IV:

	Son Born	Total Life
Adam	23.0	81.0
Seth	20.5	79.2
Enosh	19.0	78.5
Kenan	17.0	79.0
Mahalalel	16.5	77.5
Jared	16.2	84.2
Enoch	16.5	36.5
Methuselah	16.7	84.9
Lamech	18.8	63.3
Noah	ca. 33.0	83.0

Table IV

The numbers in Table IV are more plausible than the numbers in Table III, because about five times as many men today live to be 78–85 years old than 90–97 years old. All of the adjustments in Table IV appear in the Total Life column because all of the numbers 60 or greater in Table III are in the Total Life column. The 36.5 years of Enoch is unchanged because 36.5 is less than 60. A chronology based on the numbers in Table IV is given in Table X in Appendix B.

The "six hundred and first year" of Genesis 8:13 was an error for "sixty-first year" (when Noah was 49) according to this modified Septuagint chronology. This was a date calculated by the Priestly editor P whose received text for Genesis 5 and 7:11 was already corrupted with tenths of years mistranslated as years, years as tens of years, and tens of years as hundreds of years. Correcting for these translation errors, the flood occurred when Noah was 48 years old and he died at the age of 83.

Sumerian king lists

Attempts to justify the large numbers of Genesis 5, even by those who dismiss them as mythical, are often based on the still larger numbers found in the Sumerian King Lists[29] which have tens of thousands of years for each king before the flood. These cuneiform tablets give the numbers in *shar*, the cuneiform sign for 3600. For example Ziusudra, the Sumerian Noah, ruled for 10 *shar* years, usually translated as 36,000 years. The Weld Blundell tablet (WB–444) has eight kings[30] ruling a total of 67 *shar* or 241,200 years. The WB–62 tablet[31] lists ten kings ruling a total of more than 126 *shar* years. Berossus provided a similar list totaling 120 *shar* years.

WB-62	shar	Berossus	shar
Alulim	18+	Aloros	10
Alalgar	20	Alaparos	3
Kidunnu	20	Amelon	13
Alimma	6	Ammenon	12
Enmenluanna	6	Amegalaros	18
Dumuzi	8	Daonos	10
Ensipazianna	10	Euedorachos	18
Enmenduranna	20	Amempsinos	10
Sukurlam	8	Otiartes	8
Ziusudra	10	Xisuthros	18
	126+		120

Leaving aside questions about why these names and numbers are different, suppose you found these king lists without knowing that the numbers were in *shar* units. You knew only that they were lengths of reigns of kings of Sumer. Would you not suspect that the numbers represented years? Twenty years is a plausible length of time for a king to reign. Eighteen years and three years are also plausible. If we had not been told that *shar* meant 3600, we could reasonably assume that these numbers represented intervals of time between 3 and 20 years. Could *shar* have been confused with year?

As mentioned above, prior to 2100 BC, archaic numbers were formed with a round stylus. A small diameter round stylus held perpendicular to a tablet made a small circular O impression in a clay tablet and often meant ten. A larger diameter round stylus made a large circular (*shar*) impression that often meant 3600.

In cuneiform, the *shar* sign consisted of four wedges in a diamond arrangement that imitated the large circular round-stylus sign[32] for 3600. In archaic pre-cuneiform writing, years were represented by an incised diamond-shaped time-sign called U_4 by scholars.[33] The diamond-shaped cuneiform sign for *shar* was similar in shape to the U_4 time sign.

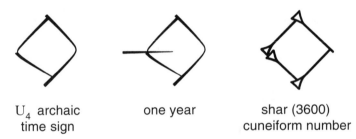

| U_4 archaic time sign | one year | shar (3600) cuneiform number |

An additional stroke or strokes to the left of the U_4 sign indicated the number of years. Since the year strokes were numeric signs, an inexperienced scribe might mistakenly read the remaining U_4 time sign as a numeric sign also. The cuneiform number sign that closely resembled U_4 was *shar*.

The stroked U_4 sign for year was used during the Jemdet Nasr period,[34] the period when Noah was king. By the Early Dynastic IIIa (Fara) period, the stroked U_4 sign for year had been replaced by the *mu* sign:[34]

mu (year)

The scribe who translated the Sumerian king list wrote a *mu* sign for each king, because he probably understood that the numbers represented years and each stroke to the left of the U_4 sign meant one. But the U_4 sign with one stroke meant one year not one *shar* of years.

For some of the kings, fractions of *shar* were represented by additional signs. In the WB–62 cuneiform king list, the first king Alulim reigned 18 *shar*, 4 *geshu*, 10 *ab* years which is usually translated 67,200 years. Having translated the year sign incorrectly as *shar*, the scribe would expect the next sign to be *geshu* meaning 1/6 of a *shar* or 600. However, what the scribe probably saw was a carelessly inscribed archaic sign for month that he read incorrectly as *geshu*.

1 month
archaic time sign[33]   1 geshu (600)
                            archaic number[33]

In the WB–62 cuneiform king list, after the 4 *geshu* signs for king Alulim is a cuneiform sign AB_2 meaning cow[35] with the sign for ten inside it. Ten cows (or any number of cows) would not be expected in a king list and are ignored in modern translations. In this context the sign seems to mean 10 days. The ancient scribe confused the archaic sign for evening with the archaic sign for cow and wrote the equivalent cuneiform sign for cow.

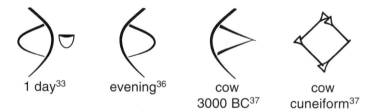

1 day[33]   evening[36]   cow
                                 3000 BC[37]   cow
                                                  cuneiform[37]

If 18 *shar* was a misreading of 18 years, and 4 *geshu* a misreading of 4 months, and 10 cows a misreading of 10 evenings, king Alulim probably reigned 18 years, 4 months, and 10 days.

From about 2600 BC to about 2000 BC archaic numerals coexisted with cuneiform numerals.[38] This is approximately the same time that Sumerian cuneiform characters were being adapted to the Akkadian language. But the U_4 signs for year, month and day had already been replaced by cuneiform signs before the ED III period (before 2600 BC).[34] The scribe who translated the original pre-flood king list into cuneiform and sexagesimal numerals was apparently not aware that the old U_4 diamond signs on his received tablet was the old way of writing years, because the stroked diamond had not been used for hundreds of years. He probably assumed that the U_4 signs and the horizontal strokes were separate number signs, perhaps because the old clay tablet with Jemdet Nasr signs was worn and difficult to read. The scribe was apparently unaware that the U_4 sign that resembled *shar* was not *shar* and did not mean 3600.

The Sumerian Noah reigned for 10 years, not 10 *shar* years. The Sumerian king list numbers were mistranslated by an ancient scribe, just as the Genesis 5 numbers were mistranslated by another ancient scribe.

Family genealogy

Noah or his father Lamech may have compiled a list of names of their ancestors by questioning elderly relatives who remembered many of the names and ages. The most elderly relative Noah could have questioned was Jared who could not have remembered Adam who died 15.0 years before Jared was born. Jared's father Mahalalel could not have remembered Adam, because Mahalalel was only 1.5 when Adam died. Jared's grandfather Kenan was 18.5 when Adam died and hence may have remembered Adam. But Noah or Lamech could not have questioned Kenan who died when Methuselah was only 12.8 and before Lamech and Noah were born. Mahalalel's son Jared would be the most likely source of the names of Noah's ancestors, but he would not have remembered Adam.

Jared died when Noah was 16.0 years old and Lamech was 34.8 years old. Noah's sons were born long after Jared died and their births were not recorded in the ancestor list of births and deaths because Noah's sons had not yet been born at the time information was obtained from Jared.

Lamech's age at Noah's birth was recorded as 18.8 which is the first time in Genesis 5 that a fractional year was not a quarter year. This suggests that Noah's birth was recorded in years and lunar month truncated to tenths of years during Noah's lifetime, perhaps when he was a teenager.

Calculation of the Genesis 5 numbers from the ancestor list of births and deaths was done after Noah's death, because the numbers included Noah's age at death recorded in Genesis 9:28. Noah's death was probably recorded routinely by Shuruppak scribes in the same archives where deaths of Noah's ancestors and other nobles were recorded. A later scribe who searched the official death records for data on Noah and his ancestors and who calculated the Genesis 5 numbers probably lived during the Early Dynastic III period, three hundred years after Noah's death, when oral traditions of the flood were first committed to writing.[21]

Eight hundred years after the flood traditions and the Genesis 5 numbers were first written in clay, Sumerian literature was collected and systematically translated into Akkadian by the scribal schools of Babylonia[39] during the

Old Babylonian period (1800–1600 BC). This was the period when the Atrahasis version of the flood story was written, or at least the copy that has survived to the present. This period was the most likely time for the original Sumerian version of the flood story to be translated into Akkadian. At the same time, the archaic genealogy numbers that accompanied the flood story were probably also translated – actually mistranslated – into cuneiform in the sexagesimal number system.

Land and tax records

Information on Noah's ancestors may have been recorded by the Shuruppak government along with information on other major Shuruppak land owners. About 3000 BC, land sales in Sumer began to be recorded on stone monuments and clay tablets.[40] These tablets were stored in the government (temple) archives along with tax and administration records. Most of the earliest records were not dated and would therefore be of little use in constructing a numeric genealogy. During the Ur III Period (about 2100 BC) land sale documents were routinely dated with the regnal year, month, and day.[41] During the pre-Sargonic (Early Dynastic IIIb) period, documents recording land and slave sales were dated with years, but not with month and day.[42]

Perhaps earlier in Noah's time, some land documents were already being dated by regnal year or year name, although this is unattested in the Jemdet Nasr period. By comparing the recorded year names to a king list, an ancient scribe could reconstruct a cumulative chronology showing the passing of title from father to son to grandson. This is assuming that whenever a landowner died, a government scribe prepared a new tablet giving the death year and the name of the rightful heir so that the current owner would be on record as the person responsible for paying taxes. Although taxes were often collected in the form of days of forced labor, the merchant class and major landowners would pay in commodities. The tax collectors would need to know exactly who was responsible for payment and when a taxpayer died who the successor taxpayer was. The land and tax records thus became a depository for genealogical information especially for wealthy families whose ancestral land was passed down from father to son for several generations. Land records often included the names of the paternal grandfather and father in addition to the name of an heir. For example, a deed from the Akkad Dynasty gave the name of one seller as Sin-alshu, son of Ayer-ilum, son of Pu-balum the shepherd.[43]

In addition to registering land transfers, births were sometimes registered.[44] Although registering births is not attested during the Jemdet Nasr period when Noah and his ancestors lived, a Shuruppak temple may have recorded some births of nobles and priests who had a special relationship with the temple, just as people in recent centuries who were members of a church or synagogue had their births or baptisms recorded. In addition, some of the genealogy information may have come from stories told by Jared who may have recalled how old some ancestors were when they inherited the ancestral land, or how old some of them were when their sons were born, and the regnal year or year name when some of these events occurred. Fragments of this data may have been compiled by Lamech, Noah, or one of their scribes and stored in the Shuruppak archives.

Centuries later, a scribe constructing a genealogy based on regnal years would need an accurate king list. Such a list may have included the exact number of years, months and days that each king reigned. Suppose the scribe calculated that an ancestor's birth occurred during the reign of king W and his death occurred during the reign of the next king Z. To calculate how old the ancestor was when he died, the regnal year of the ancestor's death date would be calculated and added to the number of years and months in the reign of king W. Then the regnal year of the ancestor's birth date would be subtracted from the total. To simplify these calculations, the scribe might convert months and seasons to tenths of years of the kings' reigns.

By including fractional years of each king's reign in the calculations, the scribe would introduce a distortion into the time scale whenever a new king began his reign. No such distortion would occur between two dates within the same king's reign. In the following example, assume that king W reigned 20.5 years and Abcde's birth occurred in year 10 of king W and Abcde's death occurred in year 36 of king Z.

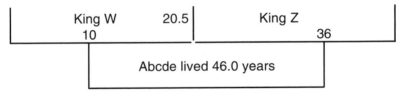

Abcde's calculated age at death would be $36 + 20.5 - 10 = 46.5$ years, with a distortion of half a year. But in the following example where king W reigned for say 40.5 years, both the birth and death occur during the reign of the same king and no distortion results. Abcde's age at death would be $36 - 10 = 26.0$ years.

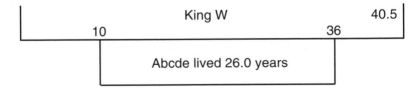

In the following Genesis 5 extract from Table X in Appendix B, the fractional years provide evidence of the distortions explained above. The fractional years (.0 or .2 or .5 or .7) are in the original sequence, but occur in pairs or triplets. The ages in each pair or triplet have the same fractional year because they occurred during the same king's reign.

0.0	Adam born
23.0	Seth born

43.5	Enosh born
62.5	Kenan born
79.5	Mahalalel born

81.0	Adam died
96.0	Jared born

102.2	Seth died
112.2	Enoch born

141.5	Kenan died
145.5	Lamech born

164.2	Noah born
180.2	Jared died

In one of these groups, the fractional year is the same for three consecutive births: Enosh (43.5), Kenan (62.5), and Mahalalel (79.5). This is the result of the ages at birth for Enosh and Kenan being round numbers. But after Mahalalel's birth, the fractional year shifts back to .0 because Mahalalel was 16.5 when his son Jared was born. Assuming that the birth and death dates were recorded only in regnal years with no months or days, the shift from a .5 series to a .0 series was an artifact of calculations made by an ancient scribe who used fractional years from the king list. Enosh, Kenan, and Mahalalel were born during the reign of the same king. The king's reign ended before Jared was born and his reign was recorded in years plus half a year. This half year was included in the ancient scribe's calculation of how old Mahalalel was (16.5) when Jared was born.

Assuming that most or all of the birth and death dates were recorded in regnal years or year names without months or days, then any fractional years that appear in the Table X chronology would be the result of distortions from using fractional years in king list numbers. If this assumption is correct, then the fractional year should change in Table X whenever the length of a reign includes a nonzero fractional year. When we compare the Sumerian king lists to the chronology of Table X, the periods of time corresponding to pairs or triplets in Table X should approximately match the lengths of the kings' reigns. And that is what we find.

Matching Genesis 5 to the King List

The Sumerian King Lists WB-444[29,30] and WB-62[29,31] and the corresponding list from Berossus provide the number of years for each of the kings who reigned during the lives of Noah's ancestors. Other fragmentary king lists have been found.[45] In the following table, some of the kings have been rearranged to correspond with the sequence in WB-444:

WB–444		WB–62		Berossus	
Alulim	8	Alulim	18:4	Aloros	10
Alalgar	10	Alalgar	20	Alaparos	3
omitted	–	…kidunnu	20	omitted	–
omitted	–	…alimma	6	Ammenon	12
Enmenluanna	12	Enmenluanna	6	Amelon	13
Enmengalanna	8	omitted	–	Amegalaros	18
Dumuzi shepherd	10	Dumuzi shepherd	8	Daonos shepherd	10
Ensipazianna	8	Ensipazianna	10	Amempsinos	10
Enmenduranna	5:5	Enmenduranna	20	Euedorachos	18
Ubartutu	5:1	Sukurlam	8	Otiartes	8
omitted	–	Ziusudra	10	Xisuthros	18

The above three king lists have been consolidated into the following Table V with fractional years restored. Since the Genesis 5 chronology in Table X begins 98.2 years earlier than the Sumerian king list, three nameless kings in the early Jemdet Nasr period have been added to the beginning of the king list to fill the gap. There may have been more than three. These nameless kings are not necessary to match the king list to the Table X chronology from the death of Seth to the flood. Since the three versions of the king list give greatly different numbers for each king, the numbers in Table V were chosen because they result in a match with the chronology of Table X. The names of the two Larsa kings Kidunnu and Alimma are partly illegible.[31] They did not reign from Larsa because Larsa was not a city during the Jemdet Nasr period.[46] Perhaps one king (called Ammenon by Berossus) from Nippur was listed, but the city and king name was illegible on the original tablet and later a Larsa scribe inserted his own city name[47] and a legendary name (Alimma) that resembled the nearly illegible name on the original tablet.

	kinglist	theory	theory cum.	city
nameless king X		30.5	30.5	
nameless king Y		49.5	80.0	
nameless king Z		18.2	98.2	
Alulim	18:4	18.7	117.0	Eridu
(Aloros)	8	7.7	124.7	Eridu
Alalgar (Alaparos)	10	9.7	134.5	Eridu
Alimma (Ammenon)	12	12.2	146.7	?Nippur[47]
Enmenluanna (Amelon)	6	6.2	153.0	Badtibira
Enmengalanna	8	8.2	161.2	Badtibira
Dumuzi the shepherd	10	10.0	171.2	Badtibira
Ensipazianna	8	8.0	179.2	Larak
Enmenduranna	18	18.5	197.7	Sippar
Sukurlam [Lamech]	5:1	5.0	202.7	Shuruppak
Ziusudra [Noah]	10	9.7	212.4	Shuruppak

Table V

Names in parentheses in Table V are from Berossus.

When the cumulative numbers from Table V are combined with the Genesis 5 numbers from Table X, the two sets of numbers fit together nicely. Horizontal lines divide the following chronology into reigns of kings in Table VI. The regnal years are one greater than the calculated years because a king's first year is year one rather than year zero.

Era Year	
0.0	Nameless king X reigning
0.0	Adam born
23.0	Seth born in year 24 of king X.

30.5	Nameless king Y began reign
43.5	Enosh born in year 14 of king Y.
62.5	Kenan born in year 33 of king Y.
79.5	Mahalalel born in year 50 of king Y.

80.0	Nameless king Z began reign
81.0	Adam died in year 2 of king Z.
96.0	Jared born in year 17 of king Z.

98.2	Alulim began reign at Eridu.
102.2	Seth died in year 5 of king Alulim.
112.2	Enoch born in year 15 of king Alulim.

117.0	Aloros began reign at Habur/Eridu.
122.0	Enosh died in year 6 of Aloros.
124.7	Alalgar began reign at Eridu
128.7	Methuselah born in year 5 of Alalgar
134.5	Alimma (Ammenon) began reign
141.5	Kenan died in year 8 of king Alimma.
145.5	Lamech born in year 12 of king Alimma.
146.7	Enmenluanna (Amelon) began reign at Badtibira.
148.7	Enoch died in year 3 of king Amelon.
153.0	Enmengalanna began reign at Badtibira.
157.0	Mahalalel died in year 5 of king Enmengalanna.
161.2	Dumuzi the shepherd began reign at Badtibira.
164.2	Noah born in year 4 of king Dumuzi.
171.2	Ensipazianna began reign at Larak.
179.2	Enmenduranna began reign at Sippar.
180.2	Jared died in year 2 of king Enmenduranna.
197.7	Sukurlam (Lamech) began reign at Shuruppak.
202.7	Ziusudra (Noah) began reign at Shuruppak.
208.7	Lamech died in year 7 of Noah's reign.
212.4	the six-day flood occurred in year 10 of Noah's reign.

Table VI

Except for the reign of Noah's father Lamech, the birth and death dates were all recorded in regnal years without month or day. Many of the reign lengths in the king list were recorded in quarter years (seasons) with some reigns at the end having years and months. Quarter years are truncated to tenths of years in the above table.

The chronology in Table VI ends with Lamech (SU.KUR.LAM in Sumerian)[48] and his son Noah (Ziusudra) who were both kings of Shuruppak according to the Sumerian king list WB–62.[50] The combined chronology in

Table VI spans almost the entire Jemdet Nasr period which ended with the river flood of 2900 BC.

Occupation of Shuruppak is not attested prior to the Jemdet Nasr period[51] and therefore building of Shuruppak probably began during the Jemdet Nasr period. This suggests that the Table X numbers begin with Adam about 3113 BC because prior to 3113 BC there were no individual property owners at Shuruppak and therefore no Shuruppak real estate records existed prior to Adam. The Adam of Genesis 5 was not the first man; he was the first of Noah's paternal ancestors to own recorded Shuruppak real estate. His actual name has been lost.

Personal names of Noah's ancestors may have been represented on stone markers (ancient *kudurru*) or land sale tablets, but some of the names may have been illegible or untranslatable. Adam's name may have been represented as a unique sign or pictograph that resembled ⟨⟨⟩⟩ the Sumerian pictograph for man and was copied as if it were the sign for man. Later this sign was copied as a proper name and translated into Hebrew as *adam*, a Hebrew word for man. Likewise Enosh was another Hebrew word for man or men or mortal and may have originated with a unique pictographic name that scribes were unable to translate. Alternatively, the name Adam may have been *A-da-mu* that was already being used during the third millennium, both as a personal name and as a divine name.[52]

Why the numbers were not lost

Although most of the flood story was transmitted orally until syllabic writing was sufficiently developed to record narratives, the genealogy details in Genesis 5 are so precise that it is unlikely that they were passed down by oral tradition through several generations. Ancient Sumer was a cosmopolitan society, not an isolated tribe conducive to fidelity of oral transmission. Either the numbers of Genesis 5 were recorded before the death of Jared or they were fiction. If not fiction, then the source data for the Genesis 5 genealogy was probably recorded on contemporaneous clay tablets or stone monuments. The place where birth and death records would have the greatest chance of survival was the Shuruppak archives where other government and temple records were stored and where government archivists were committed to preserving old records.

Before the flood, Noah or Lamech could have requested that a temple scribe do a search for records on their ancestors. Most of the names and numbers of Genesis 5 could have come from land ownership records in the archives that was supplemented with birth and death information from Jared's memory when Noah was still a teenager. The scribe may have combined this genealogy data and recorded the year of birth and death for each of Noah's ancestors back to Adam. The scribe would keep a copy of this genealogy in the archives, which may be how the information in Genesis 5 survived.

Another possibility is that a title search was done after the flood by a government scribe when Noah's ancestral land was sold to pay his taxes and debts. To establish whether anyone else had claim to Noah's ancestral land, the scribe may have searched the land records back as far as the chain of title could be traced. The chain of title went back more than 200 years to the beginning of the Jemdet Nasr period, but was broken at Adam's record because the previous owner's record could not be found. Prior to Adam's record, land owners may not have been recorded in Shuruppak because Shuruppak had not yet been built.

Ancestor names and death years from a land title search, along with birth years from temple and family records would have been made part of the official record of a flood-related court decision to sell Noah's ancestral land. Instead of being lost with the other real estate records that probably existed only as single copies, the list of Noah's ancestors may have survived because it was stored with other court records related to Noah and the flood and later scribes made copies of these records.

After the flood story was written in clay and the numbers in Noah's ancestor list were calculated during the Early Dynastic IIIa period, the tablets may have remained in the Shuruppak archives for several centuries. From time to time these old tablets were recopied, translated, edited, rearranged, combined, extracted, and summarized. Some of these extracts were carried to other cities before Shuruppak was abandoned. During the Old Babylonian period after 1800 BC, when Sumerian literature was collected and translated into Akkadian, the calculated genealogy data was probably translated from archaic Shuruppak number signs into cuneiform sexagesimal notation by a Babylonian scribe. The scribe mistranslated the genealogy numbers and his cuneiform mistranslation was stored in the Babylonian archives.

In the late sixth century BC during the exile period, a Judean priest who was collecting material for Genesis or the Toledoth Book[53] probably found these genealogy records in the Babylonian archives, perhaps with the help of a friendly Babylonian priest who provided a translation of the clay tablet records, including the source of Genesis 5 and a summary of the flood story. Transmission of the flood story is discussed more fully in Chapter 8 herein.

Conclusions

If the numbers in Genesis 5 represent ages of real people, then the Septuagint has the primary version of Genesis 5, because it is the only version (after adjusting by ten and other corrections)[12] that is consistent with human life as we know it. The Masoretic and Samaritan versions of Genesis 5 are secondary and reflect attempts by their respective editors to correct what they believed to be errors. Although we cannot be certain that the people mentioned in Genesis 5 were real people, there is nothing in the Septuagint version that strains credulity once the notational system is understood.

The excessive size of the numbers is the result of a scribe during the Old Babylonian period confusing archaic number signs in two different Shuruppak number systems. This mistake resulted in ages at death being inflated by twelve, and tenths of years being changed to years, years changed to tens of years, and tens of years changed to hundreds of years .

The original birth and death data was recorded on clay tablets stored in Shuruppak archives during the Jemdet Nasr period before the Euphrates River flood of 2900 BC and shortly after Noah's death. About three hundred years after the flood, during the Early Dynastic IIIa period, a scribe calculated the Genesis 5 numbers from the archival records. He used the Shuruppak SHE–GUR–MAH number system to record his calculations using archaic round-stylus numbers. The Early Dynastic IIIa period was the only period when a *gur* was equal to eight *barigs* and this peculiar SHE–GUR–MAH number system is attested only in Shuruppak[20] where the archival records of Noah's ancestors were most likely to be stored.

Several hundred years later, during the Old Babylonian period, a scribe who was translating the flood story into cuneiform, misread the SHE–GUR–MAH number signs as proto-sexagesimal signs. The Septuagint Genesis 5 numbers were based on that mistranslation. The numbers were furthered altered in the Masoretic and Samaritan versions of Genesis 5. After corrections are made for mistranslated Shuruppak number signs, the Septuagint version of Genesis 5 appears to be an ordinary family genealogy, subject to the same problems and uncertainties that modern family genealogists face when writing about their great-grandfather's great-grandfather.

Noah lived to be 83 years old and Methuselah lived to be 85. All of the antediluvians except Noah fathered their first sons in their late teens or early twenties just as young men do today. The river flood of 2900 BC occurred when Noah was 48 years old and had been king for ten years.

The numbers in the Sumerian king lists were also mistranslated by an ancient scribe who confused the archaic sign for year with the cuneiform sign for 3600.

References

1.   Scholars often treat the names in Genesis 5 as fictional eponyms similar to the eponymous names in the Genesis 10 table of nations and Genesis 11 (see chapter 9 herein). I will argue that Genesis 5 was compiled by a different hand and is a surviving fragment of a real estate title search made from archival records for Noah's ancestral land in Shuruppak. The names Adam (man) and Enosh (man) in Genesis 5:3–11 were place holders for men whose names were missing or illegible in the land records and had no connection with the mythical generic man (adam) of Genesis 2–4 until a Genesis author combined parts of Babylonian myths during the exile.

2.   James A. Borland, "Did People Live to be Hundreds of Years Old Before the Flood? Yes", in *The Genesis Debate*, Ronald F. Youngblood (editor), (Nashville: Thomas Nelson, 1986).

3.   James Barr, "Archbishop Ussher and Biblical Chronology", *Bulletin of the John Rylands Univ. Libr. of Manchester*, 67(2) (Great Britain: 1985), pp. 575–608.

4.   Emanuel Tov, *Textual Criticism of the Hebrew Bible*, (Minneapolis: Fortress Press, 1992), pp. 11, 352.

5.   John Skinner, *A Critical and Exegetical Commentary on Genesis* (Edinburgh: T&T Clark, 1930), pp. 134, 233.

6.   Ralph W. Klein, "Archaic Chronologies and the Textual History of the Old Testament", *Harvard Theol Review*, 67 (1974), pp. 255–263.

7.   Gerhard Larsson, "The Chronology of the Pentateuch: A Comparison of the MT and LXX", *Journal of Biblical Literature*, 102 (1983), pp. 401–409.

8.   Charles M. Laymon (editor), *The Interpreter's One-Volume Commentary on the Bible*, (Nashville: Abingdon Press, 1971), p. 1227. See also John William Wevers, *Notes on the Greek Text of Genesis* (Atlanta, Georgia: Scholars Press, 1993), p. xv: "The LXX may [sometimes] interpret its text incorrectly; it is not a perfect document, but it is far and away the earliest, the closest in time to the original authors, that we have."

9.   Tov, op. cit., p. 9.

10.   Hans Walter Wolff, "Problems Between the Generations in the Old Testament", in *Essays in Old Testament Ethics*, James L. Crenshaw and John T. Willis (editors), (New York: Ktav Publishing House, 1974), pp. 77–95.

11.   Lloyd R. Bailey, *Genesis, Creation, and Creationism*, (New York: Paulist Press, 1993), p. 58.

12.   Before discussing how the Genesis 5 numbers were originally calculated in an archaic pre-cuneiform number system, it is first necessary to understand what the numbers mean. For ease of understanding, the numbers are represented here in modern decimal notation. But I am *not* saying that tenths of years were ever represented in a decimal system by the

Babylonians or the Judeans. And I am *not* saying that they ever represented tenths of years as decimal fractions in the sexagesimal system. The scale of the original numbers was distorted by a factor of ten because of confusion between two archaic number systems that were not decimal. This is explained in detail in this chapter under "Conflicting number systems."

13.   M. E. L. Mallowan, "Noah's Flood Reconsidered", *Iraq*, 26 (1964), pp. 62–82, especially p. 81.

14.   Georges Ifrah, *From One to Zero: A Universal History of Numbers*, (New York: Viking Penguin, 1985), pp. 371, 379. Place-value (positional) number systems are like our decimal system. Each digit has a different value depending on which place or column it appears in a multi-column number. For example, in the tens place the digit 3 means thirty, but in the hundreds place the digit 3 means three hundred. Place-value numbers were first used about 2000 BC in Babylonia based on the Sumerian sexagesimal system.

15.   Jöran Friberg, *The Third Millennium Roots of Babylonian Mathematics*, Vol. I, Research Report 1978–9 (Sweden: University of Göteborg, Department of Mathematics, 1978), p. 44.

16.   Jöran Friberg, "Numbers and Measures in the Earliest Written Records", *Scientific American*, 250 (Feb, 1984), pp. 110–118, especially p. 116.

17.   Ifrah, op. cit., p. 325.

18.   Hans J. Nissen, Peter Damerow, Robert K. Englund, *Archaic Bookkeeping* (Chicago: University of Chicago Press, 1993), p. 118.

19.   Nissen, op. cit., pp. 28–29. The SHE–GUR system is summarized on page 48 of Nissan.

20.   Robert K. Englund, UCLA, personal communication.

21.   Mallowan, op. cit., pp. 69–70. Fara period is Early Dynastic IIIa.

22.   Denise Schmandt–Besserat, *Before Writing, From Counting to Cuneiform*, Vol. I (Austin, Texas: University of Texas Press, 1992), pp. 192–194, especially 193.

23.   *Barig* is sometimes spelled *bariga* or *nigida*.

24.   Friberg, *The Third Millennium Roots*, op. cit., p. 43.

25.   Jöran Friberg, *The Early Roots of Babylonian Mathematics*, Vol. II, Research Report 1979–15 (Sweden: University of Göteborg, Department of Mathematics, 1979), p. 16.

26.   Nissen, op. cit., pp. 48–49.

27.   Schmandt–Besserat, op. cit., p. 153.

28.   Friberg, *The Third Millennium Roots*, op. cit., p. 42.

29.   Gerhard F. Hasel, "Genealogies of Gen 5 and 11 and Their Alleged Babylonian Background," *Andrews University Seminary Studies*, 16 (1978), pp. 361–374, especially 366.

30.   Thorkild Jacobsen, *The Sumerian King List* (Illinois: University of Chicago Press, 1939), pp. 69–77.

31.   S. Langdon, "The Chaldean Kings Before the Flood", *Journal of Royal Asiatic Society* (1923), pp. 251–259.

32.   Nissen, op. cit., p. 140.

33.   Nissen, op. cit., pp. 28, 37. The U_4 sign was originally a pictogram of the rising sun.

34.   Robert K. Englund, "Administrative Timekeeping in Ancient Mesopotamia", *Journal of the Economic and Social History of the Orient*, 31, pp. 121–185, especially p. 183.

35.   Langdon, op. cit., p. 256.

36.   Englund, op. cit., pp. 166–167.

37.   Nissen, op. cit., p. 124, Fig. 106 in Jemdet Nasr and ED III columns, rotated 90 degrees.

38.   Ifrah, op. cit., pp. 174–176.

39.   Mallowan, op. cit., p. 66.

40.   J. N. Postgate, *Early Mesopotamia*, (London: Routledge, 1994), p. 66.

41.   Ignace J. Gelb, Piotr Steinkeller, Robert M. Whiting, *Earliest Land Tenure Systems in The Near East: Ancient Kudurrus*, (Chicago: Oriental Institute of the Univ. of Chicago, 1989), Plates 155–166.

42.   ibid. Plates 131, 133.

43.   Postgate, op. cit., p. 95.

44.   Postgate, op. cit., p. 281.

45.   J. J. Finkelstein, "The Antediluvian Kings: A University of California Tablet," *Journal of Cuneiform Studies*, 17 (1963), pp. 39–51. King list UCBC 9–1819, that has missing names, misspelled names, and numbers that are missing digits, was probably written by a student scribe from memory.

46.   Robert McCormick Adams, *Heartland of Cities*, (Chicago: University of Chicago Press, 1981), Fig. 18.

47.   Jacobson, op. cit., p. 72, note 17.

48.   Langdon, op. cit., p. 258, line 15 and note 5. Langdon in note 5 says "Written SU–KUR–LAM" but in line 15 of the tablet translation he has "Aradgin son of Uburtutu" instead of "SU–KUR–LAM son of Uburtutu". This Aradgin interpretation is disputed by Jacobsen.[49]

49.   Jacobsen, op. cit., p. 76, last sentence of note 32.

50.   Langdon, op. cit., pp. 258–259; see also Chapter 9 herein.

51.   J. N. Postgate, "The transition from Uruk to Early Dynastic", in *Gamdat Naṣr Period or Regional Style?*, Uwe Finkbeiner and Wolfgang Röllig (editors), (Wiesbaden: Dr. Ludwig Reichert Verlag, 1986), Fig. 1, Fig. 9.

52.   Cyrus H. Gordon, "Notes on Proper Names in the Ebla Tablets" in *Eblaite Personal Names and Semitic Name–Giving*, editor Alfonso Archi, (Rome: Missione archeologica italiana in Siria, 1988), pp. 153–158, esp. p. 154.

53.   Antony F. Campbell and Mark A. O'Brien, *Sources of the Pentateuch*, (Minneapolis: Fortress Press, 1993), pp. xvii, 23.

8

Transmission of the Flood Story

*"No passion in the world is equal to the
passion to alter someone else's draft."*

H. G. Wells

In Chapter 2, many similarities were noted between the six surviving Ancient Near East versions of Noah's flood story:

Ziusudra Epic (in Sumerian)
Atrahasis Epic (in Akkadian)
Gilgamesh Epic (in Akkadian)
Genesis 6–9 (in Hebrew)
Berossus version (in Greek)
Moses of Khoren version (in Armenian)

The strong similarities between these six versions indicate a large degree of literary dependency or affinity. The six versions are editions of the same story. The similarities are most impressive when comparing Gilgamesh XI with Atrahasis, because the editor of Gilgamesh XI copied much of the material from the epic of Atrahasis,[1] and even used the name Atrahasis at line 187. The six versions share common story elements and distinctive words and phrases. For example, the phrases "seven days and seven nights" or "forty days and forty nights" are found in four of the six versions. In three of the six versions birds are sent out and returned. In three versions the hero saves "the breath of life" or "the seed of life" or "the seed of mankind." In five versions the hero offered a sacrifice after the barge grounded. In three versions the hero's name is very similar: (Ziusudra, Xisuthros and Khsisuthros).

As discussed in Chapter 2, the flood story originated in the Early Dynastic I period about 2900 BC.[2] In 2900 BC, writing was used mostly for accounting and was not yet able to record the whole syllabic structure and flow of spoken language until the Early Dynastic III period (about 2600 BC).[3] Syllabic writing continued to evolve before and after the flood, but three hundred years passed before it was possible for the full flood story to be written in narrative form. During this period of oral transmission, story tellers, epic poets, bards and minstrels apparently mythologized mundane events in the story.

Three hundred years is a long time for a legend to be transmitted orally. Most disasters are forgotten within a few generations unless the details of the disaster are turned into a memorable song or a ritual such as an annual commemoration by which the young people are taught about the event that initiated the ritual. The flood of 2900 BC would have been quickly forgotten had it not been described in a mythical story about a king who was friendly with the gods and who saved "the seed of mankind" from destruction.

It is also possible that details of the flood story were remembered during these centuries of oral transmission because primitive outlines of the story were written in clay by story tellers using pictographs, numbers, and rebus-like syllable signs, not to record every word, but as a memory aid to remind the story teller of what story element came next in the story sequence.

Shortly after the flood there were probably several stories about the flood because different witnesses would give different (and to some degree conflicting) versions of events. It would be expected that each witness would include details not known by the other witnesses. After Noah's barge grounded near Eridu and his sons went to Sippar and Noah and his wife went to Dilmun, there would be at least three different versions of the flood story:

Noah's story at Dilmun

Shem's story at Sippar

a priest's story at Eridu

Some of these witnesses were present at the same events. But there were also some events where all witnesses were not present. For example, Shem's journey on foot up the Tigris River to Mount Judi could not have been witnessed by Noah or the priest at Eridu because Noah and his sons separated when they left Eridu. And it is not likely that Noah and his sons later agreed on one version of the story, because according to Berossus, after the family separated, the flood hero never saw the others again.

After each witness told and retold his own version of the flood story, a body of oral tradition was probably recited in each city where the witnesses lived. As years passed, these bodies of oral tradition were partially merged by story tellers who collected new story details from travelers from the other cities. Some of the details became garbled during this merger of traditions, especially after witnesses were dead and unable to correct misunderstandings.

Noah's story

Of the three eyewitness versions of the flood story, the Dilmun version from Noah would be the most detailed, although it would be lacking details from the Eridu priest and from Shem's journey up the Tigris. The sequence of events in the flood story probably came from Noah's memory, although the precise chronology of dates by month and day in Genesis 7:11, 7:24, and 8:3–5, etc. were probably reconstructed more than two thousand years later.[4]

Barge construction details probably also came from Noah, although these were recollections of a chief executive who had never built a boat, and not the technical knowledge of an architect or shipwright.

A Dilmun story teller may have interviewed Noah and his wife and recorded in clay some pictures and numbers for the datable events that Noah and his wife could remember. The story teller would want to interview Noah for the same reason reporters interview celebrities today. Noah had a very full and interesting life that would make a good story.

Noah probably told the interviewer that he had escaped a flood, and after the barge grounded he had offered a sacrifice at the top of a hill. But as the story was orally transmitted, later story tellers left their listeners with a false impression that Noah offered the sacrifice at the top of a mountain not a hill, and that Noah's barge had grounded on the mountain.

Shem's story

As with Noah, his son Shem is a legendary character because there is no archaeological evidence that he existed. But if Shem was a real person he was a witness to some events that occurred after Noah's family separated. The second version of the flood story may have come from Shem and his brothers and wives at Sippar and included details of their "roundabout" journey on foot from Eridu to Sippar. These details would not have been known to Noah who never saw his relatives again. However, it is possible that Shem's story came from Noah, who may have reported what Shem was instructed to do, not what he actually did.

The apparent conflict between Genesis 6:19 and 7:2 regarding the number of animals on the ark may have resulted from Shem's story being different from Noah's story. The conflict need not be resolved by disregarding one or the other estimate because both may be correct. The "two pairs of every kind" of Genesis 6:19 may be the animals that Noah gave to Shem at Eridu and which Shem and his brothers and their wives took to Sippar. Shem's story would say two, while Noah's story would say seven.

As discussed in Chapter 5 in connection with a legend recorded by Moses of Khoren,[5] after the barge grounded, Shem and his brothers and their wives traveled northwest on foot, probably with some of the animals. They traveled from Eridu up the Tigris River to a "small plain at the foot of an extensive mountain" which was probably Mount Judi in the mountains of Ararat. Later at Sippar, Shem mentioned that they had floated for a year on his father's cattle boat and came down from the heights of Mount Judi. This led some story tellers to falsely assume that the boat had grounded on Mount Judi in the mountains of Ararat. This misunderstanding became a permanent part of Shem's story and erroneously linked the grounding place to the mountains of Ararat.

Later, when a Sippar story teller heard a traveler from Eridu mention that Noah had sacrificed on top of a hill, the story teller would naturally assume that the traveler was referring to a hill/mountain in the mountains of Ararat. This would reinforce the earlier error that the barge had grounded on Mount Judi in the mountains of Ararat. Shem knew that the barge had grounded on a mud flat near the shore of the "Lower Sea" near Eridu, but after Shem was dead he was no longer able to correct the story teller's mistakes.

Shem apparently did not contribute any new genealogy data, because his own birth date as defined by his father's age was not included in the surviving text. Shem did not become king of Shuruppak and did not inherit Noah's ancestral land, and therefore the scribe who calculated the Genesis 5 numbers omitted Shem from the list. The 500 years of Genesis 5:32 and the 100 and 500 years of Genesis 11:10–11 are round numbers which suggests they are estimates made many years after Shem died.

In 2900 BC, Noah's family genealogy was not yet written and would not be written for another 300 years. However, the birth and death records of Shuruppak nobles on which Noah's genealogy would be based were probably stored safely in the temple archives at Shuruppak. When news of Noah's death reached the temple, a scribe recorded Noah's death on a new tablet that he stored in the archives along with the birth and death records of Noah's ancestors and other Shuruppak nobles. The Genesis 5 numbers would have been forgotten if left to oral transmission.

However, most or all of the names and genealogy information on Shem's descendants in Genesis 11:10–26 appear to be fictitious (see Chapter 9, pp. 152–153). The numbers were fabricated, the names were eponymous, and there are no stories attached to these names which suggests that many generations passed before anyone among Noah's descendents took an interest in collecting family stories, names and ages. Family history, even of modern origin, typically survives only if family members take an interest in it every few generations and record the memories of the old people before they die. If this was done by Noah's descendants, little or none of it has survived prior to Abraham. The genealogical data linking Noah to Abraham is not reliable.

Shem's contribution to the flood story seems to have been solely his version of events during the roundabout journey to Sippar by way of Mount Judi after the barge grounded near Eridu. Some of Shem's story about this journey survived long enough to be included in a book about the flood referred to by Moses of Khoren,[5] and alluded to by Berossus, although this part of the story was not included in Genesis or the Babylonian epics. Shem's orally transmitted story from Sippar may have merged with Noah's orally transmitted story from Dilmun prior to 2600 BC.

A priest's story

The third version of the flood story may have came from a priest of Enki at Eridu who gave a supernatural slant to the facts. This Eridu version would not have been known to Shem at Sippar nor to Noah at Dilmun because some of the described events occurred after Noah and his sons had left Eridu. This Eridu priest's version was known to the author of Atrahasis, the editor of Gilgamesh and to Berossus, and included the following material:

• fear expressed by the gods (priests) during the flood, mentioned in Atrahasis;

• hunger and thirst of the gods (priests) after the flood, mentioned in Atrahasis;

• the god (soldier) inspecting the barge and asking "Has anyone escaped alive?" in Atrahasis and Gilgamesh; and

• the oracle mentioned by Berossus: "a voice came from the air, telling them that they must respect the gods."

The details supplied by the Eridu priest had a mythical form and the distinction between priests and gods was blurred. Just as gifts to the priests were called sacrifices to the gods, priests were called gods in the priest's version of the flood story. By mythologizing ordinary people and events, the Eridu priest also undercut our ability to determine whether the mythical material was fiction or mythologized legend. The priest's contribution to the story is therefore the least credible of the three eyewitnesses.

The archetype flood story

By 2600 BC, at the beginning of the Early Dynastic III period, the surviving written records of Noah's flood story were probably still scattered fragments at various cities, in various libraries, archives, and private collections and in different parts of each collection. Some of these records survived because they were collected, copied and translated by archivists who stored the results of their research along with administrative records and other records from before the flood. These records may have included the following:

> Transcriptions of story tellers' and bards' recitations.
> Chronology of flood events by month and day
> Birth and death records for Shuruppak kings and nobles.
> Land and tax records.
> Archivists' summaries of extant records.

The above fragments are suggested as probable sources (many existing as single copies) that were collected and combined by the writer of an archetype flood story, the story that later spawned the six versions that have survived to the present. The writer of this archetype flood story may have been a temple scribe and probably wrote the story in the Sumerian language about 2600 BC.

Woolley[6] described such scribes and remarked that "some even indulged in original research and might collect and copy out the old inscriptions on brick [clay] or stone which threw light upon the past history of their own city. It is to the labours of these that we owe most of what we have learnt concerning the life and thoughts of their time."

Archaeologist Max Mallowan[10] wrote that he was "tempted to believe that the significance of the name of Gilgamesh in the context of the Flood Story is that it was in his time that the memory of the Flood was committed to writing... At last perhaps the scribes were becoming sufficiently literary to commit the record of the event to writing, and although it seems unlikely that they had yet achieved the expertise required for the composition of an epic, the Fara texts [Early Dynastic III period] which may have been written ... c.2600 B.C. and later, perhaps indicate that they were on the way there."

The Shuruppak scribe who recorded stories about Ziusudra (Noah) and the flood of 2900 BC may have searched for all of the extant records and oral traditions on past floods, after a later flood that occurred in the scribe's own time (about 2600 BC) at the beginning of the Early Dynastic III period. This later flood was the latest and most violent of a series of four floods that left four flood strata in Kish.[7] The earliest of the four flood strata resulted from Noah's flood of 2900 BC. The fourth flood of 2600 BC intervened between the Early Dynastic II period and the Early Dynastic III period.[8]

The Shuruppak scribe combined orally transmitted flood traditions and written records into one archetype flood story which may have included a conflation of traditions from more than one flood. Although hundreds of flood traditions may have been circulating in Sumer by the time the scribe wrote down the story, the written form of the archetype story standardized the story elements and distinctive phrases he collected from oral tradition. This scribe was probably the same scribe who calculated the Genesis 5 numbers from archaic birth and death records he found in the Shuruppak temple. For calculating, he used the SHE–GUR–MAH number system that was peculiar to Shuruppak during the Early Dynastic III period.[9]

Hundreds of years later, during the Old Babylonian period (1800–1600 BC), when Sumerian literature was collected and systematically translated into Akkadian by the scribal schools of Babylonia,[11] one of the scribes, perhaps a student scribe, translated the Sumerian archetype flood story into Akkadian. He mistranslated the archaic SHE–GUR–MAH number signs into cuneiform sexagesimal numbers (see Chapter 7) which effectively multiplied the numbers by ten in what later became Genesis 5.

The archetype flood story included various eyewitness reports, but also included myths, misunderstandings and mistakes that had become attached to the story during the oral transmission phase. Although the source material for this archetype story began as oral tradition, after the story was written in clay tablets, copies could survive almost unchanged for more than two thousand years in Sumerian and Babylonian archives.

The Epic of Ziusudra was extracted from this archetype flood story. Although the fragmentary copy of Ziusudra found at Nippur was dated to around 1600 BC, it was probably an abridged copy of a much older poem based on still older material. Since the Ziusudra epic was written in Sumerian about a Sumerian king and the archetype flood story was first written about 2600 BC at the beginning of the Early Dynastic III period when Sumerian was still the dominant written language in the southern Euphrates valley, the archetype flood story was probably also written in Sumerian.

Various extracts were made from the archetype story by later writers, editors, poets, bards and story tellers. Although these extracts retained many of the original distinctive words and phrases that can still be found in the surviving versions, the unity of the story was blurred as various people selected different parts of the archetype story and modified them to suit their needs.

One of these extracts was the epic of Atrahasis. According to Atrahasis III,iv,6–9 the storm caused a river flood: "They [dead bodies] have filled the river... Like a raft they have moved to the riverbank." About 1200 BC the flood myth from Atrahasis was added to the epic of Gilgamesh.[1] Gilgamesh XI,123 has "They [dead bodies] have filled the sea." We can see the mythmaker's hand at work here, changing a local river flood into an ocean deluge.

Another extract from the archetype flood story was the Genesis version.

The Genesis version

According to the Documentary Hypothesis, also called the Source Hypothesis,[12,13] the Genesis flood story is a composite of two sources written by two different authors or series of authors: J (Jehovist) and P (Priestly) that were combined by a post-exilic editor who is given the siglum R[jp] (Redactor) by scholars.[14] This theory is based on stylistic differences, duplication of story elements and the fact that some sentences use *Yahweh* (Lord) for the divine name while other sentences use *elohim* (God). For example:

J	P
So the Lord said, "I will blot out man whom I have created from the face of the ground." (Genesis 6:7)	And God said to Noah, "I have determined to make an end of all flesh." (Genesis 6:13)
And Noah and his sons and his wife and his sons' wives with him went into the ark" (Genesis 7:7)	Noah and his sons, Shem and Ham and Japheth, and Noah's wife and the three wives of his sons with them entered the ark. (Genesis 7:13)

In recent years the Documentary Hypothesis has been challenged by several scholars.[15] Wenham[16] argued that the Genesis flood story had one unified epic source and repetition of story elements in Genesis 6–9 was done by one author for literary purposes, to give the story a symmetrical palistrophic or chiastic structure in which elements in the second half of the story resemble elements in the first half. Emerton[17] pointed out weaknesses in Wenham's analysis. In rebuttal, Wenham[18] agreed that a proven contradiction within or between narratives would make it highly probable that there are different sources present, but Wenham remained unconvinced that such contradictions had been demonstrated. The Documentary Hypothesis is discussed at length by Garrett[19] who questions the methodology used by its supporters. It is beyond the scope of this book to attempt to resolve this issue as it applies to the Genesis flood story or to explore the details of transmission paths of different portions of the flood story.

The following Genesis quotes are attributed to J:

"coming of the flood on the seventh night" Atrahasis,III,i,37
"after seven days the waters of the flood came" Genesis 7:10

"I opened the window" Gilgamesh XI,135
"Noah opened the window of the ark" Genesis 8:6

"The dove went out and returned" Gilgamesh XI,147
"sent forth the dove and the dove came back to him" Genesis 8:10

"The gods smelled the sweet savor" Gilgamesh XI,160
"The Lord smelled the sweet savor" Genesis 8:21a

The following Genesis quotes are attributed to P:

"[Enki] told him of the coming of the flood" Atrahasis III,i,37
"God said to Noah ... I will bring a flood" Genesis 6:13,17

"pitch I poured over the inside" Gilgamesh XI,66
"cover it inside and out with pitch" Genesis 6:14

"Like the *apsû* you shall roof it" Gilgamesh XI,31
"Make a roof for the ark" Genesis 6:16

"he touched our foreheads to bless us" Gilgamesh XI,192
"And God blessed Noah" Genesis 9:1

"I shall remember these days and never forget them" Gilgamesh XI,165
"I shall remember my covenant ... I may remember" Genesis 9:15–16

Although the J material is believed by some scholars to have been authored about 1000–900 BC, and the P material was authored centuries later during the Babylonian exile, the J material was actually a product of the exilic period according to Hans H. Schmid.[20] Portions of flood text attributed to J or P were both derived from Babylonian sources.

Since the parts of the Genesis flood story attributed to P or J both have close parallels in Gilgamesh and Atrahasis and all share very similar story elements and distinctive words and phrases, both the J and P versions (which contain additional story elements not found in either Atrahasis or Gilgamesh) were probably derived from the earlier archetype flood story. Whether the Genesis version was authored by two exiled priests working separately whose writings were later combined by R^{jp}, or by one priest who mixed his own commentary with verbatim quotations from earlier works, is of little importance in reconstructing Noah's story. Either way, the surviving versions of the Genesis flood story were derived indirectly from one written archetype flood story compiled centuries earlier from oral traditions based on three or more eyewitness accounts of the 2900 BC river flood.

The poets who authored the epics of Ziusudra, Atrahasis and Gilgamesh did not use the detailed chronology found in the Genesis version. However, Berossus gave the month and day of the flood and therefore he had access to at least this part of the chronology, whether it was true or not. Hence, a short chronology was probably included in the archetype flood story or as a separate document stored along with the archetype story in the Babylonian archives. Since genealogy data was not used in the other surviving versions of the flood story, the Genesis 5 genealogy and the archetype flood story were probably separate documents in the Babylonian archives.

Some scholars have suggested that one of the sources used by P was a collection of genealogies called the Toledoth Book.[21] *Toledoth* is Hebrew for births, generations, genealogical line, and included family stories in addition to genealogy data. Family genealogy is cumulative and new material is usually added every few generations. Otherwise gaps occur in the story sequence.[22]

The priests of Yahweh who obtained the flood story details and Noah's genealogy during the exile (probably after the capture of Babylon by Cyrus II in 539 BC) added them to the Toledoth Book. Genealogy data were added later at appropriate places in the flood story (e.g. Genesis 9:28–29).

Chain of translations

The priests who authored Genesis used material that is also included in Atrahasis (and hence in the archetype story) but not in Gilgamesh. The seven day waiting period before the flood (Genesis 7:4 and 7:10) is found in Atrahasis,III,i,37: "coming of the flood on the seventh night." But in Gilgamesh XI there is no reference to a seven day period before the flood and only a vague reference to when the flood began: "That time arrived." Moreover, the expression "forty days and forty nights" in Genesis 7:12 corresponds to "seven days and seven nights" in Atrahasis III,iv,24 and "seven days and seven nights" in Ziusudra 203. But the corresponding line at Gilgamesh XI,127 has "six days and seven nights," not seven days and seven nights. The editor of Gilgamesh XI changed the number of days and nights to be unequal when he copied the flood story from Atrahasis, a change not reflected in Genesis 7:12. Hence, it seems likely that the Genesis authors did not use material from Gilgamesh, although the fragmentary condition of Atrahasis and Ziusudra makes such an inference uncertain.

The following flowchart shows possible transmission paths of versions of the flood story from the eyewitnesses by way of the archetype flood story to the present surviving editions.

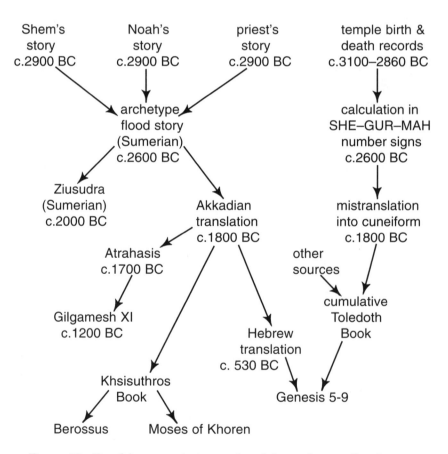

Figure 12. Possible transmission paths of the archetype flood story

Atrahasis,III,iv,6–9 describes the flood as a river flood: "Like dragonflies they [dead bodies] have filled the river... Like a raft they have moved in to the riverbank." But Genesis 7–8 describes the flood as an ocean flood. It therefore seems likely that the Genesis flood story was not derived from the Epic of Atrahasis. If not from Atrahasis nor from Gilgamesh, the Genesis flood story came from another source, perhaps a lost Akkadian or Aramaic version of the archetype flood story that included several details preserved only in Genesis.

Genesis was not the only version that preserved details not preserved in other versions. As discussed in Chapter 5, there was a legend recorded by Moses of Khoren[5] regarding "a book about Khsisuthros and his sons, which has not survived to the present." Moses of Khoren used substantially the same name Khsisuthros for the flood hero as the Ziusudra epic, which increases the probability that both had a common origin, i.e. the Sumerian archetype flood story. The Khsisuthros Book was probably a translation of the archetype story. This lost book, later revised to refer to Assyria, mentioned Shem's journey on foot northwest and later southeast, apparently along the Tigris River. Berossus also knew about this "roundabout way" by which Shem traveled to Sippar and also retained the name Xisuthros, thus increasing the probability that the source used by Berossus was a version of the archetype flood story which mentioned Shem's journey along the bank of the Tigris.

The flood hero was named Ziusudra in the archetype story. The surviving Ziusudra Epic does not mention the birds going out and returning, even though the lines where they would have been mentioned are still intact on the Ziusudra tablet. Likewise the boatman is not mentioned in the Ziusudra Epic. Hence, the Ziusudra Epic is an abridged version and was not the source used by the authors of Atrahasis or Genesis, or by Berossus.

An Akkadian translation of the archetype flood story was probably the source used by Berossus (about 270 BC) when writing his history of Babylonia. Although it is possible that Berossus made use of a Sumerian text of the archetype flood story, it seems more likely that he used an Akkadian translation, because Sumerian was a dead language by the time of Berossus and important Sumerian records had already been translated into Akkadian.

During the second millennium BC, the Hurrians spread Sumerian and Akkadian literature westward to the Hittites and to the Mediterranean coast of Syria. The Gilgamesh Epic was available in both Hittite and Hurrian translations.[23] The Hurrians came from the mountains of Armenia (the mountains of Ararat) in what is now eastern Turkey, north of northern Mesopotamia. When people from northwest Mesopotamia moved west into Canaan, they carried the Hurrian version of the flood story with them. A fragment[24] of Atrahasis dated from the 14th century BC was found at Ras Shamra, the site of the ancient Canaanite city of Ugarit on the coast of Syria.

And since a fragment of Gilgamesh was also found at Megiddo in Israel,[25] it is likely that both of these flood stories were known to Judeans long before the Babylonian exile in the late sixth century BC.

The archetype flood story probably included the Ararat name because Mount Judi was in the mountains of Ararat. Hence, the Ararat name would probably be included in any Hurrian version of the flood story. The Niṣir and Ararat regional names and the Judi mountain name were probably all mentioned in the archetype flood story.

According to Lambert,[23] borrowing by the Hebrews of the flood and creation myths from Babylonian sources occurred no earlier than 1500 BC and the myths probably reached the Hebrews in oral form about 1200 BC. Thus the story about Noah and the flood may have been part of the pre-exilic Hebrew tradition, even though details were lost during oral transmission before the time of the exile.

Although copies of the epics of Atrahasis and/or Gilgamesh may have been available to Hebrew writers about 1200 BC, it is not likely that genealogy and chronology tables accompanied copies of Atrahasis or Gilgamesh in popular story telling. Also it is not likely that distinctive words and phrases and precise details such as "in the second month, on the seventeenth day of the month" would have survived centuries of oral transmission before P wrote them down. Such details could have come from a collection of written flood records compiled by the author of the archetype story and stored in the Babylonian archives. The archetype flood story in the Babylonian archives would be far more detailed than oral tradition and was probably the source for most of the Genesis flood material in both the P and J versions.

There are linguistic clues in Genesis that suggest a Babylonian source rather than a long period of oral tradition. The Hebrew word *kopher* used at Genesis 6:14 means pitch and was similar to the Akkadian word *kupuru* meaning pitch that is used in both Atrahasis III,ii,13 and Gilgamesh XI,65. The usual Hebrew word for pitch is *zepheth* not *kopher*, and *kopher* means pitch only in Genesis 6:14. This suggests that the part of the flood story attributed to P was not transmitted orally in Hebrew for hundreds of years, but was translated from an ancient Babylonian source during the exile. Otherwise the common word *zepheth* would have been substituted for *kopher* during the long period of oral transmission. Similarly, the word Shinar (Genesis 11:2), attributed to J, as the name for the southern Mesopotamian region, occurs in the Bible outside of Genesis only in texts from around the exile period, (Isaiah 11:11, Daniel 1:2, Zech. 5:11). This suggests that the part of Genesis attributed to J was also augmented from Babylonian sources during the exile.

Except for Genesis, there is no reference to Noah in the pre-exilic books in the Hebrew Bible. The genealogy data in I Chron 1:4 mentions Noah, but this book was written or updated during the time of Ezra, after the exile.[26]

Isaiah 54:9 mentions Noah in connection with the flood, but this is in Second Isaiah written during or shortly after the exile.[27]

One or two Hebrew extracts of the Babylonian material survived into the post-exilic (Persian) period. These included a Yahvist extract written in the style of J and a more complete P extract reflecting the vocabulary of the post-exilic period.[28] Both extracts omitted parts of the archetype story (e.g. Shem's journey on foot up the Tigris River) and each extract included material not included in the other. Additional fragments, some transcribed from memory (e.g. Genesis 4:17–18), may have been added when Genesis was assembled into its present form during the post-exilic period by R[jp] a Judean editor.[29]

Genesis 6:7 where Yahweh warns Noah of the coming disaster, was based on the archetype flood myth in which the god Enki warns the flood hero. As discussed in Chapter 5, the Sumerian Noah sacrificed at the temple of Enki, a story element that was adapted for Genesis 8:20: "Noah built an altar to Yahweh … and offered burnt offerings on the altar." Likewise the Genesis 11:6–7 story where Yahweh said "let us go down and confuse their language, that they may not understand one another's speech" was adapted from the Golden Age myth:[31] "Enki, the lord … of Eridu, changed the speech in their mouths, [bringing] contention into it, into the speech of man that had [previously] been one." Likewise the story about eating forbidden fruit in Genesis 2:17, 3:1–19 was adapted from the myth *Enki and Ninhursag*.[32]

The Sumerian god Enki played an important role in the creation myth, the forbidden fruit myth, the confusion of speech myth, and the flood myth, which suggests that archivists had already collected several myths about Enki in the Babylonian archives, and these were made available to Judean priests during the exile.

Babylonian archives

The oldest Sumerian tablets were accounting records: land sales, tax administration, costs of construction projects, etc. Although writing was not advanced enough in 2900 BC to record narratives, it was advanced enough to record accounting facts, including months and days in a flood chronology, and was also advanced enough to record memory aids for story tellers.

In addition to temple birth records from the Jemdet Nasr period, land sales, tax administration and other government records, commercial accounting records, promissory notes, missing person lists, genealogies, etc. related to the flood may have been stored on shelves in various Sumerian archives, libraries, and private collections. These were later collected and combined by a Sumerian scribe who authored the archetype flood story about 2600 BC. Most of his unedited source documents probably existed only as single copies and have therefore not survived.

As discussed in Chapter 7, Noah's original genealogy data that was written in clay before the flood and was compiled and calculated about 2600 BC, was translated from round-stylus Shuruppak number signs into cuneiform sexagesimal signs about 1800 BC by a Babylonian scribe, perhaps the same scribe who translated the Sumerian archetype flood story into Akkadian. This scribe did not do his work in Shuruppak which had been abandoned before the Old Babylonian period.[30] His translation was probably saved in one or more of the Babylonian archives. From time to time archivists probably edited, copied, excerpted, summarized and translated the archetype flood story and Noah's genealogy, and these edited versions were also saved in one or more archives where they remained for centuries.

In parallel with these written records, the oral traditions continued, but chronological details were forgotten, barge construction details were forgotten, quotations were forgotten, and personal names and place names were changed to local names in the oral versions. During the exile, Judean priests of Yahweh who were already aware of these oral traditions, searched for further information on the flood in the Babylonian archives where they found a copy of the archetype flood story, genealogies, and a collection of myths about Enki. The Judean priests may have made use of this collection when they authored the first draft of Genesis 1–9, perhaps with the help of a friendly Babylonian priest who provided a translation.

Conclusions

After the river flood of 2900 BC, at least three different stories about the adventures of Noah and his sons were told in the cities where eyewitnesses lived: Noah's story at Dilmun, Shem's story at Sippar, and a priest of Enki's story at Eridu. Three bodies of oral tradition spread from these three cities, but errors accumulated in the stories. Story tellers and bards mythologized the stories and included misunderstandings and mistakes in their recitations. About 2600 BC during the Early Dynastic IIIa period, these oral traditions and written records related to the flood were collected and combined into one archetype flood story by a Shuruppak scribe writing in the Sumerian language. This archetype story was the "book about Khsisuthros and his sons" referred to by Moses of Khoren. Excerpts from this lost book spawned the six editions of the flood story that have survived to the present. This book was translated into Akkadian about 1800 BC by a Babylonian scribe who mistranslated the numbers in Noah's genealogy. During the Babylonian exile in the late sixth century BC, the Judean authors of Genesis extracted the flood story and Noah's genealogy from a translation of the archetype flood story along with other Enki myths stored in the Babylonian archives.

References

1. Jeffrey H. Tigay, *The Evolution of the Gilgamesh Epic* (Philadelphia, PA: University of Pennsylvania Press, 1982), p. 237.

2. M. E. L. Mallowan, "Noah's Flood Reconsidered", *Iraq*, 26 (1964), pp. 62–82.

3. Hans J. Nissen, *The Early History of the Ancient Near East*, 9000–2000 B.C. (Chicago: University of Chicago Press, 1988), pp. 137–138.

4. Lloyd M. Barré, "The Riddle of the Flood Chronology", *Journal for the Study of the Old Testament*, 41 (1988), pp. 3–20.

5. Moses of Khoren, *History of the Armenians*, translation by Robert W. Thomson, vol. 4 of Harvard Armenian Texts and Studies, (Harvard University Press, 1978) pp. 79–80 (near end of section 6). Another translation is quoted in Bailey,[13] p. 194. Moses of Khoren cited Olympiodorus as his source.

6. C. Leonard Woolley, *The Sumerians* (New York, W.W. Norton, 1965), p. 110.

7. L. Watelin and S. Landon, *Excavations at Kish*, (Oxford University, 1934), vol 4, pp. 41, 53. The layer marked "clay" is also labeled "Flood 4".

8. Mallowan, op. cit., p. 79.

9. see chapter 7, pp. 112–116.

10. Mallowan, op. cit., pp. 69–70.

11. Mallowan, op. cit., p. 66. This translation was not done at Shuruppak which was abandoned before the Old Babylonian period.[30]

12. Antony F. Campbell and Mark A. O'Brien, *Sources of the Pentateuch* (Minneapolis, Fortress Press, 1993) pp. 2–9.

13. Lloyd R. Bailey, *Noah: The Person and the Story in History and Tradition*, Studies on Personalities of the Old Testament (Columbia, SC: University of South Carolina Press, 1989), pp. 135–151.

14. Frank M. Cross, "The Priestly Work," *Canaanite Myth and Hebrew Epic* (Cambridge: Harvard University Press, 1973), p. 305. Cross argues that P and R were the same person.

15. Campbell and O'Brien, op. cit., pp. 10–15.

16. Gordon J. Wenham, "The Coherence of the Flood Narrative," *Vetus Testamentum*, 28 (1978), pp. 336–348.

17. J. A. Emerton, "An Examination of Some Attempts to Defend the Unity of the Flood Narrative in Genesis, Part II," *Vetus Testamentum*, 38, 1 (1988), pp. 1–21.

18. Gordon J. Wenham, "Method in Pentateuchal Source Criticism," *Vetus Testamentum*, 41, 1 (1991), pp. 84–109.

19. Duane A. Garrett, *Rethinking Genesis: The Sources and Authorship*, (Grand Rapids, Michigan: Baker Book House, 1991), pp. 25–28, 113–119.

20.   Hans Heinrich Schmid, *The So-Called Yahwist* (1976), discussed by Campbell and O'Brien, op. cit., pp. 10–11, note 24.

21.   Campbell and O'Brien, op. cit., xvii, 23.

22.   For *toledoth* theories see Garrett, op. cit., pp. 93–106.

23.   W. G. Lambert, "A New Look at the Babylonian Background of Genesis," *Journal of Theological Studies*, N.S., Vol 16, part 2 (October 1965), pp. 287–300, especially p. 299–300.

24.   W. G. Lambert and A. R. Millard, *Atrahasis: The Babylonian Story of the Flood* (Oxford, Clarendon Press, 1969), pp. 24, 131–133.

25.   A. Goetze and S. Levy, *Atiqot*, II (1957), pp. 108–115, (English edition (1959), pp. 121–128.

26.   Charles M. Laymon (editor), *The Interpreter's One-Volume Commentary on the Bible*, (Nashville: Abingdon Press, 1971), p. 209a.

27.   ibid. p. 329.

28.   Keith R. Crim, et al (editors), *The Interpreter's Dictionary of the Bible*, Supplementary Volume, section 2, "The Completion of P," (Nashville: Abingdon Press, 1976), p. 685.

29.   Niels Peter Lemche, "The Chronology in the Story of the Flood", *Journal for the Study of the Old Testament*, 18 (1980), pp. 52–62.

30.   Robert McC. Adams, *Heartland of Cities* (Chicago: University of Chicago Press, 1981), Fig. 33 compared with Fig. 21.

31.   Samuel Noah Kramer, "The 'Babel of Tongues': A Sumerian Version," *Journal of the American Oriental Society*, 88 (1968), pp. 108–111. Reprinted in *I Studied Inscriptions from before the Flood*, Richard S. Hess and David Tsumura (editors), (Winona Lake, Indiana: Eisenbrauns, 1994), pp. 278–282, especially p. 281.

32.   Samuel Noah Kramer, *History Begins at Sumer,* third edition, (Philadelphia, PA: University of Pennsylvania Press, 1981), p. 142.

9

Noah's Relatives

"Ancestor, ancestor, why be elusive,
when all that I seek of you is proof conclusive."
Winston De Ville

Noah's father Lamech

Genesis 4:19–24 gives us very little information about Noah's father Lamech, other than Lamech had two wives, that he killed (or will kill) a man who injures him, and that he had three other sons besides Noah. The story of Lamech was embellished with fiction by later writers, for example in the book I Enoch 106:1–7.[1] But additional legendary information on the flood hero's father is provided by the Sumerian King List and the Epic of Gilgamesh.

According to the Sumerian King List WB–62, the father of Ziusudra (Noah) was SU.KUR.LAM.[2] Noah's father was named Lamech in Genesis 5:28. Therefore SU.KUR.LAM was Lamech, Noah's father. The King List also indicates that SU.KUR.LAM immediately preceded Ziusudra (Noah) as king of Shuruppak. Both Noah and his father Lamech were kings of Shuruppak. The logogram SU.KUR.LAM[KI] was also another name for the city Shuruppak.[4] KI was a determinative meaning a place name. Another name for Shuruppak[5] was LAMxKUR.RU[KI]. Shuruppak[6] was also the name of the father of Ziusudra (Noah) and a document reads "Shuruppak, son of Ubartutu gave instructions to his son Ziusudra".[7] Cities are often named or renamed after famous people and the city known as Shuruppak was apparently named after Noah's father Lamech or vice versa. Shuruppak (the person) was a sage in Sumerian tradition, a Sumerian Solomon.[6]

According to the Sumerian King List WB–62, SU.KUR.LAM was a "son of UBUR.TU.TU." According to Gilgamesh XI,23, Utnapishtim (Noah) was a "son of ^{P}UBARA^{d}TU.TU." Lamech and Noah were both a "son of" this unknown entity. UBARA can mean protégé[8] or protection. ^{d}TUTU was an epithet of a deity[9] and TU_6TU_6GÁL referred to incantation priests at the temple of Enki at Eridu,[10] although the signs TU and TU_6 are different. Lamech and Noah could both be a "son of" a common ancestor named ^{P}UBARA^{d}TU.TU, but "son" could also indicate affiliation with a religious organization in which "son of" meant being a member, as in "Sons of Saint Patrick." As members,

Lamech and Noah would be protégés of a highpriest and under the protection of the temple. The logogram UBARA^{d}TU.TU was sometimes written with the personal name determinative as ^{P}UBARA^{d}TU.TU.

According to the Sumerian King List (see chapter 7 herein), SU.KUR.LAM (Lamech) was king of Shuruppak for 5 or 8 years and was succeeded by his son Ziusudra (Noah) who was king of Shuruppak for 10 years.

Noah's grandfather Methuselah

The conventional chronology based on the Masoretic Text has Noah's grandfather Methuselah dying in the year of the flood, presumably by drowning. But the present chronology based on the Septuagint (see chapter 7 herein), has Methuselah dying about 3 months after the barge landed. If Methuselah lived through the flood, it is curious that he is not mentioned at Genesis 7:7 and 7:13 among the people who went into the ark. Likewise he is not mentioned at Genesis 8:18 among the people who disembarked. Even Berossus, who mentions Noah's daughter and boatman and close friends on the ark, does not mention Noah's grandfather. Where was Methuselah? And why did he die shortly after the barge grounded?

According to Atrahasis III,ii,41 the storm a year earlier interrupted a family banquet on board the barge. Apparently Methuselah did not attend the banquet and when the levees burst he was not on the barge. Methuselah was probably where any 84 year old man would be – at home. Methuselah may have lived in the same compound with Noah. Noah's home may have been on high ground in or near Shuruppak where other wealthy people lived, an area of the city that was not flooded or at least not as deeply as the lowland near the river and behind the levees.

After the river flood subsided, Methuselah would still be living at Shuruppak, probably mourning the presumed death of his grandson Noah and his family. A year later when Noah's creditors learned that Noah was still alive and had fled to a foreign country, that the barge was still intact, but the cargo had disappeared, the Shuruppak government may have sold Noah's property to pay his taxes and debts. Although Noah may have been personally immune from prosecution because of his special relationship with the temple of Enki, his property could still be sold to pay his taxes and debts. This foreclosure sale may have occurred about 3 months after the barge landed or about the same time as Methuselah's death.

As a member of Noah's family who could not pay the debts, Methuselah would be forced into slavery. Long time friends would shun him, because they would not want to be suspected of condoning tax evasion and theft of government property. What would probably happen to any man who was evicted from his home, stripped of his clothes and personal possessions, with no family or friends, impoverished and enslaved at the age of 85?

Noah's sons

According to Genesis 5:32, Noah had three sons Shem, Ham, and Japheth. Shem was the oldest according to Genesis 10:21. These names appear to be fictitious eponymous names derived from Genesis 10, the table of nations.[11] Mr. Shem was the supposed ancestor of all semites. Mr. Ham was the supposed ancestor of the Egyptians, and Mr. Japheth was the supposed ancestor of Indo-Europeans including the Greeks. Shem, Ham, and Japheth are therefore fictitious demigods.[12] However the legend preserved by Moses of Khoren[13] about Shem's journey northwest near a river agrees with a similar legend from Berossus about the flood hero's relatives who "went by a roundabout way" to Sippar. Hence, there is enough legendary content in Shem's story to treat him as a legendary character, even though his name may be fictitious. The archetype flood myth may have mentioned unnamed sons of Ziusudra whose births were not recorded in the archives of Shuruppak and therefore only an estimate of the times of their births appear in Genesis 5:32. The names Shem, Ham, and Japheth may have been selected later from the fictitious eponymous names in the table of nations.

There seems to be a conflict between Genesis 5:32 and 7:6 in view of Genesis 11:10b:

5:32	After Noah was 500 years old, Noah became the father of Shem, Ham and Japheth.
7:6	Noah was 600 years old when the flood waters came upon the earth.
11:10b	When Shem was 100 years old, he became the father of Arpachshad 2 years after the flood.

This conflict is discussed at length by Cryer[14] who points out that if we deduce that Shem was 100 years old 2 years after Noah's 600th year, that is in 602, Shem must have been born when Noah was 502. But Genesis 5:32 has Shem being born after Noah was 500. This small conflict between the numbers is more significant if the year 600 of Noah (60.0 with decimal point inserted) originally meant year 48 (corrected for the nonstandard Shuruppak meaning of GUR). If we assume that GUR (48) was mistranslated as 600 for Noah's age when the flood occurred, 500 years would have no meaning because any year count greater than or equal to 480 (48.0) would jump to 600 (60.0) or more. No value would exist in the gap between 480 and 600, because numbers 48 and greater were mistranslated as 600 and greater. This suggests that the 500 years of Genesis 5:32 was an estimate or a calculation made by a later scribe such as P, just as the 601 of Genesis 8:13 was calculated by adding one to 600. For the same reasons, the remainder numbers in Table I in chapter 7 are calculations made by a later scribe such as P.

We can accept at face value the 2 years after the flood mentioned at Genesis 11:10b, because misplacing the decimal point[15] would probably not be a problem with single digit integers. We cannot insert a decimal point in the 100 years of Genesis 11:10b because that would make Shem ten years old when he fathered his son Arpachshad. The 100 years of Genesis 11:10b was probably also an estimate by P who subtracted his 500 estimate from 602 and got approximately 100.

The formula of Genesis 5 which gives the age of each father when his son was born and then the remaining years before his death is not used in Genesis 5:32 and Noah's time of death is given in Genesis 9:28 as years after the flood rather than years after the birth of Shem. When the original archaic numbers were calculated from archival records by a scribe during the Early Dynastic IIIa period (see Chapter 7), about 300 years after the flood, the scribe probably did not record when Shem was born, because the scribe was probably interested only in the births of Noah and his ancestors. Hence, P working with the mistranslated numbers more than two thousand years later, would have no information on when Shem was born and therefore estimated that Shem was born when Noah was about 500 years old.

If we add the 2 years after the flood to Noah's age 48.0 when the flood occurred, the total is 50.0. Removing the decimal point yields 500. So now we have 500 in three places including the round numbers 500 in Genesis 5:32 and 500 in Genesis 11:11 which are probably estimates made by P. Perhaps the 500 [50.0] of Genesis 5:32 was Noah's age when his grandson Arpachshad was born rather than when his three sons were born. Perhaps Genesis 5:32 originally read something like: "When Noah was 50 years old, 2 years after the flood, Noah's firstborn fathered a son."

A plausible estimate of Shem's age when Arpachshad was born would be about 17, two years after the six-day flood. That would make Shem about 15 at the time of the flood. Hence Shem was born when Noah was about 33. Shem could not have been much younger than 16 when his son was born, because that would make him too young to father a child. Likewise, Shem was probably not much older than 16 at the time of the flood, because if his wife was old enough, he would have fathered his first child during the months of isolation in the barge. Perhaps he did father a child while on the barge, but it was not counted as his first son because it may have been a daughter. His first son would then be his second child, born less than two years later.

Noah's descendents were fictitious

Although the antediluvians of Genesis 5 can be understood as ordinary men who lived to ages comparable to modern people, it does not follow that the names listed in Genesis 11:10–32 refer to ordinary people. Noah's descendents would have lived during the period covered by the Table of Nations in Genesis 10, a artificial construction of eponymous names.[11] Apparently the priests who compiled the Toledoth book could not find any genealogy records for individuals in the time period between Noah and Abraham and they therefore filled the gap with fictitious names.

The Septuagint version of the Shemite numbers from Genesis 11:12–22 shown above in Chapter 7, Table II are repeated in Table VII below using modern decimal notation:

	Son born	Remainder	Total (calculated)
Arpachshad	13.5	43.0	56.5
Shelah/Kenan	13.0	33.0	46.0
Eber	13.4	37.0	50.4
Peleg	13.0	20.9	33.9
Reu	13.2	20.7	33.9
Serug	13.0	20.0	33.0

Table VII

Shemite data corrected for missing decimal points[15]

The first clue that the names and numbers in Table VII are fictitious, are the numbers 13.0 which occur every two lines for Shelah, Peleg, and Serug. It is unlikely that every two generations a man fathered a son at exactly the same age. In the numbers for Arpachshad through Serug, there is not enough variation in the ages when their first sons were born, considering that the first child is often a daughter. A second clue is Peleg and Reu having identical life spans of 33.9 years. Not likely. A third clue are the low ages when each man fathered a son. It is very unlikely that these men became fathers at the age of thirteen (conception at age 12.2) if decimal points are restored as in Table VII.

Even if Masoretic numbers are used and decimal points are not restored (see Table II in chapter 7), there is still the problem of why these men waited so long to father children and then fathered sons at exactly the same age. It should be clear that the numbers in Genesis 11:12–22 are a fictitious genealogy constructed by a family genealogist or scribe who filled in the missing data with estimates for the numbers and copied names from the table of nations in Genesis 10. There is a tendency among family genealogists to estimate numbers that have been lost. Later generations have to guess about which data were estimates and which data were obtained from earlier sources.

Analysis of the Genesis 11 numbers and names after Serug is beyond the scope of this book, but they too appear to be a fictitious construction based on tribal names, appellatives, and place names. For example the names Serug, Nahor, and Terah are place names attested in neo–Assyrian documents as Sarugi, Nahiri, and Turahi.[16]

Mistakes in Genesis 4 genealogy

The genealogy of Genesis 4:17–18 is similar to the genealogy of Genesis 5 and many of the same names or similar names appear in both lists, but in a different sequence. Rearranging Genesis 4 to conform to Genesis 5:

Genesis 4	rearranged	Genesis 5
Adam	Adam	Adam
Cain	Cain	Seth
–	–	Enosh
–	Cain	Kenan
Enoch	Mehuyael	Mahalalel
Irad	Irad	Jared
Mehuyael	Enoch	Enoch
Methushael	Methushael	Methuselah
Lamech	Lamech	Lamech
–	–	Noah

It should be clear that the person who supplied the Genesis 4 information had a faulty memory. He not only got the sequence Mahalel, Jared, Enoch backwards, he also confused Kenan (Cainan) with Seth's brother Cain. The numbers of Genesis 5 are not present in Genesis 4 which suggests that Genesis 5 is primary and Genesis 4 was recorded from memory. Recalling a list of names or words in the wrong sequence is a common memory error.

References

1.   M. A. Knibb (translator), *The Ethiopic Book of Enoch: A New Edition in the Light of the Aramaic Dead Sea Fragments*, 2 volumes, (Oxford: Clarendon Press, 1978), volume 2, pp. 244–245.

2.   S. Langdon, "The Chaldean Kings Before the Flood", *Journal of Royal Asiatic Society* (1923), pp. 258–259, lines 15–16 and note 5. Langdon in note 5 says "Written SU–KUR–LAM" but in line 15 of the tablet translation he has "Aradgin son of Uburtutu" instead of "SU–KUR–LAM son of Uburtutu." This Aradgin interpretation is disputed by Jacobsen.[3]

3.   Thorkild Jacobsen, *The Sumerian King List* (Illinois: University of Chicago Press, 1939), p. 76, last sentence of note 32.

4.   Langdon, op. cit., p. 256, line 17, and 259, line 17.

5.   Rykle Borger, *Akkadische Zeichenliste*, (Germany: Verlag Butzon & Bercker Kevelaer, 1971), p. 77.

6.   Samuel N. Kramer, "Gilgamesh and the Land of the Living," *Journal of Cuneiform Studies*, 1 (1947), pp. 3–46, especially p. 33, end of note 208.

7.   Samuel Noah Kramer, "Reflections on the Mesopotamian Flood", *Expedition*, 9, 4 (summer 1967), pp. 12–18, especially 16.

8.   Langdon, op. cit., p. 259, note 6. See also Labat, sign 152.4.

9.   Douglas B. Miller and R. Mark Shipp, *An Akkadian Handbook* (Winona Lake, Indiana: Eisenbrauns, 1996), p. 69.

10.   Margaret Whitney Green, *Eridu in Sumerian Literature*, Ph.D. dissertation, (University of Chicago, 1975), p. 226.

11.   Lloyd R. Bailey, *Genesis, Creation, and Creationism*, (NY: Paulist Press, 1993), pp. 78–82.

12.   Cyrus H. Gordon, "Notes on Proper Names in the Ebla Tablets" in *Eblaite Personal Nams and Semitic Name–Giving*, Alfonso Archi (editor), (Rome: Missione archeologica italiana in Siria, 1988), pp. 153–158, esp. 154.

13.   Moses of Khoren, *History of the Armenians*, translation by Robert W. Thomson, vol. 4 of Harvard Armenian Texts and Studies, (Harvard University Press, 1978) pp. 79–80 (near end of section 6). For Shem's route see Figure 3 in Chapter 5 herein (page 66).

14.   Frederick H. Cryer, "The Interrelationships of Gen 5,32; 11, 10–11 and the Chronology of the Flood (Gen 6–9)", *Biblica*, 66, #2 (1985), pp. 241–261.

15.   I am *not* saying that tenths of years were ever represented in a decimal system by the Babylonians or the Judeans. See Chapter 7 herein under "Conflicting number systems."

16.   Abraham Malamat, "King Lists of the Old Babylonian Period and Biblical Genealogies," *Journal of the American Oriental Society*, 88 (1968), pp. 163–173, reprinted in *I Studied Inscriptions from Before the Flood*, Richard S. Hess and David Tsumura (editors), pp. 183–199, especially p. 189.

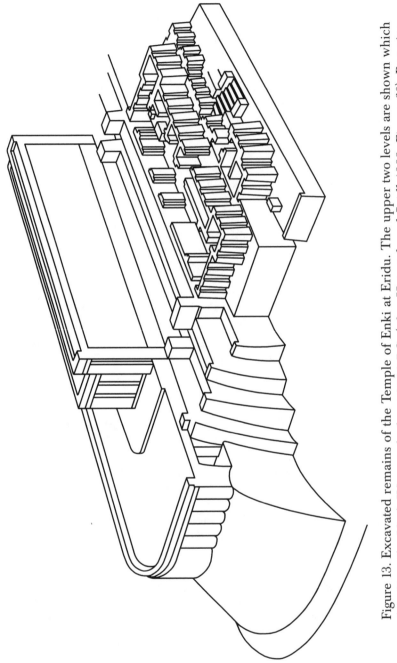

Figure 13. Excavated remains of the Temple of Enki at Eridu. The upper two levels are shown which date from the Uruk IV period, about 3500 BC. (after Heinrich and Seidl 1982, Figure 60). Remains from the Early Dynastic period and the altar on which Noah sacrificed at this temple have not survived.

10

The Basic Theory

*"Everything should be made as simple
as possible, but not simpler."*

Albert Einstein

In this chapter a theory about the flood story is presented with a minimum of arguments and references. This theory repeats some of the facts and plausible conjectures presented in other chapters based on legendary material. Material that is obviously mythical and conjectures based on mythical material are omitted. The legendary parts of the story are corrected for exaggerations, overgeneralizations, translation errors, logic errors and misunderstandings. Although this core legend cannot be proved to be historical, the events discussed in this chapter would have been physically possible and may have happened. Some of these legendary events may have been fiction. Readers who have doubts about some of the items in this chapter are referred to Chapters 2–8 where this material is argued in detail.

The scope of words used in this reconstructed flood story is limited to Noah's personal knowledge. "All animals" means all the animals Noah had custody of. "Every person" means every person that Noah could see. "The earth" means the land within Noah's visible horizon.

Versions of the Flood Story

The six surviving versions of the Noachian flood story are the myths and legends about Ziusudra, Atrahasis, Utnapishtim, Noah, Xisuthros and Khsisuthros. The six stories about these heroes are derived from earlier flood stories that originated in ancient Sumer, in the southern Tigris–Euphrates River valley in what is now southern Iraq. These stories were based on a historic river flood that occurred about 2900 BC at the end of the Jemdet Nasr period and the beginning of the Early Dynastic I period. This river flood deposited about 60 cm of yellow sediment directly above Jemdet Nasr strata in Shuruppak, a commercial city then on the Euphrates River. Many people probably died in the flood of 2900 BC, but most of the people survived it and the flood was not severe enough to interrupt the continuity of civilization in the Tigris–Euphrates valley.

Although the hero in the six versions of the flood story was given different names, they are the same person because the six versions have a common origin. For convenience, the name Noah is used for this hero, regardless of the version of the story. The possibility that Noah was a fictional character set in a real river flood setting cannot be ruled out, but is not explored here. The focus here is on what the original archetype flood story may have been and what facts it was based on, not whether the story was true or not.

Noah king of Shuruppak

Noah was a king or chief executive of the city-state Shuruppak during the end of the Jemdet Nasr period. He was a respected leader and probably a wealthy land owner. Noah's ancestral land was probably located at Shuruppak, because that is where both Noah and his father Lamech were chief executives. Noah owned gold and silver at a time when these metals were used largely by professional merchants and those involved in caravan trade, and therefore Noah was probably a merchant or trade official before becoming king of Shuruppak. Noah lived at about the same time as the first dynasty of Egypt, two hundred years before the pyramid builders.

Being involved with trade on the Euphrates River, Noah routinely transported cargo on the river. Noah's Ark was a commercial river barge for hauling livestock, grain, beer, wine and other cargo between cities on the river. These cities included Shuruppak, Uruk and Ur. Towing a barge downriver from Shuruppak to Ur took about three days and towing it back up the river from Ur to Shuruppak took about ten days.

The Atrahasis Epic mentions barley as one of the goods in the flood hero's boat. Barley was a major export and Noah's barge probably transported thousands of baskets of barley from Shuruppak to the port city Ur, then near the shore of the Persian (Arabian) Gulf, for export on foreign sailing ships. Wherever barley is grown, beer is usually brewed and Noah supplied beer for consumption by the boatbuilders. Noah's barge probably transported thousands of clay jars of beer for sale at cities on the Euphrates River and for export. A shipment of this barley and beer would later serve as food and drinking water for the people and animals during the year the barge was drifting on deep water.

The barge was probably used many times to transport cargo, but only the final voyage was reported in the flood story, because that may have been one of the few times or the only time that Noah rode on the barge. Noah's boatman Puzur–Amurri was also on board during the flood. Noah "entrusted the great structure including its contents" to Puzur who was probably Noah's general manager in charge of the barge operation. Puzur managed the people who steered the barge through the channels of the river and the servants or slaves who hauled or drove oxen hauling the barge down and then up the river for a few weeks each year in June and July.

The river barge and the cargo

Modern artists traditionally draw Noah's Ark as a rounded-hull seagoing vessel with a projecting keel. But the vessel on which the story of Noah's Ark was based was probably an assembly of dozens of flatboats, not one huge keelboat, and was designed for use in the calm water of the lower Euphrates river. It was a commercial river barge and each unit had a nearly rectangular cross section to maximize clear space for the cargo. The barge was constructed using the technology of 2900 BC.

Noah's barge was less than half as long as it is normally described. In Gilgamesh XI,58 the length of the barge is given as 120 cubits. The Sumerian cubit was about 20 inches. Hence the barge had a length of about 200 feet. The Genesis 6:15 dimensions were originally recorded in hand spans rather than cubits. The barge was 300 spans long, 50 spans wide, and 30 spans high. This converts to 200 feet long, 33 feet wide, and 20 feet high. The Genesis length in hand spans agrees with the Gilgamesh length in cubits. Comparable barges with a length of 150–200 feet were used in the Old Kingdom of Egypt.

Noah's barge was constructed of reeds and wood. The lower part of the barge consisted of dozens of woven reed quffas covered inside and out with pitch and lined with wood. The wood lining was like a hull that was built shell-first inside each quffa. The framing was inserted after each shell was constructed. Dozens of these pontoon-like quffas were roped together and carried thousands of sealed jars of beer, wine, and vegetable oil.

Although there is no evidence that such a multiple quffa barge design was actually used in 2900 BC, it would have been physically possible, practical to build and operate, and consistent with the primitive technology used during the period in which Noah lived.

The "gopher wood" of Genesis 6:14 was probably cypress or a tree known in Sumerian as GI.PAR, although other kinds of wood and reeds were also used. More information on the river barge may be found in Chapter 6 herein.

The popular myth of an ark containing millions of species is not supported by Genesis 7:2–3 which describes the herd as seven pairs (fourteen) of each clean animal (i.e. animals used for temple offerings and food for the priests), one pair of each unclean animal and bird and seven pairs of clean birds. Deuteronomy 14:4–5 lists 10 species of clean animals, which implies 140 clean animals in Noah's barge. Deuteronomy 14:7–18 lists about 30 species of unclean animals and birds. The total deck area required for an estimated 270 animals was 2200 square feet or about one third of the 6600 square foot deck, leaving the other two thirds of the middle deck for baskets of grain and walkways.

The broad words of Genesis 6:19: "And of every living thing of all flesh, you shall bring two of every kind into the ark" is an overgeneralization and may be interpreted narrowly to mean every living thing of importance that Noah owned or had custody of. This means only that he did not leave any of the animals behind, not that he took every living species on the planet. According to Gilgamesh XI,82 "All I had of living creatures I loaded aboard." Yes, all he had, and only those he had.

Noah's barge transported about 270 animals for sale at ports on the river. These included cattle, sheep, goats, oxen and poultry. They were his inventory, his stock in trade. But exotic zoo animals such as elephants, giraffes, hippos, lions, apes and kangaroos were not included in Noah's inventory. Since it would be impossible for Noah to attract millions of animals from all over the planet, he did not do so. The animals came to the barge because their owners' herdsmen brought them to the barge to be shipped as cargo.

Atrahasis mentions "wild creatures of the steppe that eat grass." Noah transported hay to sell to his customers to feed the hay-eating animals they bought from Noah. He also carried additional hay in his barge to feed hay-eating animals during the few days they were being transported to market. The hay, being light, was probably piled on the flat roof which served as an upper deck. Some of the animals were fed grain rather than hay.

Heavy cargo would not be stored on the roof or upper deck, because that would make the barge top heavy. The heavy clay jars of beer, wine, dried fruit and vegetable oil were stored on the lower deck below the water line. The middle deck was probably where the animals were transported. Baskets of grain were probably also transported on the middle deck. The door of the barge (Genesis 6:16) was in its side and opened onto the middle deck, probably a few feet above the water line when the barge was fully loaded. This is the usual place for a door in large river boats designed for calm water. Such a door allowed the animals to be loaded and unloaded onto wharves from the middle deck using a short horizontal gangplank.

The estimated 152 large animals and people consumed less than 44,000 gallons of beer and wine in 382 days. If the jars were stacked two deep, less than 5500 square feet of deck area would be required to store the jars. Well water was not hauled as cargo, because drinking water for the expected three–day voyage was available from the river.

As a wealthy merchant and chief executive of Shuruppak, Noah had access to the labor and materials needed to build a large commercial barge. Since a large river barge would have economy of scale, Noah probably commissioned building of the largest barge that would be practical with the technology that existed then. Noah admitted "I have never built a boat" and he therefore hired skilled boatbuilders. Noah "butchered bulls for the people and killed sheep every day. Beer, oil and wine I gave the workmen to drink... until the ark was completed."

Noah's workers built the barge at a construction site next to the Euphrates River. The workers first had to demolish a house that previously stood on the construction site. The barge was built next to the river so that it could be launched and used for hauling cargo. "The launching was difficult; there was shifting of load above and below, until two-thirds of the structure was submerged".

Mountain or mound?

According to the conventional interpretation of the Genesis version of Noah's story, the sea level rose for 150 days until it covered the tops of all mountains and then subsided for another 150 days. This would have been physically impossible. If the sea level rose to the 16,946 foot peak of "Mount Ararat" for 150 days, the oceans would have had to triple in volume and then shrink back to normal in only 300 days. If the oceans rose 8,600 feet to cover the mountain Pir Omar Gudrun that is often identified as the Mount Niṣir of Gilgamesh, then 1.5 quintillion tons of water would have to appear and disappear in 300 days. A worldwide mountain-covering deluge lasting 300 days is impossible.

The high mountains nearest to Shuruppak where Noah lived were the Zagros mountains which are not visible from Shuruppak because of the curvature of the earth. The Zagros mountains to the east and the Armenian mountains to the north are beyond the horizon. There are no mountains in the southern Tigris–Euphrates valley, only higher or lower hills on a flat alluvial plain. Noah could have seen hills in the Euphrates valley.

The ambiguous Hebrew word *hār* translated as "mountain" in Genesis 7:20 and 8:4 can also mean "hill" and is so translated in many other places in the Old Testament. The Akkadian word for hill/mountain was *shadû* which was also ambiguous and could mean a low hill only ten feet high. There is no unequivocal evidence in the received versions of the flood story that Noah had ever seen a real mountain. The "high hills/mountains" of Genesis 7:19 may have been the high ground in the Euphrates valley that usually remained dry during annual inundations, but could have been flooded by unusually high water that rose about 15 cubits and overflowed the levees. Noah could have seen some of this high ground being flooded, but Noah would not have been able to see all of the hills in the Euphrates valley, because most of the hills were beyond the horizon. Likewise the Zagros and Armenian mountains were beyond the horizon and Noah was not able to see them from Shuruppak or from the Euphrates River.

River flood caused by a thunderstorm

Each spring the Euphrates river flow increases several fold from melting snow in the Armenian mountains. The river crests in May and remains at crest stage through July. According to Berossus, Noah's flood occurred on the fifteenth day of Dasios corresponding approximately to our month of June. Noah's flood occurred in June when the river was at crest stage and when the average rainfall in the Euphrates valley during dry years is zero.

Gilgamesh XI,92–102 clearly describes the conditions that immediately preceded the flood. First there was a thunderstorm and heavy rain and then a river flood that breached the dams and levees along the Euphrates River: "...the weather was fearful to behold... A black cloud arose from the horizon. Adad [the storm god] thundered within it... Erragal tore out the dam posts, Ninurta made the dikes overflow." Atrahasis III,iv,7–9 also refers to the flood as a river flood: "[Dead bodies] have filled the river...Like a raft they have grounded on the riverbank."

The thunderstorm occurred in June when the river level was still at crest stage from the annual spring inundation. When heavy rain began to fall, Noah was greatly alarmed, because heavy rain, when the river was still at crest stage, meant imminent failure of the levees.

The flood was not expected

If Noah had been expecting a great flood, he would not have left behind the library of clay tablet writings that he wanted dug out of the mud at Sippar after the flood (according to Berossus). Noah "provided punting poles" which were needed by his crew to keep the barge headed in the right direction and away from sandbars in the river. Punting poles would be useless in deep water, which indicates that Noah was not expecting a deep flood. The barge was built next to the river so that it could be launched and used for hauling cargo. If the barge had been built solely as a lifeboat, there would not have been any need to launch it into the river.

On the tenth day of the second month (seven days before the storm began), Noah's workers began loading cargo into the barge for another June voyage on the Euphrates River. This was a routine task they did every year in June after a fresh crop of barley had been harvested, packaged in baskets, and hauled to the wharf where Noah's barge was moored. Local ranchers had also sent their livestock to be shipped as cargo on Noah's barge. Seven days later (Genesis 7:10), on the seventeenth day when the storm began, most of the cargo was already loaded.

According to Genesis 7:12–13 Noah entered the ark on the very same day that abnormally heavy rain began to fall. According to Atrahasis III,ii,41 the storm interrupted a family banquet on board the boat: "He invited his people to a banquet. He sent his family on board. They ate and they drank.

But he was in and out. He could not sit, could not crouch, for his composure was broken and he was vomiting gall." Before the storm began, Noah could not have known that a storm and a flood was coming. But when the storm began, Noah recognized that a flood was imminent and he and his workers worked frantically to get the remaining livestock and cargo on board before the rising river overflowed the levees and destroyed unloaded cargo.

The flood lasted only six days

Gilgamesh XI,108–131 describes the storm: "For one whole day the south wind blew, gathering speed as it passed over the land like a battle. One person could not see another... For six days and seven nights the wind blew, and the storm and flood overwhelmed the land. When the seventh day arrived, the storm subsided...The sea grew calm; the wind abated; the flood ceased."

According to Genesis 7:20, "The waters rose fifteen cubits higher and covered the hills." Fifteen cubits defines the magnitude of the river flood. It was not a deluge, but it was deep enough to breach the levees and cover the lowlands and a few hills with water for more than a hundred miles in all directions. Fifteen cubits was how much the water rose above flood stage, not how deep the water was. Depths were different at different locations.

The flood ended after six days, but according to Genesis 8:13 water was on the earth for more than a year. There is no conflict between the river flood lasting six days and deep water lasting a year, because this happened in two phases. The second deep water phase was not really a flood. The water was deep because during the storm the river carried Noah's barge down the river and out into the deep water of the Persian Gulf.

Months of deep water in the Gulf

According to Atrahasis III,ii,55, the flood hero cut the mooring lines during the storm. The swollen river carried the runaway barge downstream and several miles out into the deep water of the Gulf. Noah did not see this during the six-day storm when "one person could not see another." After the storm, Noah was not able to determine where he was, because no land was visible. The horizon to horizon water in the Gulf was visually indistinguishable from the horizon to horizon flood in the river valley.

Noah or Puzur probably measured the depth of the water with a sounding line. They knew the water was getting deeper. But the water was not rising in the Gulf. The water continued to get deeper only because the current and wind carried the barge into deeper water. The barge drifted about the Gulf for five months beyond sight of land and could easily have drifted there for many more months.

For five months Noah could see only horizon to horizon water in all directions from his barge. Noah reported only what he could see and he could not see any dry land as far as the horizon. This was not because all land was flooded, but because the nearest dry land was more than ten miles away and was therefore beyond the horizon.

Fortunately for Noah and his family, the wind mentioned in Genesis 8:1 blew the barge back toward shore where the water was shallow. The wind did not blow the water away. The wind blew the barge into shallow water.

The barge grounded in an estuary

According to Genesis 7:11b "all the fountains of the great deep burst forth" and remained open for five months according to Genesis 8:2. This was a story teller's way of saying that salt water from the deep ocean surrounded Noah's barge for five months. The water was salty because the barge was in the Gulf. After five months the barge was surrounded by brackish water at the mouth of the river where wind and eddy currents near the river mouth had moved the barge. This is confirmed in Gilgamesh XI,195 (line 203 in recent translations) that locates the Babylonian Noah and his wife "at the mouth of the rivers" after the barge grounded.

According to Gilgamesh XI,140: "Upon *KUR nişir* the boat grounded". *KUR nişir* is usually translated as Mount Nişir, but it could also mean Nişir Land or country Nişir. The word *nişir* may have been derived from the Akkadian word *nişirtu* that meant secret or hidden or inaccessible. In the original story, the barge may have grounded in a marshy estuary named Nişir Land because it was inaccessible to shipping. The boat grounded on the 17th day of the 7th month (November) according to Genesis 8:4.

Although story tellers assumed that the water was subsiding, the water depth actually remained about the same for months after the barge grounded and the water was only several feet deep. If the water had continued to subside after the barge grounded, there soon would have been plenty of dry land around the barge. Instead, the barge was surrounded by water for more than two months. The barge grounded several miles from shore in a shallow estuary that was always under water, even at low tide when the river was low. Dry land was beyond the horizon and therefore not visible.

Noah sights land

Two months later in January, Noah's ninth month, the river was rising again as it normally does in January from winter rain in the valley. Noah's barge refloated on this rising water at high tide and drifted close to some islands which later story tellers assumed were tops of mountains/hills. Noah saw these islands on the first day of the tenth month (Genesis 8:5). "I looked for coastlines in the expanse of the sea. Twelve times an island emerged" (Gilgamesh XI,138–139). Noah saw the islands, not because the water was subsiding; it was actually rising from the winter rain. He saw the islands because the barge had drifted near enough to them that he could see them.

More than a month passed (Genesis 8:6) and still all Noah could see was horizon to horizon water. He sent some birds out in hopes that they might see land, but the first birds did not see any, because the islands were already beyond the horizon. The barge was still drifting and had drifted too far away from these islands for Noah or the birds to see them.

Second grounding

During high tide in May, the wind blew the barge closer to shore where the estuary was normally dry at low tide during most of the year, but was temporarily under water during a "spring" tide in the Gulf and when the river current was at its maximum. Again the barge grounded in the mud of the estuary in the first month (May) of the second year near low hills of the delta. There actually were legends that the ark grounded and refloated and then grounded again. Noah could see dry land at a distance, but the barge was still in several feet of water where it grounded. Noah had to wait nearly two months for the river current to subside and for a neap tide in the Gulf so that the part of the estuary where the barge had grounded was no longer under water at high tide. He also had to wait for the surface of the mud flat to bake dry in the hot summer sun.

Noah and family disembark

After the spring inundation subsided, the part of the estuary where Noah's barge grounded was no longer under water and it "lay flat as a rooftop" according to Gilgamesh XI,135. The mud flat was dry enough to walk on. Noah and his family took the animals, grain and other cargo to nearby hills. Noah then built an altar and offered a sacrifice (Genesis 8:20). He did this at the top of a hill-like ziggurat according to Gilgamesh XI,156. The barge was not at the top of a hill; the altar was at the top of a hill.

Here we can see how story tellers got the mistaken notion that the barge grounded on the top of a mountain. By interpreting *shadû* as mountain instead of hill, when they read that Noah had built an altar at the top of a mountain, the story tellers assumed that the barge, being nearby, must also have been at the top of the mountain. But the barge was not near the top of a mountain or even the top of a hill. The barge grounded at sea level in the mud of the intertidal zone of an estuary near the shore of the Persian Gulf.

Other survivors

The overly broad words in Genesis 7:21–23 are myth: "All flesh died that moved upon the earth...and every man... Only Noah was left and those that were with him in the ark." These are a story teller's generalizations based on the fact that his received story did not mention other survivors. But there were other survivors not mentioned in Genesis.

In addition to the eight people mentioned at Genesis 7:13, the boatman and flood hero's daughter were also on the barge during the flood according to Berossus. Since the Euphrates River flood of 2900 BC was only a local flood that lasted six days, there were many survivors and Noah met some of them after he disembarked. In the original version of Noah's story, some of these people were probably mentioned. But with retelling of the story, references to these people were dropped because they conflicted with the story teller's objective of portraying Noah as a super hero who accomplished what nobody else had accomplished. It is not the job of a story teller to discuss people who are beyond the scope of the story.

The barge grounded in the mud of an estuary at the mouth of the Euphrates River. According to Gilgamesh XI,195 (new line number 203) the flood hero and his wife lived "at the mouth of the rivers." After arriving safely at a port at the mouth of the rivers, ship captains were expected to make donations to the local temple in gratitude to the gods. The flood hero "offered burnt offerings on the altar" according to Genesis 8:20b. These offerings were made "at the top of a hill-like ziggurat" according to Gilgamesh XI,156. This ziggurat was a raised platform at the temple of the god Enki in the city of Eridu, then near the shore of the Persian Gulf at the mouth of the Euphrates River. According to Atrahasis fragment RS 22.421, the flood hero said "I lived in the temple of Ea, my lord." The god Ea was known in Sumerian as Enki. The temple of Enki was called the *apsû*–house and included a ziggurat. The altar on top of the ziggurat where Noah made his sacrifice was a fireplace for cooking food that Noah was donating to the temple. The sacrificial food was eaten by the priests of Enki at the Eridu temple.

Noah's family separates

The people from Noah's barge divided into two groups according to Berossus. Noah, his wife, their daughter and the boatman went to live on the island of Dilmun. Noah's sons and their wives went to Sippar, a city then about 190 miles up the Euphrates river from the Gulf coast. According to Berossus, they were requested to "recover the writings from Sippar." They "went by a roundabout way" to Sippar and "dug up the writings at Sippar." This "roundabout way" refers to a journey on foot when they traveled up the west bank of the Tigris River to Mount Judi in the mountains of Ararat and then back down the Tigris River and overland to Sippar. The writings (a library of oven-baked tablets of inscribed clay) that Noah's sons salvaged in Sippar were buried in mud by the heavy rain and overflowing rivers in a place where the tablets could be found in spite of the flood damage. The relatives never saw the flood hero again according to Berossus.

Noah's legal problems

Noah did not return to Shuruppak or resume his duties as king. He could not tow the barge back up the river because it would take years to rebuild all the damaged levees along the river with towpaths on top for barge-towing oxen or human towing teams. The estuary where the barge grounded may have been many miles from the nearest navigable channel. Moreover, it was the wrong time of year for river traffic and the water level was low. Even if Noah were willing to abandon his barge and move the animals overland, there were other reasons why Noah did not return to Shuruppak.

More than a year had passed since the flood and Noah had been presumed dead. Noah was responsible for government grain in his custody, much of which he and his family and the animals had eaten. And Noah had not paid any taxes for more a year. Sumerian kings were trustees, not autocrats and were not exempt from the law. People who failed to pay their taxes were forced into slavery. Noah had been king of Shuruppak before the flood, but another king was ruling there now and Noah would be viewed as a rival. Ziusudra iv,160 mentions "the overthrowing of the kingship" in connection with the flood. Atrahasis III,i,44 mentions that the flood hero was "expelled." Gilgamesh XI,39–41 has the flood hero admitting that a god "hates me. I dare no longer walk in his land nor live in his city."

Soon after the barge grounded, Noah probably sold most of the animals, grain and the remaining cargo at Eridu. Noah's animals did not restock the entire world or even the entire valley. Only Noah's sons, the temple at Eridu, and local ranchers near Eridu benefitted. News of Noah's arrival at Eridu quickly reached his creditors who probably came to Eridu to repossess all of the remaining cargo and Noah's assets. Noah probably stayed at Eridu, at the mouth of the rivers, only long enough to dispose of the barge and the cargo and then left Eridu before his creditors arrived.

With his job gone and his merchanting business ruined, Noah probably wanted only to retire in comfort in a land where his creditors and the Shuruppak government would not bother him, i.e. in a foreign country where he had no debts. According to Ziusudra vi,260, the flood hero went to live in the land of Dilmun. Dilmun was a port on an island in the Persian Gulf and is identified by scholars as Bahrain.

Mount Judi and the mountains of Ararat

The "mountains of Ararat" mentioned in Genesis 8:4 have long been identified with the Armenian mountains in what is now eastern Turkey, a region called Uruatri or Urartu by the Assyrians. But since the land where Noah's barge grounded was not in a mountainous region, the barge could not have grounded on an Ararat/Urartu mountain. Story tellers who believed that Noah's barge grounded in the mountains of Ararat misunderstood the story told by Noah's son Shem (see Figure 3, page 67).

After the barge grounded on the Gulf coast, Shem and others traveled on foot from Eridu northwest up the west side of the Tigris River through the region later named Assyria to the "plain at the foot of an extensive mountain" which was probably Cudi Dagh (Mount Judi) in the Armenian mountains of Ararat. Two months later they traveled back down the west side of the Tigris River on foot in a southeast direction to about where Baghdad is today and crossed overland to Sippar on the Euphrates River. This describes how Noah's sons "went by a roundabout way" to Sippar.

After arriving at Sippar, Shem probably told the people there about his adventures, including floating on his father's barge for a year and coming down from the heights of Mount Judi. Years later, some story tellers misunderstood Shem's story and assumed that the barge had grounded on Mount Judi. This falsely linked the barge grounding spot to Mount Judi in the mountains of Ararat.

How old was Noah?

Most of the names and numbers of Genesis 5 may have been derived from land tax records in the temple archives for Noah's ancestral land and from a few birth records in the temple. Whenever a landowner died, a new clay tablet would be prepared to record who was responsible for paying the taxes and these tablets were stored in the archives. The tax archives thus became a depository for genealogical information on families where ancestral land was passed down from father to son for several generations.

The tax records did not record the ages of each man when his son was born, but may have recorded the year name when the previous owner died. In many instances the previous owner was the new owner's father. Temple archives may also have recorded the births of the children of nobles and other people connected with the temple, including Noah's ancestors. Extracts from these tax and birth records were recorded on clay tablets and survived because copies of the records related to the flood story were collected and stored in archives in various cities where other government records were stored and where archivists were committed to preserving old records.

The year numbers in Genesis 5–9 were recorded in years and tenths of years, not hundreds of years, using archaic pre-cuneiform round-stylus number signs. In several instances, seasons were rounded to tenths of years. The numbers were distorted by three errors made by ancient scribes.

Three hundred years after Noah's flood, about 2600 BC, during the Early Dynastic IIIa period, a Shuruppak scribe calculated the Genesis 5 numbers for Noah's ancestors from the tax records and birth records collected before the flood. The Shuruppak scribe did his calculations in the SHE–GUR–MAH number system originally designed for counting volumes of grain. About 1800 BC, when a Babylonian scribe translated the archaic numbers into cuneiform, he incorrectly assumed that the numbers were written in the Sumerian proto-sexagesimal number system designed for counting discrete objects such as animals. By confusing the number signs of the two systems, the scribe effectively converted tenths of years into years and tens of years into hundreds of years, although these numbers were not decimal numbers. Mistaking fractions for integers was the first error.

In 2600 BC there was no single standard number system in Sumer. In Shuruppak where Noah lived, a nonstandard number system was used in which the *gur* sign meant 48 instead of the standard 60. In 1800 BC, when the Babylonian scribe translated the archaic number signs into the sexagesimal system, he assumed that standard signs were being used. As a result, he read 48 as the number 60 and inflated by 12 all numbers greater than 48. This was the second error.

The numbers were further altered about 300 BC after the Babylonian exile by a Judean scribe who subtracted 100 from many of the numbers and made other alterations to the Proto-Masoretic Text selected by the Masoretes. This was the third error. Most modern translations of the Bible are made from later editions of the Masoretic Text with the altered numbers.

The Genesis 5–11 numbers in the Septuagint (a Greek translation from Hebrew) are closest to the original numbers. When the Septuagint scholars translated the Hebrew Pentateuch into Greek at Alexandria, Egypt about 280 BC, they used a Hebrew text that was edited in the 5th and 4th centuries. This was an older source than the Proto-Masoretic Text selected during the first century CE.

The "six hundred and first year" of Genesis 8:13 should be read as "sixty-first year" (when Noah was 49). This was a date calculated by the priest P who wrote Genesis 5 and 7:11 based on a Babylonian text that was already corrupted by mistranslated archaic numbers.

In 2600 BC, when the Shuruppak scribe calculated the Genesis 5 numbers from land tax records, the chain of title in these tax records went back more than 130 years, but was broken at the tax record of "Adam" because the previous owner's record could not be found. The oldest tax record in the extract may have included the name of the land owner, but this name may have been an untranslatable pictograph that resembled the Sumerian sign for "man." The scribe probably copied the pictograph as "man." Later this sign was copied as if it were a proper name and still later translated into Hebrew as "adam" a Hebrew word for man. Likewise Enos (enosh) was another Hebrew word for man or men and was used because the original untranslatable pictographic name in the tax record was copied as "man".

Noah's ancestors fathered their first sons when they were in their late teens or early twenties and they died in their late seventies or early eighties. Noah's grandfather Methuselah lived longer than the other ancestors and died a few months after the barge grounded at the age of 85. The flood occurred when Noah was 48. Noah lived to be 83. More information on the Genesis 5 numbers may be found in chapter 7 herein.

Transmission of the flood story

Noah was chief executive of Shuruppak during the end of the Jemdet Nasr period and his story began to circulate during the Early Dynastic I period that followed the flood of 2900 BC. During the Early Dynastic I period, the art of writing was not yet sufficiently advanced for recording every word of a narrative. Three hundred years passed before the flood story was written in clay in narrative form by a scribe at the beginning of the Early Dynastic III period (about 2600 BC). During these three centuries of oral transmission, story tellers and epic poets mythologized mundane events in the story and made various mistakes.

Shortly after the flood of 2900 BC, there were at least three oral traditions about the flood:

> Noah's story at Dilmun
> Shem's story at Sippar
> a priest's story at Eridu

As years passed, these bodies of oral tradition were partially merged by story tellers who collected new story details from travelers from the other cities. Some of the details apparently became garbled during this merger of traditions, especially after the witnesses had died and were no longer available to correct misunderstandings.

Of the three eyewitness versions of the flood story, the Dilmun version from Noah was the most detailed. The chronology of the flood probably came from Noah's memory of the main events that he could recall by month and day. Barge construction details probably also came from Noah.

The second version of the flood story came from Shem at Sippar. Shem's story was about his roundabout journey on foot from the Gulf coast up the Tigris River to Mount Judi and back down the Tigris River on foot and overland to Sippar on the Euphrates River.

The third version of the flood story probably came from an Eridu priest of Enki who gave a supernatural slant to the story. This version was known to the author of Atrahasis, the editor of Gilgamesh and to Berossus. The priest's story told of the temple oracle mentioned by Berossus: "a voice came from the air, telling them that they must respect the gods." The priest's contribution to the story is the least credible of the three eyewitnesses, because he or later story tellers mythologized events he witnessed.

Three oral traditions evolved from these three eyewitness reports and were combined into one archetype flood story authored by a Shuruppak scribe writing in Sumerian during the Early Dynastic IIIa period. This archetype flood story spawned the six surviving versions of Noah's flood story and influenced several lesser versions. The six surviving versions describe similar events using similar words and phrases because they were all derived from this one archetype story written by one scribe. The archetype story also included myth, misunderstandings and mistakes that had become attached to the story during the oral transmission phase. Although the source material for this archetype story began as oral tradition, after the archetype story was committed to clay tablets, it survived almost unchanged for more than two thousand years in various Sumerian and Babylonian archives.

Several extracts were made from the archetype story by later writers, editors, poets, and story tellers. Although these extracts retained many of the original distinctive words and phrases that can still be found in the surviving versions, the unity of the story was blurred as several people selected different parts of the archetype story and modified them to suit their needs. The Genesis version was one of these extracts.

Both the J and P Genesis versions of the flood story were derived from the archetype story found in the Babylonian archives during the exile, probably after the capture of Babylon by Cyrus II in 539 BC. Judean priests obtained extracts of the flood story from a translation of the archetype flood story in the archives. These Hebrew extracts were later combined during the post-exilic period.

In addition to the archetype flood story, the Judean priests also found in the Babylonian archives a genealogy of Noah's ancestors which became Genesis 5.

Later, in the third century BC, Berossus used a copy of the archetype flood story when writing his history of Babylonia.

The lost "book about Khsisuthros and his sons" referred to by Moses of Khoren was probably a translation of the archetype flood story. Khsisuthros was Ziusudra, the Sumerian Noah.

More discussion of the transmission of the flood story may be found in chapter 8.

Mutually reinforcing errors

Several errors were made by ancient story tellers that turned the flood legend into myth. These errors resisted correction because the errors reinforced each other.

For example, after the barge grounded, Noah built an altar at the top of a ziggurat hill at the temple of Enki in the city of Eridu. The barge was at sea level and the altar at the top of the hill was dozens of feet above sea level. By misinterpreting the ambiguous word for hill as mountain, story tellers assumed that the nearby barge was also at the top of a mountain. They made this error because Noah's sons visited a real mountain, Mount Judi, after the barge grounded. But the barge did not ground on a mountain and the water never rose up onto a mountain. Because Mount Judi was mentioned in the same story with Noah's barge and his sacrifice on an altar, story tellers assumed that Noah's altar and hence the barge were both on Mount Judi.

These mistakes were reinforced because Mount Judi was in the mountains of Ararat and a country with a similar name *Aratta* had also experienced a river flood at the same time as the Euphrates River flood. To the uncritical story tellers, these separate places seemed to be the same place. The river flood in Aratta was confused with the Euphrates River flood and the mountains of Aratta were confused with the mountains of Ararat. Mount Judi in the Ararat mountains was confused with the ziggurat hill (not mountain) where Noah used the altar. The journey of Noah's sons on foot down the river to Sippar was confused with their earlier voyage on the barge during the storm. The six-day flood in the Euphrates River valley in which the river rose fifteen cubits over flood stage was confused with the deep water of the Persian Gulf.

These errors continue to the present day, especially in modern paraphrases of the Genesis flood story. Fortunately, the surviving Hebrew, Akkadian, and Sumerian fragments preserve enough of the original story that these errors can be detected and corrected.

Conclusions

The Noachian flood stories are mostly myth, but these stories also include enough legendary detail to identify Noah's flood as the historical Euphrates River flood about 2900 BC that was the basis for the flood myth. The archetype Noah was a wealthy land owner before becoming chief executive of Shuruppak. Cattle and grain were hauled in river barges on the Euphrates River and the ark was a commercial river barge. The river flood was caused by a heavy six-day thunder storm in June when the river was already at crest stage during the annual inundation.

There were fewer than 280 ordinary ranch animals on Noah's barge during the flood. The barge also contained thousands of baskets of barley and thousands of jars of beer and other cargo that were being transported to market. Noah did not know a flood was coming until he saw a thunderstorm approaching. The river rose 15 cubits over flood stage and breached the levees at Shuruppak where Noah's barge was moored. After Noah cut the mooring lines, the swollen Euphrates River carried the runaway barge down the river into the Persian Gulf.

The flood of 2900 BC lasted only six days, but Noah's barge drifted about the deep water of the Persian Gulf for several months before grounding.

This deep water was not a flood; it was just the normally deep water of the Persian Gulf. During these several months, Noah could not see land because the nearest land was more than ten miles away and beyond the horizon. The barge did not ground on a mountain top; it grounded in the mud of an estuary at the mouth of the Euphrates River.

Two months after grounding, the barge refloated and continued to drift in the estuary for four more months. During high tide in May, the barge grounded a second time in the intertidal zone of the estuary, within sight of land. Two months later, after disembarking, Noah visited the temple of Enki at the nearby city of Eridu and offered a sacrifice on an altar at the top of a ziggurat hill, a high platform at the temple. Story tellers mistranslated hill as mountain. There were many survivors of the river flood and Noah met some of them after the barge grounded.

Noah had legal problems after the barge grounded because he was in default on his taxes and debts in Shuruppak and Nippur. He could not return to these cities because he would be forced into slavery. Noah, his wife, daughter, and his boatman sailed on a small sailboat to the island of Dilmun where they lived in exile. Noah's sons and their wives traveled on foot up the west side of the Tigris River to the base of 7,000 foot Mount Judi in the mountains of Ararat. After staying there two months, they traveled on foot back down the west side of the Tigris River and crossed overland to Sippar on the Euphrates River. Story tellers misunderstood the story and assumed that the barge had grounded on Mount Judi in the mountains of Ararat. The so-called "Mount Ararat" (*Aghri Dagh* in eastern Turkey) was not involved in the original adventures of Noah or his sons.

Noah's barge was constructed of wood and reeds. The lower part of the barge probably consisted of dozens of woven reed quffas covered inside and out with pitch. Each quffa was probably lined with wood planks assembled inside each quffa using shell-first construction. The framing was inserted inside the shell of wood planks after the shell was constructed inside the woven quffas. Dozens of these pontoon-like quffas were roped together and carried thousands of sealed jars of beer, which was what Noah and his family and the animals drank while they were drifting about the Persian Gulf.

Noah did not live to be 950 years. That was an ancient mistranslation of archaic (pre-sexagesimal, not decimal) numbers that had no decimal points. The Septuagint numbers in Genesis 5 are closest to the original numbers if fractions are distinguished from integers. The flood occurred when Noah was 48 years old and Noah lived to be 83 years old.

These numbers and events in Noah's life are based on reconstructed legends and are not provably historic. The conclusions are restated in chapter 16 with percentage confidence level estimates of how likely the conclusions are to being factual.

Table VIII – Timeline of the Flood Story

MAY

month 1

Euphrates River inundation reached crest stage.

Hay and barley were harvested.

Beer was brewed.

JUNE

Ranchers brought livestock to Noah's wharf.

month 2, day 10 – Genesis 7:10

Workers began loading cargo into the barge at Shuruppak.

— 7 days later —

month 2, day 17 – Genesis 7:11

Noah's family had a banquet on the barge.

A thunder storm approached.

Noah's workers loaded remaining cargo.

Heavy rain began to fall.

The river flood rose 15 cubits above the levees.

The river flood washed out dams and levees.

Noah cut the mooring lines.

The barge floated down the river into the Persian Gulf.

— 6 days later — Gilgamesh XI,127

month 2, day 24

The storm ended.

The river flood subsided.

The sea was calm.

The barge was in the Persian Gulf beyond sight of land.

The deep salt water phase began.

The barge drifted about the Gulf.

— 5 months elapsed — Genesis 7:24, 8:3

Wind blew the barge into a shallow estuary.

The barge was in brackish water at mouth of Euphrates river.

NOVEMBER

month 7, day 17 – Genesis 8:4

The barge grounded in an estuary several miles from shore.

No land was visible.

— about 2 months elapsed —

JANUARY

month 9

The river was rising from winter rain.

The barge refloated on rising water at high tide.

The barge drifted again.

— 14 days later —
FEBRUARY
month 10, day 1 – Genesis 8:5
The barge drifted near some islands.
Noah saw several islands.
— 40 days elapsed — Genesis 8:6–7
MARCH
month 11, day 11
The barge was still drifting.
No land was visible because it was beyond the horizon.
Noah sent out raven.
— about 6 days later — Genesis 8:8–9
month 11, day 17
Noah sent out a dove.
— 7 days later — Genesis 8:10–11
month 11, day 24
Noah sent out a dove.
— 7 days later — Genesis 8:12
APRIL
month 12, day 1
Noah sent out a dove.
— 30 days later —
MAY
year 2, month 1, day 1 – Genesis 8:13
River current was at maximum during a spring tide.
The barge grounded a second time near land.
The water was several feet deep at high tide.
— 1 month later —
JUNE
month 2
The river current decreased.
— 26 days later —
month 2, day 27 – Genesis 8:14
Noah disembarked during a neap tide.
The estuary was flat as a roof top and dry.
Noah took his family and cargo to nearby hills.
month 2, day 28
Noah offered a sacrifice on the top of a ziggurat hill at the
temple of Enki at Eridu.
The priests of Enki ate the sacrifice.
Noah lived at the temple of Enki for a short time.
— about 3 days later —

JULY

month 3, about day 1

    Noah sold his barge and cargo at Eridu.

    Noah, wife, daughter, and boatman sailed for Dilmun.

    The sons and their wives traveled on foot up the Tigris River.

    — about 2 months elapsed —

SEPTEMBER

month 5

    Noah's ancestral land at Shuruppak was sold to pay debts.

    Methuselah died.

    — about 2 months elapsed —

NOVEMBER

month 7

    The sons and wives arrived on foot at the base of Mount Judi.

    — 2 months elapsed —

JANUARY

month 9

    The sons and wives begin journey on foot down the Tigris River.

    — about 2 months elapsed —

MARCH

month 11

    The sons crossed overland to Sippar on the Euphrates River.

    The sons told their story at Sippar.

    The sons dug up a library of tablets from the mud.

11

Expanded Theory

"He who would know the truth
must read between the lines."
Anon.

This chapter repeats the material in Chapter 10 and retells the flood story as a speculative narrative without evidence or arguments. Several additional conjectures are also included here. Some of these are based on source material that is clearly mythical and may turn out to be fiction. But this story has two important qualities: each event described here would have been physically possible, and was reported or suggested by the ancient sources or plausibly fills gaps in the ancient stories. The words probably, maybe, perhaps, and suppose have been omitted but are implied. Readers who want less conjecture may turn to Chapter 10 for the basic theory.

About 2900 BC, 49 centuries ago, in the land of ancient Sumer, there lived a cattle merchant who was known in his later years as Ziusudra (meaning 'long life'). He is now commonly known as Noah and that is the name he will have here. Noah was born into a wealthy family about 2948 BC. Most of Noah's known ancestors fathered their first sons when they were in their late teens or early twenties and they died in their late seventies or early eighties. Noah's grandfather Methuselah and father Lamech were among the elite in the city-state of Shuruppak where their ancestral land was located. This land was first acquired about 3090 BC by one of Noah's ancestors, nine generations before Noah, when Shuruppak was first being built about the beginning of the Jemdet Nasr period.

Shuruppak was then on the Euphrates River and the river was used for transporting cargo, especially during the annual river inundation during May through July. Merchants transported people and cargo on the river in round woven-reed boats called quffas that were coated inside and out with a mixture of bituminous pitch and oil to make them waterproof. Quffas are still being used and are sometimes more than 20 feet in diameter.

Noah ordered his own fleet of quffas to be built for transporting his livestock. After each barley harvest in late May, his quffas also hauled thousands of baskets of barley for the Shuruppak government. Noah accumulated a small fortune in gold and silver at a time when these metals were used mostly by professional merchants.

By the time Noah was 30, Noah and Lamech were prosperous merchants transporting cargo on the river. Their quffas carried cattle, sheep, goats, grain, poultry, vegetable oil, beer, and textiles down the river. They also carried imported and sea products up the river including salt, fish, lumber, stone, and metals brought in sailing ships to ports on the Persian Gulf coast.

The capital of Sumer was then at Sippar under the leadership of Enmenduranna. Lamech was 52 years old and Noah was 33 years old when Enmenduranna died about 2915 BC. A new chief executive was needed, and Lamech was elected by the leaders of Sumer. After taking office, Lamech and the other leaders moved the capital to Shuruppak which was closer to the Gulf and was on important trade routes.

Noah's cargo transporting business continued to expand. Whenever the Shuruppak government needed cargo hauled on the river, Noah's barges provide the transportation. The government had a monopoly on importing and exporting which were tied to diplomatic relations with foreign governments. Noah's fleet of quffas became increasingly involved with transporting government grain down river to the city of Ur, the major Gulf port for exporting to other countries.

As business expanded, so did labor costs. It took only 3 days to haul cargo down the river from Shuruppak to Ur, but returning back up river from Ur to Shuruppak took 10 days. The cost of feeding the quffa crews during the trip back to Sippar became excessive because four men were required to row each quffa, and hundreds of rowers were costly to feed.

Instead of rowing the quffas as separate boats, a small team of slaves and oxen could tow dozens of quffas that were joined together into large barges. Noah encouraged other city-states on the river to build tow paths on the levees along the river from Sippar south to Ur so that towing teams could tow Noah's barges. A large barge is cheaper per ton of cargo than several small barges. Thus Noah's transportation costs were lower when dozens of quffas were joined together into large barges and this economy of scale provided financial incentives for building larger barges.

Noah becomes chief executive

When Noah was 38 and his father Lamech was 57, Lamech stepped aside after 5 years as chief executive of Shuruppak because of failing eyesight. The elders of Shuruppak elected Noah to take his place. The elders were the wealthy people that Noah had known for many years. Noah was widely respected as a leader and had often spoken to the city assembly and the elders of Shuruppak. They knew that Noah was smart and charismatic, he was a successful merchant and trade official, he could organize and manage large numbers of people, he was very fair, honest, dependable, paid his debts when due, and he contributed generously to the temples.

Noah, like his father, had negotiated business deals with merchants and government officials. Noah also negotiated with high priests in the various temples in cities that traded with Shuruppak. It was especially important to Noah that temple officials in Shuruppak, Nippur, Uruk, Ur, and Eridu support his plans to increase export trade with foreign countries and with the trading port at Dilmun, an island in the Persian Gulf.

Temple priests had to keep well informed about what was happening in other cities and other countries because government officials often consulted temple oracles for advice. Noah usually offered a sacrifice at the temple in each city he visited and listened to the advice of the oracles. The high priest of Enki at Eridu was one of the temple officials that Noah consulted. Noah persuaded the temple of Enlil at Nippur to finance the cargo on his barge by lending grain and other commodities to barter for imported goods. When Noah later presented his plans to the elders of Shuruppak, the temple oracles had already told them that the gods (priests) supported his plans.

Noah's plans for a 3-deck, 200 foot barge were accepted by the city elders and construction began. As the chief executive of Shuruppak, Noah had access to the labor and materials needed to build a large commercial river barge. The elders of Shuruppak encouraged and supported building of the barge under control of their own leader Noah, because they envisioned that the barge would substantially increase the wealth of Shuruppak merchants. Noah promoted this vision and told the elders that the gods would "shower plenty on you, an abundance of birds, a profusion of fish" when the new barge became operational.

With financial support from temples, merchants and other investors, Noah could build a much larger barge than the Shuruppak budget or his personal wealth would allow. Noah's foreign supplier of cedarwood from the trading port of Dilmun helped finance the barge by supplying timber and split and hewn lumber, because when the barge was operational it would transport the lumber merchant's imported lumber and other cargo upriver from gulf ports of entry. Noah took on greater amounts of debt that was secured by his ancestral land and other property.

Building a river barge

Noah's ark was a commercial river barge designed for use in the calm water of the lower Euphrates River. The barge was assembled as a horizontal rectangular array of 63 flat-bottomed quffas arranged in 7 columns and 9 rows. Each quffa was about 22 feet long, 4.7 feet wide, and 7.5 feet deep. The entire barge was about 200 feet long, 33 feet wide, and 20 feet high. The Genesis 6:15 dimensions were originally in hand spans rather than cubits.

The barge had three decks. The upper deck was a flat roof that was piled high with tons of hay covered by an awning a cubit above the heads of the workers. The middle deck was where the animals were stored along with baskets of grain stacked several high. The lower deck consisted of the bottoms of the wood-lined quffas which were built shell-first. A single wood hull 200 feet long would have leaked excessively, but leakage was not a serious problem with small tar-coated quffas which were roped together like pontoons in a pontoon bridge. Heavy cargo, including sealed clay jars of beer, wine, and vegetable oil, were hauled in these quffa-like pontoons.

The main door of the barge was in its side and opened onto the middle deck about 2.5 feet above the water line when the barge was fully loaded. This is the usual place for a door in large river boats designed for calm water. Such a door allowed the animals to be loaded and unloaded onto wharves from the middle deck using a short horizontal gangplank.

Noah did not get personally involved with design and construction of the barges. He admitted "I have never built a boat." Noah was a chief executive and executives delegate responsibility to subordinates. He "entrusted the great structure including its contents" to Puzur–Amurri who was Noah's boatman, his general manager in charge of the entire barge operation. Among his many responsibilities, Puzur hired and managed master shipwrights and numerous skilled workmen to design and build the barge. Noah's servants "butchered bulls for the people and killed sheep every day. Beer, oil and wine I gave the workmen to drink... until the ark was completed."

The construction site chosen for the barge was on a parcel of land on which a house stood next to the Euphrates River. Noah was advised by a temple oracle to "Tear down the house, build a boat." Noah ordered the house demolished and the land cleared for the construction site. After the barge was built and launched into the river, the land was used for stockyards, warehouses, and barge maintenance facilities.

Noah had the barge built next to the Euphrates River so that it could be launched directly into the river and used for hauling cargo. "The launching was difficult. There was shifting of load above and below, until two-thirds of the structure was submerged." Noah also "provided punting poles" that were needed by his crew to keep the barge headed in the right direction and away from sandbars in the river. Punting poles would be useless in deep water, but Noah was not expecting deep water.

There were fewer than 280 animals on Noah's barge and they occupied only one third of the middle deck. Baskets of grain and other cargo occupied the other two thirds of the middle deck. Many of the animals were fed grain rather than hay. Noah said "All I had of living beings I loaded aboard." Yes, all he had, and only those he had.

Noah's clean animals included cattle, sheep and goats. His unclean animals included raven, swine and eagles. They were his inventory that he was offering for sale or had already sold and not yet delivered. But most of the world's animals were not included. Exotic zoo animals such as elephants, giraffes, hippos, apes, tigers and kangaroos were not present in Noah's cattle barge.

The animals came to the barge because their owners' herdsmen brought them to the barge to be transported as cargo. Most of the livestock, and other cargo on the barge was owned by other merchants, temples, or the Shuruppak government.

Before the flood

Each spring the Euphrates river flow increases several fold from melting snow in the Armenian mountains. The river crests in May but remains high until late July. Farmers welcomed this annual inundation because they needed the water to irrigate their fields. Transportation of cargo on the river was busiest during the inundation when the river channels were deep enough for large boats.

Each year in June, the barge and its crew left Shuruppak for a few weeks on a voyage down the river as far as the marsh land in the vicinity of Ur. The cities Ur and Eridu were then near the mouth of the Euphrates River and near the shore of the Persian Gulf. Noah scheduled the annual voyage in mid June after the spring inundation had crested and a fresh crop of barley and hay had been harvested. The return trip took place a few weeks later in July while the river was still deep enough for navigation.

Puzur supervised the people who steered the barge through the channels of the river while slaves hauled or drove oxen hauling the barge. Puzur also supervised the stevedores who loaded cargo into the barge and he supervised distribution and delivery of the cargo at port cities where the barge docked. Noah's servants and slaves did the work, and supervision of these workers was done by other servants.

Although Noah was head of the government, he was personally responsible for the safety and honest distribution of government property that he managed. This included barley that was owned by the government and earmarked for export. Barley was a major export and Noah's barge transported thousands of baskets of barley to Ur for transfer to foreign sailing ships. Thousands of jars of beer were also transported for sale at cities on the river and for export.

The barge also transported hay as cargo for sale. The amount of hay was many times more than needed to feed the animals during the week they were being transported to market. Buyers of Noah's animals also needed to buy hay to feed the animals, perhaps for several months, until the animals were ready for slaughter.

When Noah was 44, his father Lamech died at the age of 63. Noah was still chief executive of Shuruppak. His barge operation continued to be successful year after year. When Noah was 48 years old, he had been chief executive of Shuruppak for ten years and was still widely respected as a leader. His wife was raising their three sons at their Shuruppak ranch. Noah's eldest son Shem was about 15.

At the usual time in June, Noah ordered his workers to load the cattle, grain and other cargo onto his river barge for another routine voyage down the Euphrates River. Then a freak storm changed his life.

The thunderstorm and river flood

It was mid June. The river had crested more than a month ago and the channel was still deep enough for hauling loaded barges. The hay and barley had been harvested. For the past week local farm workers had been delivering thousands of baskets of barley overland to Noah's warehouse next to the wharf where his barge was moored. Also during the past week, local ranch workers had delivered a few hundred cattle, sheep, goats, poultry and other animals to Noah's stockyard next to the wharf. Likewise, hay farmers brought tons of hay to Noah's warehouse and producers of beer, wine and vegetable oil brought thousands of sealed clay jars of their products to Noah's warehouse for transporting on the barge. Noah's inspectors tagged and recorded the animals and other cargo as they were loaded into the barge.

The heavy clay jars of beer and wine were the first cargo to be stowed in the lower deck of the barge, in the quffa pontoons. Then the animals and baskets of grain were loaded onto the middle deck. Finally the hay was piled on the roof which served as a third deck. An awning was stretched above the hay to keep direct sunlight from drying out the hay and to keep sunlight from heating the barge.

Yesterday the workmen had finished loading the cargo. Later today the hauling crew and their task masters were scheduled to arrive with oxen to haul the barge and its cargo down river. If everything went as planned, the barge would stop at Uruk and other cities along the river and at the Gulf port city of Ur. But things did not go as planned.

The previous night something strange happened that had never occurred before in June, at least not that the old people of Shuruppak could remember. A small amount of rain had fallen, although not enough to do any damage. This morning the sky was still cloudy, especially near the horizon where clouds were getting increasingly dark.

Shortly after dawn, Noah and his family visited Puzur at the wharf where the barge was moored. The day was expected to be a busy one with much last minute checking and rearranging of the cargo. City officials and the high priest would be here to see the barge off. Noah was planning to give a speech during the ceremony. After the barge left port, Noah and his family were planning to return to their main house at the top of the hill in Shuruppak.

Noah was not planning to ride on the barge. He had more important things to do than ride on a cattle barge. But he was present today to make last-minute decisions if any were needed. Nothing could be allowed to go wrong because Noah's personal wealth as well as his reputation as chief executive of Shuruppak were at stake.

Puzur invited Noah and his family on board the barge for breakfast. Puzur's domestic servant girls prepared the food and carried it onto the barge and placed it on the table before Noah's family. For a few hours Noah could relax with his family and his old friend Puzur.

The distant clouds were getting darker. "A black cloud arose from the horizon" with "thundering within it." Noah "looked up at the appearance of the weather. It was fearful to behold." It would not have been unusual for a thunderstorm to occur during the winter. A few inches of rain often fell when the river level was low. But this thunderstorm was coming in June when the average rainfall was zero. As the thunderstorm intensified, Noah became increasingly alarmed because with the river level still at crest stage from the annual spring inundation, continual heavy rain meant the river would soon rise high above flood stage and overflow the levees.

When Noah realized that a flood was imminent, he ordered his family members to remain on the barge. If they were on shore they might get trapped in rapidly rising water. Noah's stockyards and warehouses near the wharf were on the flood plain just behind the levee next to the river and contained goods and livestock he had not planned to transport on the barge. These goods and livestock included cargo he had just received for sale in Shuruppak and would be destroyed when the river overflowed the levees. Noah and his workers worked frantically to get this cargo onto the barge before the levees overflowed. Noah "could not sit, could not crouch, for his composure was broken and he was vomiting gall."

Noah's family was already on board for the breakfast, but his 85 year old grandfather Methuselah was still across town in Noah's house at the top of the hill. He was safe because the river would not rise that high.

The woven reed awning that kept direct sunlight off the barge would blow away in the storm. Noah ordered it lowered and lashed to the deck. It was porous and would not keep rain off the hay, but it would prevent the hay from blowing away. When the rising river overflowed the levees, Noah ordered the gangplank removed and the main door bolted and sealed. Although his commercial barge was never intended as a life boat, it served that function well. The severity and duration of the storm and flood came as a surprise to Noah, but by acting decisively at the last moment, he was able to save his livestock and cargo. By the time it was clear that a flood was coming, it was too late to move all the cargo to high ground.

The storm came up from the Arabian Sea from the south and lasted six days. "For one whole day the south wind blew, gathering speed as it passed over the land like a battle. One person could not see another person."

As the heavy rain continued, torrents of water flowed down from the mountains and raised the water level in the river valley. The river rose fifteen cubits in Shuruppak and breached the levees, just as Noah had feared. As the water rose, there was a danger that the barge would heel over as the mooring lines that were still attached to mooring poles held down one side of the barge. Noah ordered the mooring lines cut and the barge was set adrift. The swollen river carried the runaway barge downriver toward the Persian Gulf and Noah lost contact with potential rescuers.

"For six days and seven nights the wind blew and the storm and flood overwhelmed the land." The barge was completely at the mercy of the current and during the six day storm the swollen river carried the barge 70 miles down the river and several miles out into the Persian Gulf. Noah was not able to see the barge entering the Gulf, because all of the landmarks were under water or were too far away to see during the storm when "one person could not see another." The river current and wind at the mouth of the river carried the barge into the deep water of the Gulf and beyond sight of land.

"When the seventh day arrived, the pounding storm flood [weakened]. The sea grew calm. The wind abated. The [river] flood ceased." The sky became clear again and bright sunlight warmed the barge. Noah opened a hatch and climbed up on the deck, expecting to see the river banks and the valley where he lived. Instead all he saw was endless water from horizon to horizon in all directions. The barge was drifting slowly in the Persian Gulf and dry land was just beyond the horizon, but Noah did not know this. It looked to Noah as if his whole world was flooded.

Dead bodies were floating about in the water. Noah "sat down and wept. Tears ran down over his face." He looked in all directions for land. Nothing. Puzur, being an experienced river barge operator, repeatedly measured the water depth with a sounding line. The water was deeper than anything in their experience, although the water was not too deep to measure. Noah and Puzur assumed that deeper water meant rising water, because earlier they had seen the river rising as the water became deeper at Shuruppak. But the water continued to get deeper only because the current and northwest wind carried the barge into deeper water in the Gulf.

The woven reed awning was still holding down the hay, but the hay was soaking wet. Noah and his sons untied and rolled up the awning so that the hot sun would dry the wet hay that would otherwise become moldy.

There was something very strange about the water surrounding the barge. River water sometimes was brackish, but this water was salty. Story tellers later assumed that the salty water near Noah's barge must have come from an underground ocean. Therefore, the sources of salt water, which they called fountains, must be open and these fountains were gushing salt water all over the land. If only the gods would shut off the fountains of salt water, the water would drain off the land, so they thought.

Deep water in the Persian Gulf

Of course, the story tellers were mistaken about this. The land was not covered by salt water and the salt water surrounding the barge was not going to drain away. This deep body of salt water was an arm of the Persian Gulf and had been there all along and would continue to be there. Noah's only chance of survival was to reach dry land just beyond the horizon. A passing sailboat might be able to rescue Noah and his family, but no boats came near enough to see the barge.

Then the rain returned. Each day and night some rain would fall. Not as heavy as during the 6-day thunderstorm, but the rain continued off and on for forty days and forty nights. That would only prolong the flood, Noah thought. He was mistaken about this too. The flood had ended weeks ago. The barge was not floating in flood water. But to Noah, more rain meant more flooding. At least the rain was fresh water that he and his family could collect for use as drinking water.

The only other things in the barge they could drink were beer and wine. Even the animals had to drink beer. There were thousands of jars of beer stored on the bottom deck. Noah and the others were in no danger of dying from dehydration. Since nobody knew how long the deep water would last, they collected as much rain water as they could in empty beer jars.

The rain also helped cool the barge. On bright sunny days it got uncomfortably hot inside the barge. Noah kept the hatches open all day and night when it was not raining. This provided air circulation and light, although the awning kept direct sunlight out of the hatches so the barge would not overheat. Noah and his family slept on deck except on rainy nights. The night air was cooler than that inside the barge.

Each day the animals had to be fed and watered, and the manure hauled out. Also each day, bilge water and animal waste in the quffas had to be bailed out. The 270 or so animals were cared for by the nine people and everyone worked from sunrise to sunset. Noah's sons and the servant girls were kept busy caring for the animals.

Every day, Noah's sons climbed up onto the top deck to air out the hay and throw down bundles of hay to the middle deck for the animals. There was plenty of hay for the cattle, sheep and goats to eat, although Noah put the animals on short rations, because he had no idea how long the deep water would last.

The barge stank from animal waste that dripped down from the middle deck onto the jars of beer on the bottom deck. But the beer was not spoiled, because the jars were sealed. The outsides of the jars were washed in clean water before the jars were opened. The baskets of barley were stored on the middle deck and were separated from the animals by woven-reed walls. The poultry were fed barley and Noah and his family also ate barley.

There were thousands of baskets of barley in the barge to be delivered at Ur for export. The barley was owned by the temples and the Shuruppak government and Noah was personally responsible for it. He and his family were not allowed to eat the grain, but they did what they had to do. Noah had also planned to sell the live poultry at Ur. Some were laying hens that provided fresh eggs for Noah and his family.

The barge continued to drift slowly from the tide and currents in the Gulf and from the wind. Every day Noah and Puzur scanned the horizon for land, but every day they were disappointed. The barge drifted about the Gulf for five months beyond sight of land and could easily have drifted there for many more months.

Fortunately for Noah and his family, the wind began to blow from the south again and blew the barge back toward the mouth of the river where the water was shallow. Noah knew that the water was becoming more shallow because Puzur measured the depth. But without visible landmarks they did not know *why* the water was becoming shallow. Story tellers erroneously assumed that the wind caused the water to go down because the water became shallow after the wind blew. But the wind did not blow the water away. The wind blew the barge into shallow water.

More good news: the water around the barge was no longer salty. It was brackish, but it was drinkable. Story tellers reasoned that the gods must have closed the fountains of salty water that had been gushing out onto the land. They did not understand that the barge was surrounded by fresh water because the wind and eddy currents had moved the barge into an estuary at the mouth of the river. The estuary was more than ten miles wide and marshy delta land along the shore was only a few feet above the water at low tide. At high tide the marsh land was submerged. Noah was too far away from the delta and marshes to see any land, even at low tide.

The barge grounds in an estuary

The barge grounded in the shallow estuary in November, Noah's seventh month. Noah assumed that flood water was receding, because the water was becoming shallow. The water should continue to recede and the land should be dry in a few days. But weeks passed and the water was not receding. The water would get shallow for several hours and then it would get deeper for several hours. The water seemed to go down for awhile and then rise back up, twice a day, week after week. Later story tellers assumed this was flood water that should recede as the annual river inundations had always receded. After a few weeks, there should have been plenty of dry land around the barge. Instead, the barge continued to be surrounded by water because the barge was stuck in the mud of an estuary that was always under water, even at low tide when the river was low.

Noah was worried, but the truth would have worried him even more. If the barge were to remain grounded several miles from shore in an estuary that was always under water, Noah would never be able to leave the barge and he would never again reach dry land, unless he were seen by people on a passing sailboat. The barge remained grounded in the estuary because in November the river was near its lowest level.

Two months later in January, Noah's ninth month, the river was rising again as it normally does in January from winter rain in the valley. Noah's barge refloated on this rising water and drifted close to some islands which later story tellers assumed were tops of mountains. Noah saw these islands on the first day of the tenth month. Although story tellers assumed that the land was becoming visible because the water was going down, the water was actually rising from the winter rain. Noah saw the islands because the barge had drifted near enough to the islands that he could see them.

More than a month passed (Genesis 8:6) and still all Noah could see was horizon to horizon water. He was getting anxious because his supplies of fodder and food were getting smaller every day. Soon he would have nothing to feed the animals and he would have to begin slaughtering them. He sent some birds on a reconnaissance mission in hopes that they might see land, but the first birds did not see any.

If the water was still subsiding from the islands that Noah had seen 40 days earlier, the islands should still be visible. But for reasons that Noah did not understand, the islands could no longer be seen. The birds could not see any land either. The barge had drifted many miles away from the islands which were now beyond the horizon and too far away for the birds to see.

During high tide in May, wind from the south blew the barge closer to shore where the estuary was normally dry at low tide during much of the year, but was temporarily under water because the river current was at its maximum and the tide was high. The water had become shallow after the south wind blew and later story tellers assumed the wind gods had blown the water away. Actually, the wind blew the barge closer to shore in the intertidal zone of the estuary. Again the barge grounded in the estuary in the first month (May) of the second year near low hills of the delta. Noah could see this dry land (Genesis 8:13) at a distance, but the barge was still in several feet of water where it grounded.

The muddy bottom of the estuary began to appear whenever the tide went out, but later each day the tide returned and the area of the estuary where the barge grounded was submerged again. Noah had to wait nearly two months for the river current to subside. Finally, near the end of July during a neap tide, the estuary bottom was dry and "lay flat as a rooftop."

The surface of the mud baked dry under the hot summer sun and was dry enough to walk on. The low hills of the delta could still be seen at a distance where they had been visible for two months. Noah could not risk losing this opportunity. He opened the main door of the barge and placed the gangplank in the doorway on the middle deck as a ramp down onto the dry mud flat. Noah, Puzur and the family members slid the animals down the ramp in cages or baskets and had to make many trips carrying the small animal cages to the nearby hills. They also drove the cattle, sheep, goats and other larger animals across the dried mud flat to the hills where grass was available for grazing.

The barge had grounded on the shore of the Persian Gulf in the intertidal zone of an estuary at the mouth of the Euphrates River several miles south of Ur and several miles east of Eridu. Climbing to the top of a hill, Noah could see a cluster of distant buildings that were part of a coastal port town where fishing boats and merchant sail boats unloaded cargo and travelers disembarked at high tide. Noah recognized the town.

The temple of Enki at Eridu

After storing most of the animals and other cargo in the port town, Noah and his family drove several of the animals west on the road to Eridu. Jars of beer were tied to the backs of the animals. After 2 or 3 hours on the road, they arrived at the center of Eridu where Noah was given an enthusiastic welcome by the priests of the temple of Enki. Noah understood what his obligations were to the temple. After arriving safely at Eridu, ship captains were expected to make a donation of cooked food to the temple in gratitude to the gods for a safe arrival.

After the flood a year earlier, the temple had fallen on hard times because the local farmers, ranchers and fruit growers, who used to enrich the temple with their offerings, saw their crops and stock destroyed by the flood. Trade routes had also been disrupted because roads and bridges were washed out, canals silted up, pack animals drowned, and storage facilities destroyed.

Dozens of villages in southern Sumer were abandoned. Fresh meat and beer were very scarce. Noah was greeted at the temple of Enki by the priests who had not eaten fresh meat for a year.

The priests carried Noah's animals to the top of a "hill-like ziggurat," a raised platform at the temple of Enki, where the animals were sacrificed on an altar. The altar was a fireplace for cooking food that Noah was donating to the temple of Enki. The fire was kindled using scraps of oily cedar wood. When Noah offered the sacrifice, he was surrounded by priests from the temple. The priests "smelled the sweet savor and gathered like flies about the sacrifice." Temple rules required them to wait for permission from a temple official to begin eating.

After the meat was cooked, a highpriestess arrived at the altar. She held up her blue lapis lazuli badge of office, that was carved in the form of flies, and gave a short speech saying "As surely as I shall not forget this lapis lazuli around my neck, I will be mindful of these days, and never forget them." She then told the priests they could "approach the offering." Noah's arrival at the temple was the occasion for a banquet with Noah supplying the roast beef and beer. By the end of the banquet the priests "had eaten the sacrifice."

Noah sacrificed the animals on an altar "on the top of a hill-like ziggurat." Many years later when the words "hill-like ziggurat" were translated, the ambiguous word *shadû* for hill/mountain was misinterpreted and the phrase was understood to mean "on the top of a mountain." Since the barge was only several miles from the altar that was built on what the translators thought was the top of a mountain, they assumed that the barge must also be near the top of the mountain. But the barge was actually at sea level, grounded in the mud of an estuary. The altar was several miles to the west, on top of the ziggurat, at the temple of Enki, in the city of Eridu. Hundreds of years later, about 2100 BC, this platform was enlarged into a step pyramid.

Noah and his family lived at the temple of Enki for a few days. This gave rise to the story that they were living "at the mouth of the rivers." But Noah stayed there only long enough to sell the barge, the animals and other cargo. He had to do this quickly because he could not stay long at Eridu.

Noah did not return to Shuruppak. He could not tow the barge back to Shuruppak because it would take years to rebuild all the damaged levees along the Euphrates river with towpaths on top for barge-towing oxen or human towing teams. The estuary where the barge grounded may have been many miles from the nearest navigable channel. Moreover, it was the wrong time of year for river traffic. The water level was low. Even if Noah abandoned his barge and moved the animals overland to Shuruppak, there were other reasons why Noah did not return to his ranch.

More than a year had passed since the six-day flood and the people of Shuruppak assumed that Noah and his family were dead. Noah had mortgaged some of his land at Shuruppak to finance the barge and had pledged the land as security for the cargo loaned by the temples or merchants. During his absence, some of his land was sold to pay his debts. He could not travel on foot to Sippar, because to travel on roads near the Euphrates River, Noah would have had to pass through Shuruppak and Nippur where he would have to face the remaining debts he owed to merchants and the temples, debts that were now in default and which he could not repay. Noah was responsible for government grain in his custody, much of which he and his family and the animals had eaten. And Noah had not paid any taxes for more than a year.

Sumerian kings were trustees, not autocrats and were not exempt from the law. People who failed to pay their taxes or defaulted on their debts were forced into slavery. Noah had been chief executive of Shuruppak before the flood, but another chief (GA.UR of Kish) was ruling there now and Noah would be viewed as a rival. Noah said that a god "hates me. I dare no longer walk in his land nor live in his city." The Shuruppak border guards were watching for Noah and would jail him for fraud, unpaid debts and unpaid taxes if he entered Shuruppak.

Noah may have sold the barge to another merchant or to an agent of the Dilmun company that supplied the cedar for building the barge. Thus Noah's debts to the Dilmun company would be paid off. Noah probably sold most of his animals, grain and the remaining cargo to Eridu merchants or to the temple of Enki soon after the barge grounded, because news of his landing would quickly reach his creditors who would then come to repossess all of the remaining cargo and Noah's assets.

Noah naked

In Genesis 9:21–25 Noah is said to have been drunk from wine and lay naked in his tent. Ham, his youngest son saw Noah naked and told his older brothers Shem and Japheth about it. Shem and Japheth then covered their father. When Noah awoke and knew what Ham had done, Noah cursed Ham's future son Canaan and said Canaan would be a slave of slaves to his brothers. The only thing Ham was said to have done was to see his father naked. Since this innocent act does not seem to warrant Noah's rage, some commentators have conjectured that Ham may have injured Noah. But Noah's overreaction becomes understandable when one considers what nakedness meant in ancient Sumer.

Pottery from third millennium Sumer shows several naked people doing menial tasks. Except during temple rituals, naked people were slaves and slaves were not allowed to wear clothes. A Sumerian word for slave SUBAR literally meant "skin body." People who failed to pay their taxes or captured enemies who were not killed were punished with compulsory nakedness which labeled them as slaves. This practice continued into the first millennium BC in Assyria (Isaiah 20:4).

Noah had been a respected and powerful king and a wealthy land owner before the flood. After the barge grounded he learned he was no longer a king, his business was ruined, his property had been sold to pay his debts and he and his family would soon be slaves unless they fled to a foreign country. Since nakedness was a badge of slavery, we can understand how overly sensitive Noah was about being seen naked.

Noah cursing Ham's future son and predicting that he would be a slave is understandable if this episode occurred immediately after the barge landed. Hearing the bad news from the priests of Enki and seeing no way out of the mess he was in, Noah was probably despondent and became drunk. He was facing slavery for himself, his wife, his children and grandchildren (who had not been born yet). He probably told his sons that they and their children would become slaves. But since Noah's prediction proved to be overly pessimistic, the only part of the prediction they remembered years later was that one of their sons would be a slave.

Noah's family separates

Noah was emotional over losing his business and kingship and fearful of being forced into slavery as punishment for tax evasion and failure to pay his debts. He also had a disagreement with his sons over whether the sons and their wives would accompany Noah into exile. Noah was probably exasperated with his sons for not understanding the great danger they were in. They reached a compromise. The sons would not accompany Noah into exile, but they and their wives promised to avoid Shuruppak and Nippur, hide out in the mountains for at least two months, and then travel to Sippar to live with their friends or relatives. To insure that the friends would accept them, Noah gave two pairs of each kind of the clean animals to his sons. They would not have to work as common laborers after arriving in Sippar.

The people from Noah's barge divided into two groups according to Berossus. Noah, his wife, their daughter and the boatman went in a different direction than Noah's sons and their wives who "went by a roundabout way" to Sippar.

Noah hurriedly sold the barge and cargo and prepared to leave for a foreign country in a sailboat. With his job and land gone and his merchanting business ruined, Noah probably wanted only to retire in comfort in a land where his creditors and the Shuruppak government would not bother him, i.e. in Dilmun, a foreign country where he had no debts. Noah sailed as soon as possible after he sold his cargo and barge. The abandoned barge remained grounded in the estuary.

After Noah and his wife boarded the sailboat that would take them to Dilmun, the highpriest of Enki performed a religious ceremony in which Noah and his wife were given the status of honorary gods (priests). Holding Noah by the hand, the highpriest of Enki took Noah aboard the sailboat. He then took Noah's wife aboard and had her kneel by Noah's side. Standing between them, he touched their foreheads to bless them. The priest of Enki said "…now Noah and his wife are associates; they shall be like gods to us." According to Berossus, Noah "was gone to live with the gods [priests] and his wife, his daughter, and the boatman shared in the same honor."

Noah and his wife and daughter and Puzur went to live in the land of Dilmun. Dilmun was a port on an island in the Persian Gulf and probably the trading port through which Noah obtained the cedar for building his barge. Being a former merchant, Noah probably knew some of the Dilmun merchants. Since Noah had to live in exile, a foreign country where he already had friends would be an attractive place for him to live. Dilmun was also described as a paradise: "The land Dilmun is pure; the land Dilmun is clean… The old man says not 'I am an old man'… Her sweet water flows from the earth… Its houses are good houses", etc. This sounds like an ancient advertisement for a retirement community. Noah and his wife and their daughter lived in retirement and in exile in Dilmun.

When Noah arrived at Dilmun he told the people of Dilmun about his adventures; how he and his family survived the flood a year earlier in a river barge loaded with cattle and grain and how his barge had drifted in deep water for more than a year. Noah also told his listeners about the altar where his animals were sacrificed at the top of a hill. As his story was repeated over the centuries, story tellers confused the river flood with the deep water of the Persian Gulf and mistranslated the word for hill as mountain.

Shem and the mountains of Ararat

While Noah and his wife, their daughter, and Puzur were traveling by sailboat to Dilmun, Shem and his younger brothers and their wives (perhaps the servant girls) were traveling on foot from Eridu, east to the Tigris River. They could not travel up the Euphrates River through Shuruppak, because their father had been king there and they would be recognized and arrested by Shuruppak border guards. As Noah's sons, they were liable for Noah's unpaid taxes and debts and would be forced into slavery.

Instead, they traveled northwest on foot up the west side of the Tigris River through the region later known as Assyria to a "plain at the foot of an extensive mountain" which was probably at the base of the 7000 foot mountain Cudi Dagh (Mount Judi) in the Armenian mountains of Ararat. The young group lived next to the river for two months. Then Shem led the group in a southeast direction back down the west side of the Tigris River to about where Baghdad is today and where they crossed overland to Sippar on the Euphrates River. This describes how Noah's sons "went by a roundabout way" to Sippar, in the words of Berossus.

While they were at Mount Judi, Shem and his brothers may have climbed the mountain or part way up the mountain, because it was probably the highest mountain, perhaps the only mountain, they had ever seen. Later after arriving at Sippar, Shem told the people about his adventures, including floating on his father's barge for a year and descending from the heights of Mount Judi just before traveling to Sippar. Shem's listeners or subsequent story tellers misunderstood Shem's story and assumed that the barge had grounded on Mount Judi. This falsely linked the flood story to Mount Judi in the mountains of Ararat.

A library at Sippar had been partly buried in mud by the heavy rain and overflowing rivers. Noah's sons dug through the ruins of the library and retrieved oven-baked tablets of inscribed clay buried in the mud.

Meanwhile, news of Noah's barge grounding near Eridu reached officials at Shuruppak and Nippur. Although the lowlands and low hills next to the river at Shuruppak had been flooded during the storm a year earlier, most of the people of Shuruppak survived by climbing to the high hills. Before the barge grounded, Shuruppak and Nippur officials assumed that Noah was dead and the barge and its cargo were destroyed during the storm. When news reached them that the barge was still intact and grounded near Eridu and Noah was still alive but the cargo had disappeared, they naturally suspected fraud and were angry with Noah. Noah's political rivals accused Noah of taking advantage of the confusion during the flood to conceal theft of government property. The officials sent a squad of soldiers to the place where the barge grounded with an order for Noah's arrest. If they found Noah they would take him into custody and transport him back to Shuruppak and Nippur to stand trial for fraud and tax evasion.

As soon as the squad leader arrived and saw the boat, he asked witnesses: "Has anyone escaped alive? No man was to survive the destruction!" It would be natural for the squad leader, a military officer, when inspecting Noah's barge and finding it in good condition, to ask nearby witnesses routine questions that any investigator would ask: "Has anyone [from this barge] escaped alive? Nobody [from this barge] was supposed to have survived the destruction." The military officer was referring only to the people in the barge who had been presumed dead, but later story tellers assumed the soldier was a god and exaggerated the scope of the soldier's questions to include all the people of the world, who the story tellers also presumed were dead.

By the time the soldiers arrived at Eridu, Noah's sons were safely on their way up the Tigris River, and Noah, his wife, their daughter and the boatman were in Dilmun. The soldier was advised to speak with the god

Enki. A priest at the temple of Enki spoke to the soldier through a reed wall as an oracle. The oracle's "voice came from the air, telling them that they must respect the gods." The soldier must follow the advice the oracle gives to him. The oracle then gave the soldier general advice about punishing criminals and commented on the unfairness of the flood. The oracle told the soldier that Noah "was gone to live with the gods [priests], and his wife, his daughter and the boatman shared in the same honor." This put the soldiers on notice that Noah was exempt from prosecution because he was a "god." He was also beyond the reach of the law because he had gone to a foreign country to live with the gods (priests). The soldiers were satisfied; nothing would be gained by pursuing Noah further.

When the storm began a year earlier, Noah and his family were already on board the barge. But Noah's 84 year old grandfather Methuselah was not on the barge. He was still at Noah's house in Shuruppak where he had lived much of his life. Methuselah's age of 969 (Genesis 5:27) was an ancient mistranslation. Noah's house was on a hill where other wealthy people lived and was not submerged by the river flood. While the barge was drifting about the Persian Gulf, Methuselah was still in Shuruppak, mourning the presumed death of his grandson Noah and his family. A year later when Noah's creditors learned that Noah was still alive and had fled to a foreign country, that the barge was still intact, but the cargo had disappeared, the creditors and the Shuruppak government forced a sale of Noah's ancestral land to pay the overdue taxes and debts. This court action occurred about 3 months after the barge grounded.

As a member of Noah's family who could not pay the debts, Methuselah was forced into slavery. Long time friends shunned him, because they did not want to be suspected of condoning tax evasion and theft of government property. Methuselah was evicted from his home and stripped of his clothes and personal possessions. With no family or friends, no house to live in, with failing eyesight, impoverished and enslaved at the age of 85, Methuselah died soon afterwards.

12

Answers to Objections

*"If the key opens the lock,
it is the right key."*

Anon.

In this chapter, actual and anticipated objections from skeptics are answered. Creationist arguments and beliefs are answered in Chapter 13. Most objections that skeptics raise against the flood story are valid ones. The flood story as it is commonly understood could not have happened. But by assuming a few mistranslations and scribal errors here and there, the legendary basis for the flood story can be reconstructed, although such a reconstruction cannot be proven historic without contemporaneous artifacts.

Most scholars view the Genesis stories as myths. Myth expert Joseph Campbell said the Genesis myths "could not possibly be read today by anybody in his right mind as referring accurately to historical events." The Noah's Ark myth is not a suitable subject for serious scholarship, except as an example of a popular delusion.

I agree with the objection but not with the *non sequitur*. True, the Genesis stories are myths and the events of Noah's flood story as they appear in the received texts could not possibly have happened. And even after being demythologized, the flood story is not provably historic. But as the King Arthur stories illustrate, some myths evolve from an archetype legend about a possibly real person. Noah can be included on a list of legendary candidates for historicity, along with King Arthur, Helen of Troy, and Saint Nicholas. Even though Noah is not yet (and may never become) a historic person, he is just as suitable for serious scholarship as other legendary characters.

You iron out the differences between various versions of the flood myth at the cost of assuming that the Biblical version completely garbled the Mesopotamian tradition, which was in turn confused. Trying to make sense of such garbled texts is futile.

The Genesis version is not completely garbled. It faithfully reproduces many of the Mesopotamian story elements using the same or similar words. Moreover, the Genesis version provides additional details that supplement the other versions. Many of the errors in the Genesis flood story, e.g. that the ark grounded in the mountains of Ararat, were made by ancient story tellers and Genesis faithfully copies those errors.

You are so sure that you have the truth about the flood story and everyone else is wrong. How can you possibly be certain when your theory is based on myth, fantasy, superstitions and guesses, which you admit were altered and mistranslated.

I am not certain that Noah was a historic person or that my interpretation of the flood story is correct. But I am absolutely certain that the sea level did not rise to cover mountains in the third millennium BC, because that would be physically impossible. This belief is based on physics, not ancient myth. Even if Noah was a fictional character and some of the details were fictional, the original story tellers based part of their stories on real events they experienced or heard about, just as every story teller does. I never said my theory was the only possible one. There may be other possible interpretations of the same sources. I have put the pieces together in a new arrangement to produce an understandable picture that is different than the conventional picture. Perhaps others may put the same pieces together into an equally plausible arrangement that is different than mine.

You admit that your theories cannot be verified from contemporaneous artifacts and are therefore unproven conjecture.

My theories have some basis in archaeology, e.g. strata from the Euphrates River flood at the end of the Jemdet Nasr period in Shuruppak and other cities. The chronological backbone of my theory is based on known facts about the annual rising and falling of the Euphrates River. Although there is no way to prove the historicity of Noah or his cattle barge, several of my hypotheses were confirmed by my looking in the archaeological literature and finding what I was looking for. For example, when I went looking for an ancient number system that would explain why the Genesis 5 ages were too large by a factor of ten (see Chapter 7), I found a nonstandard number system that reduced the ages by the expected factor. But there were unexpected bonuses: this nonstandard number system was used only at Shuruppak, the very place where Ziusudra (Noah) lived, the nonstandard numbers were used only during the Early Dynastic III period, the same period in which the flood myth was first written in clay, and the nonstandard signs explained why the death ages were inflated by twelve. These and other confirmations were more than I expected or could have hoped to find.

You argue that the ark could not have landed on the 16,946 foot "Mount Ararat", but scholars are already aware that association of this mountain with the biblical "mountains of Ararat" began no earlier than the 11th century CE. The country of Urartu did not extend that far north until the 9th century B.C.

I mentioned "Mount Ararat" *(Aghri Dagh)* only because many people who refer to the conventional ark story are not aware that "Mount Ararat" is a recent misreading of Genesis 8:4. I also argued that Noah's barge could not have grounded in the mountains of Ararat or on any other mountain. It therefore does not matter whether one chooses Ararat or Urartu or Judi or Nişir. They are all physically impossible as a grounding spot.

The Akkadian Gilgamesh Epic XI,140–144 says quite explicitly that Utnapishtim's ship landed on Mount Nişir, a 8,600–foot peak in the Zagros Mountains that was mentioned by name in the annals of Ashur–nasir–pal II of Assyria. You prefer your hypothesis that a Sumerian word in a missing portion of the Ziusudra Epic may have been mistranslated into Akkadian, but you ignore the actual textual evidence in Gilgamesh.

Mount Nişir is not the only possible translation of *shadû nişir* in lines 140–141 of the Gilgamesh text. The determinative on *nişir* is KUR in Sumerian which can be read as *mātu* in Akkadian and means land or country. Hence, KUR *nişir* in Gilgamesh XI,140–141 could mean Nişir country. The mountain referred to in the annals of Ashur–nasir–pal II is not necessarily the place referred to in Gilgamesh. Confusing different places with similar names is a common problem.

There is no way to get around the fact that Mount Nişir is referred to as a mountain in Gilgamesh XI,140–144. Whenever the KUR sign is followed by a phonetic complement -u the reading must be shadû which means mountain. Reading the determinative KUR (without -u) as country would not make sense while the adjacent lines are consistently referring to "mountain Nişir".

Shadû-ú can also mean a hill or a mound less than ten feet high. But even if *shadû* meant mountain in this context, it would merely reflect a choice by a Gilgamesh editor to exaggerate mound into mountain, just as he exaggerated the river flood into an ocean deluge. By about 1200 BC, when the editor added the flood story to the Gilgamesh epic, he confused the grounding spot at the mouth of the rivers with the mountain Judi that Shem visited. We should look beyond the mythmaker's mistakes and alterations and look for clues about the original stories in which the grounding place and the mountain were probably distinguished. In the context of a river barge grounding on a mud flat, the word *shadû-ú* can mean a small mound that was normally submerged at the bottom of an estuary. My conjecture that *shadû-ú* ^{KUR} *niṣir* should be read "mound, Niṣir country" is more credible than identifying *niṣir* with a mountain, because it would be impossible for the ocean to cover a mountain.

Your theory about Noah offering a sacrifice in front of a group of priests at the temple of Enki is fantasy. There is no mention of priests or temples in the flood myths.

Five versions of the flood myth have the hero offering a sacrifice after the boat grounded. Gilgamesh XI,156 identifies the offering place as a ziggurat. A ziggurat was part of a temple and prior to 2000 BC there were ziggurats at temples in Ur, Eridu, Uruk, and Nippur. We don't have to reach very far to determine which ziggurat the poet meant. The hero went "down [the river] to the *apsû* to live with my lord Ea." And "I lived in the temple of Ea, my lord." The temple of Ea/Enki at Eridu was known as the "*apsû*–house" and it had a ziggurat. The *apsû* was a real place, a deep water arm of the Persian Gulf where Lake Hammar is now. Eridu was a real city a few miles west of this arm of the Persian Gulf. The temple of Ea/Enki was a real temple with a real ziggurat and these have been excavated by archaeologists in the ruins of Eridu. The flood hero offered the sacrifice on an altar at the top of the ziggurat at the temple of Enki at Eridu. Since a sacrifice at a temple was really a donation of food to support the priests, and there were real priests working at the Eridu temple of Enki about 2900 BC during the period when Noah offered the sacrifice, priests were probably present at Noah's sacrifice and were probably mentioned in the archetype flood story. In the Epic of Atrahasis the damaged tablet does not say who ate the sacrifice, but in a real temple real priests ate sacrifices. All of this can be plausibly inferred from the sources, even though priests and a temple are not explicitly mentioned.

When we look in the epics of Atrahasis and Gilgamesh, wherever we would expect to find some mention of priests, instead we find references to "gods." In the Epic of Gilgamesh, the "great goddess" who accepted the flood hero's offering was called a DINGIR.MAH. The high priestess of Enki, a real woman, who accepted food offerings at the temple of Enki at Eridu was called a NIN.DINGIR. It should be obvious that an ancient story teller modified his received story slightly to deify people in the story. By assuming that some of the references to "gods" in the epics of Atrahasis and Gilgamesh were originally references to priests, several disconnected pieces fit together and the story makes more sense. The sacrifice scene is not in my basic theory because the characters are called gods. But even if you disregard the priests, the text has sufficient clues that identify the place of sacrafice as the ziggurat at the temple of Enki in Eridu.

There is nothing new in your statement that the Hebrew word *har* can be translated as hill instead of mountain. That has been known by Hebrew scholars for millennia. The word *harê* is translated as "mountains of" because the Ararat region, the ancient Urartu, is in a mountain range. *Har* can only mean mountain in the context of Genesis 8:4. Your argument that a mountain would be impossible does not make it a mistranslation.

Translating the landing place as "mountain" was a very ancient mistranslation made long before the Judeans obtained the flood story from the Babylonians. Although the Hebrew was faithfully translated, it was a faithful translation of a mistranslation. An ancient error does not become less of an error by being ancient or by being faithfully retranslated.

The notion that Noah's flood was a local flood in the Mesopotamian region has been suggested before, but is generally rejected today, because none of the Mesopotamian floods appear to have been so impressive that it could inspire the Flood story.

Although the flood of 2900 BC was unusual, it was relatively insignificant compared to Bangladesh flooding. In spite of this, Noah's flood story became famous, not because the flood itself was impressive, but because of the mythology that grew up around Noah. The editor of the Epic of Gilgamesh salvaged the old Atrahasis myth by working it into another myth about immortality. His listeners were interested in the immortality story, but as a side effect, they learned about the flood story. The myth about the flood hero was what made the story famous, not the magnitude of the flood.

None of the sources you cite mention Noah being a merchant or being a cargo agent for grain exporters. These additions you made to the flood story are fiction.

To understand the flood stories, we must infer things that are not explicitly stated. Noah owned gold and silver when those metals were used mostly by merchants. Noah transported animals and grain in his river barge, which implies he was either a merchant or government trade official, or was closely associated with merchants. The idea that he may have been an agent for grain or livestock exporters was mentioned as one of several possibilities, but is not a firm conclusion.

My theory consists of a framework based on known facts about rivers and barges plus explicit details in the received texts. I fleshed out the story with plausible conjectures based on what merchants usually did in the Persian Gulf region and what one could reasonably expect a king or chief executive to do and not do, given his leadership and commercial skills suggested by the sources.

Your theory misrepresents or ignores the plain language of the sources. In Genesis 6:17–18 Noah is warned by God that a flood was coming and to build an ark to escape destruction. Noah was clearly motivated to build the ark by being forewarned of the flood. Likewise in Gilgamesh XI,25–28 and 47 Utnapishtim is warned by Ea to expect a heavy rain and to build a ship to save the seed of life. Likewise in Atrahasis III,i,37 Ea warns Atrahasis that the flood is coming. Likewise in Ziusudra iv,156–157 Enki warns the hero that a flood will destroy mankind. The sources are unanimous on this point and yet you brush them aside and allege that Noah had no forewarning of the flood and built the ark for purely commercial reasons.

One should always be skeptical of reasons and motivations attributed to characters in a story. Even today, story writers and reporters for tabloid newspapers routinely attribute knowledge and impute motives without knowing what a person was actually thinking. How would a story teller, who lived centuries after Noah, know if Noah had prior knowledge of the flood? Motives, intentions, knowledge, emotions, doubts, and other mental states are the stuff of fiction writers. What we want is a report about what Noah did and experienced, not what he thought. After his attributed thoughts are removed, what remains is a story of a man who got caught up in an unexpected disaster. He survived it because he acted decisively when he recognized at the last moment what was about to happen. The sources are unanimous because they are editions of one archetype story in which the story teller imagined what Noah was thinking.

You have been misled by the ancient mythmakers. Every myth has little bits of fact to make the fiction more believable. But these bits of fact are no more connected than the names in a telephone book. By stripping away the obvious fiction you have uncritically accepted these unconnected facts as if they were part of some factual whole, which is exactly what the mythmakers wanted gullible listeners to do. The "facts" that you find in the myth are nothing more than a sugar coating to trick you into swallowing the fiction.

If that is what the mythmakers were doing, they made the sugar coating hard to digest. I do not deny that the legendary portion of the flood myth could have been entirely fictitious. But it is also probable that the legend was more or less based on real events. The pieces do fit together with known facts. If that was a fiction writer's trick, he did his job well.

Instead of confirming each hypothesis, you build speculations on speculations and the possibility of error multiplies.

That is why I give low ratings to some of my conclusions in Chapter 16.

Since you are so sure that Noah's Ark existed, next you will be organizing searches for remains of the Ark on the shore of the Persian Gulf or wherever you believe that it grounded.

I never said I was sure that the ark existed, only that there was a historical basis for the flood stories. When a story teller spins tales about a king who built a river barge, the story teller probably saw a real river barge that he based his story on. Even if the ark were historical, there is no chance of finding it in what was then the shore of the Persian Gulf. If it existed, it rotted away millennia ago in the marshes at the mouth of the river.

One cannot understand a myth without considering the mythmaker's agenda. The mythmaker may have been promoting certain ideas, e.g. that immortality is not attainable or that overpopulation is a social evil. You disregard the mythmaker's intent and must therefore fail to understand the myth. It is not surprising then, that you distort the clear meaning of something you do not understand.

There can be no doubt that the author of the Epic of Gilgamesh was promoting certain ideas about immortality, but these are of no interest to us. Only the flood story in Tablet XI is relevant to this book and in that part only the legendary basis for the flood story is of interest. The mythmaker's bias is relevant, but only for understanding how it distorted his selecting and editing of the legendary material. I am not trying to understand the myth as myth. I have tried to remove the myth and the mythmaker's agenda, because it obscures the legend.

Some of your quotations are taken out of context. For example, in Gilgamesh XI, 40–41 when Utnapishtim says "I dare no longer walk in his land nor live in his city" he was speaking to the elders of Shuruppak before the flood. But you have Noah saying this after the flood.

This change in the chronological sequence is based on Atrahasis III,i,44 that the flood hero was "expelled," and on Ziusudra iv,160 that mentions "the overthrowing of the kingship." Time sequences of some elements in the story were probably already rearranged by story tellers and poets and the received texts reflect such redacting.

Noah must have saved all the kinds of plants or their seed on the earth, because salt water would have killed them.

Many plants and seeds were probably destroyed by the flood in the Euphrates valley, but that freshwater flood lasted only six days and destroyed only a small part of the vegetation. The six-day river flood should not be confused with the barge floating for a year in the deep salt water of the gulf.

Isaac Asimov suggested that a meteorite could have landed in the Persian Gulf and created a tsunami that lifted a boat up into the nearby mountains. Isn't this possible?

The problem with a tsunami, meteor caused or otherwise, is it would be gone in a few hours. But the flood according to Genesis 8:14 lasted a full year. The Genesis authors misunderstood their received story. Noah's barge could have floated around the deep water of the Persian Gulf for a year, but that was not a flood. The flood lasted six days according to the Epic of Gilgamesh and was a river flood caused by an unseasonal and prolonged thunderstorm – like the Mississippi River flood of July 1993. Asimov did not consider the possibility that the word "mountain" was a mistranslation and the boat never got to a mountain and therefore there is no need to search for ways it could have been lifted onto a mountain.

If the Genesis flood myth were true, animals that are not now found in the near east like koalas and sloths would have had to travel from the ark to where they are found now. This would have been impossible and therefore discredits the entire story.

Most of the world's animals were not in the ark. According to Gilgamesh XI,83 "All I had of living beings, I loaded aboard." Noah loaded all the animals he had, and did not load animals he did not have. The sheep and goats that Noah loaded were already in the southern Euphrates valley and their descendants may still be in the Euphrates valley. They did not have to travel anywhere.

Many animals have special dietary needs and could not survive on hay and barley.

Noah carried only marketable animals that could eat the fodder that Sumerian ranchers normally used. Noah carried enough fodder in his barge to feed the animals during the few days on the river but also for sale to buyers of his animals who would need several month's supply of fodder during the coming year.

Genesis 7:4b says "every living thing that I have made I will blot out from the face of the ground." That includes freshwater fish that would have died in saltwater. Where did Noah put all the aquariums to save the freshwater fish?

There were no fish in Noah's barge, except those that his family caught for food from the Gulf. The animals that Noah's workers took into the barge were livestock and poultry that he was planning to transport to market. Noah took aboard "every living thing" that was in his stockyards, not every species of animal on the planet.

According to Genesis 6:19 Noah was required to bring "two of every kind into the ark." There are several hundred species of rats, nearly 300 species of squirrel, etc.

Noah took at least two of every kind of ranch animal that he was planning to sell, not two of every species. Even though his ranch had rats, who would want to buy rats? He took seven pairs of goats, not seven pairs of each species or sub-species of goat.

You say that the ark was 200 feet long, but any wooden boat that long would quickly break up from being tossed about in a hurricane and by tsunamis hundreds of feet high.

What tsunami? What hurricane? Noah's flood was caused by prolonged thunderstorm that lasted six days and nights. Although there were winds, there is no evidence that they reached hurricane velocity. For the remainder of the year the barge drifted slowly in the calm water of the Persian Gulf.

You speculate about several strange designs that Noah may have used to construct his barge. If it successfully withstood a severe storm, surely Noah's descendents would have used this same design in later boats. Yet nowhere is such a design mentioned.

If Noah and his family had been the only survivors, then his design would have been copied by his descendants. But many other people survived the Euphrates valley flood and the designs of different boatbuilders competed for acceptance. Large barges had to be towed by animals or slaves from towpaths on top of levees. But many of the levees were destroyed by the flood. Several years may have passed before all the levees were rebuilt and before large barges were again commercially practical. By then the barge builders may have wanted to distance themselves from the memory of the discredited Noah by using a different design. Noah's famous voyage may have been remembered by barge builders as a failure and that would discourage any copying of his barge design.

When the ark slammed into Mount Ararat or wherever it grounded, it would have smashed to pieces from the violently receding water. The ark could never have grounded twice as you imagine.

On two occasions the barge landed slowly and gently onto the muddy bottom of an estuary in the Persian Gulf. There is nothing in the sources that requires a "slammed" landing. During the storm the barge was in deep water and did not smash into anything. When the barge finally did ground, the water was calm. The water slowly became more shallow as the barge drifted into a shallow estuary and grounded gently onto a mud flat.

You admit that the Adam and Eve story is pure myth, so how can you seriously think that the Genesis 5 genealogy that begins with Adam can be anything other than myth?

Adam is a Hebrew word for man and is so translated in Genesis 1–2. But *adam* is usually transliterated as Adam instead of man in Genesis 3–4, thus giving readers a false impression that Adam was a proper name, when in fact it is a generic word for man. The creation story discusses a generic nameless man. The Genesis 5 genealogy begins with a nameless man whose real name was forgotten. Just because there are two nameless men in Genesis does not imply they were the same man, although the authors of Genesis may have wanted the reader to make such an inference. There is no connection between the mythical generic man of Genesis 1–4 and Seth's father whose forgotten name was replaced by the word *man* in Genesis 5.

Semitic people often created eponymous ancestors, e.g. all Assyrians were descended from Mr. Assyria; all Israelites from Mr. Israel, etc. Further back, they imagined they were all descended from one Mr. Man. One group referred to this ancestor as adam and another as enosh, both meaning "man." The names in Genesis 5 are fictitious eponymous ancestors.

The names in the Table of Nations in Genesis 10 are fictitious eponymous names and many if not all of the names in Genesis 11 were also (see chapter 9 herein), but the names in Genesis 5 were written by a different hand. Based on the deciphered numbers, some of the Genesis 5 names seem to be substitutes for forgotten names of real people.

You disregard references to other scholarly schools of thought, especially those in languages other than English and in recent journal articles.

This book is not a survey of what others have written on the flood myth and most recent articles are not relevant to the theories presented here.

Although scholars agree that the Hebrew version of the ANE flood is dependent to some extent on Mesopotamian versions, the differences are many and substantial, so that one cannot say that the Hebrew version borrowed the story outright from the Mesopotamians.

Of course there are differences. Each story teller and poet adapted and altered the story to their own needs. If one compares different versions of the king Arthur legend, there are many differences and inconsistencies, but that does not require us to conclude that these legends are about different people. The common story elements and phrases in the ANE flood stories indicate a common origin, regardless of the many differences.

The absence of marine organisms in silt excavated at Ur proves that estuarine water from the Persian Gulf did not cause Noah's flood.

Estuarine water from the Persian Gulf did not flood the valley during Noah's flood. The valley was flooded by the rivers overflowing from a six–day storm. The silt deposited at Ur and possible flooding from the Persian Gulf along the Gulf coast are not relevant to Noah's flood. Early story tellers confused the deep water of the Gulf with the river flood.

How can you rely on a story that has internal inconsistencies? Genesis 6:19 specifies two of every kind of animal, but Genesis 7:2 specifies seven pairs of every kind of clean animal. They cannot both be right. And Noah sacrificed at least one of every clean animal, apparently forgetting that he had only two of each.

They can both be right if the two and seven were at different times. Suppose that Noah took into the barge seven pairs of each kind of clean animal that he had. After the barge grounded he could sacrifice one of each kind of animal and give two of every kind (male and female) to his sons to take to Sippar and still have a few remaining of each kind to sell at Eridu.

Why have you ignored the Greek version of the flood story in which Deukalion was the hero who built an ark that landed on Mount Parnassus or Mount Othrys?

The Deukalion myth was told by Pindar and Hellanicus in the fifth century BC long after the Epic of Gilgamesh was widely known. Egyptian historian Manetho stated that Deukalion's flood occurred in the reign of king Misphragmuthosis (Tuthmosis III). In his reign there was an explosion of the volcano Thera (Santorin) which caused a tsunami in the Mediterranean. The Deukalion myth was probably based on a local Greek story about this tsunami flood, but it also included story elements adapted from the Gilgamesh epic.

You criticize creationists for indulging in guessing and wishful thinking, but your theory is loaded with "perhaps, could have, maybe, apparently" without any supporting evidence.

The major difference is my conclusions would have been physically possible and plausible, but the conclusions of the creationists are consistently impossible and implausible. There is no way to prove with hard evidence that a man saved some animals on a boat five millennia ago. Some of my conclusions are little more than guesses (e.g. that Noah mortgaged his land and Methuselah was evicted from his house). But the stronger of my conclusions (e.g. that the ark was a river barge that drifted about the Gulf) are based on the surviving texts in the light of known facts and what would have been probable in Noah's time and are therefore more than guesses.

In Gilgamesh XI,58 the boat was described as a cube 120 cubits long, wide and deep. You take one of these dimensions as a length of 120 cubits, but ignore the width and depth of 120 cubits.

It is unlikely that the author of Gilgamesh XI believed that the boat was a cube, because such a boat would have seemed weird to his listeners who were already familiar with boats. But if he did believe that the boat was a cube, then he misunderstood the archetype flood story which included the height and width that survived in Genesis 6:15. He disregarded these details or they were missing in his received text. Without the numbers for the height and width, the Gilgamesh XI text at line 58 seems to be saying that all edges were 120 cubits, both the width and length, a misunderstanding that results from the height and width numbers being missing. Instead, line 58 is not describing the deck or hull, but only the "upper part," the superstructure, the left side of which was 120 cubits and the right side was 120 cubits. This is saying that the superstructure was symmetrical and was the same length as the hull which was also 120 cubits long. The use of the word equal at line 30 is ambiguous and may mean only that the widths were equal throughout its length, i.e. the sides were straight and parallel, unlike the curved sides of variable-width sailboats.

Gilgamesh XI,58 confirms that the deck was square: "The edges of her upper part equalled each other at 120 cubits." The verb contains an inflectional element /t/ signifying reciprocity, in other words not just "equal" but "equal to each other."

Yes, the edges were equal to each other, but which edges? The text does not indicate which edges were equal and the poet may have been unclear as to which edges his received text referred. Edges can refer to the left edge and the right edge which were both 120 cubits long.

One place you say that Genesis 5 was written in clay before the flood and another place you say that centuries of oral tradition passed before the first versions of the flood story and Genesis 5 were written. Which do you mean?

Some records were written before the flood; some were not. Noah lived during the Jemdet Nasr period when writing had only recently been invented and was still in a primitive state. Writing was used mainly for accounting. Government officials who kept tax records probably were able to record the year name and the births and deaths of special people such as nobles and kings, even though this is unattested in the Jemdet Nasr period. Writing was not yet sufficiently advanced for recording narrative descriptions of events. These narratives were probably passed down through oral tradition until the Early Dynastic IIIa period when they could be written in clay.

The name Aratta appears in Sumerian texts but has nothing to do with a flood story. Your argument that story tellers confused the mountains of Ararat with Aratta is unsupported.

An Aratta flood was mentioned in "Enmerkar and the Lord of Aratta" at lines 572–577 and Aratta was the name of a god of Shuruppak, the city where Noah lived. Hence, there is an indirect connection between Noah and Aratta. However, my basic theory does not require that Aratta be confused with Ararat.

Many major floods have occurred in the Tigris-Euphrates valley and the flood of 2900 BC was only one of many. Legends from several of these floods were probably merged into one body of conflated traditions before they were written down.

Since Ziusudra was first mentioned in the Early Dynastic period and this period immediately followed the flood of 2900 BC, this flood was probably Noah's flood. Legends from the earlier flood of 4000–3500 BC may have become merged with Noah's story, especially if both flood stories had a hero, but it is not likely that oral tradition survived for more than 600 years. Since the six surviving versions of Noah's story have the same distinctive phrases and story elements, we can only assume that the story reflects the actions of one hero and not several, even though the archetype story may be a conflation of traditions. Writing was not sufficiently developed for recording narratives until about 2600 BC. Hence there is no way that we can discover which parts of the surviving flood stories came from the 4000–3500 BC flood and which from the 2900 BC flood, until tablets are discovered that explicitly distinguish events from each flood. For simplicity, we have to assume one hero, one story from the 2900 BC flood.

In one place you say the Sumerians used U_4 to mean year and another place you say they used *gur* to mean year. Which do you mean?

The stroked U_4 sign was archaic sign for indicating years but was not designed for calculating tens of years or tenths of years. The *gur* sign was part of a number system for calculating integers and fractions. This was at a time when writing and number signs had not yet become standardized. Each person could have his own peculiar way of writing, just as today each stenographer can use different shorthand strokes for the same sounds. Even if writing were standardized within a city, different cities often had different scribal schools and their standards changed with time. The Genesis 5 numbers were calculated more than three centuries after the original birth and death records were written and the number signs had changed during those centuries.

You argue that the Genesis 5 numbers were years and fractional years represented in a grain-measure system, but you cite no examples of such usage in the ancient world.

I reconstructed what one scribe did, not what his contemporaries did. Representing ages in years and factions may have been the personal notation of that one scribe who used a number system in which he already knew how to add and subtract. By assuming that this scribe used grain-measure numbers, several problems in Genesis 5 are explained or disappear.

Oceanography professors Walter Pitnam and William Ryan suggested that the Genesis and Gilgamesh flood stories were based on a massive flood of saltwater from the Aegean Sea that flowed rapidly through the Bosporus into the Black Sea about 5600 BC. In their book "Noah's Flood: The New Scientific Discoveries" Ryan and Pitman argue that professional entertainers called guslars are able to recall very long epic poems by using mnemonic formula or phrases as memory aids. Could this Black Sea flood be Noah's flood?

The archetype flood story could not have been written in clay before about 2600 BC, three thousand years after the Black Sea flood. But 3000 years of unbroken oral tradition implies more than a hundred generations of guslars, each modifying his received tradition. The probability is too great that one or more guslars in this chain would die or have memory failures before a successor memorized the tradition. Three thousand years is much too long for the details of any disaster, nomatter how dramatic, to survive in oral tradition without writing.

Ryan and Pitman provide persuasive evidence that a massive flood occurred in the Black Sea region about 5600 BC. But they do not provide credible evidence that identifys this Black Sea flood as Noah's flood. Noah lived in Shuruppak on the Euphrates River before the flood and his cattle barge grounded near Eridu at the mouth of the Euphrates River after the flood. Eridu is only about 75 miles from Shuruppak. But the Black Sea is separated from Shuruppak by more than 700 miles including 200 miles of mountains.

Ryan and Pitman cite Gilgamesh IV,5 and V,6 that refer to a "cedar mountain" located in or near Lebanon *(lab-na-nu)* and therefore closer to the Black Sea than Sumer. But cedars of Lebanon are not mentioned in tablet XI containing the flood story, and the flood story was a late addition to the Epic of Gilgamesh and hence is not related to the cedars of Lebanon. Ryan and Pitman also describe how people could navigate "the waters of death" and argue that the flood hero could have warnings of an impending flood in the Black Sea region, but not in the Euphrates River valley. That may be true, but these story elements do not unequivocally identify the Black Sea flood as Noah's flood.

Gilgamesh XI,60 uses a word derived from *rugbu* "upper floor", but your restriction of this to "uppermost, top floor" is unwarranted. In general, Mesopotamian houses had no more than two floors, thus the "upper" floor was also the "top" floor. Accordingly, there is no specific word for "intermediate floors" between the ground and the top and the term of choice would also be *rugbu* for intermediate floors. Line 60 "Six times I built an upper floor for her" cannot be disassociated from the idea of 6 decks above the base, leading to the 7 (vertical) divisions of line 61.

Lines 60–61 are ambiguous and should be read in a way that is in accord with practical boat building. The conventional image of Utnapishtim's ark as a cube 200 feet high divided into 7 stories of 28 feet each is highly unlikely. Such a boat would be very unstable and roll over in the water as any child knows who plays with a cube of wood in a bathtub. No one would build a boat that way. If one were describing a row of town houses having six attics, no one would infer that the attics were stacked vertically. The 6 upper stories in line 60 are most plausibly read as horizontal divisions. The 7 divisions in line 61 can also be read as horizontal divisions.

The Ziusudra Epic was composed in the late Old Babylonian period, probably after the Isin period and the Atrahasis Epic is dated about the same time as the reign of Ammizaduga. How then can you explain the absence of any flood stories during the hundreds of years after 2600 BC when you say the flood story was written in clay.

As with many legends, there is often a period of time during which a story is widely known through oral transmission, but not widely distributed in written form. When only a few written copies of a story are in existence, the chance of all copies from that period being lost is high.

You make the assumption that the flood tale is grounded in an actual event, but you do not prove it. There are dozens of other myths that do not have concrete events at their roots, but rather only primal fears of natural threats. That may be the case with the flood myths. For you, Noah is a real person and you describe his activities, but you do not provide any evidence to establish he was a real person. Likewise you go into details about construction of the ark, but do not present evidence that there ever was an ark, as opposed to an imaginary ark which existed only in literature.

By definition, there is no way to prove a legend. Although the river flood of 2900 BC was a real event and legends about Ziusudra circulated shortly after that flood, there is no way to prove that the ark and the animals and the altar in that legend really existed or that Noah was a real person.

Your theory about the numbers in Genesis 5 is at complete odds with what is known about Mesopotamian and Hebrew mathematics. There is no attested use of a decimal point system. They used simple fractions and fractions based on one sixtieth.

I never said that decimal points or decimal fractions were used in Mesopotamian or Hebrew mathematics. To make the numbers easy to understand, I represented them in modern decimal notation. But the ancients did not write them that way. Read the section "Conflicting number systems" in chapter 7 where I explain how the ancient scribes actually represented integers and fractions and how they represented the Genesis 5 numbers.

According to Adams' *Heartland of Cities* Fig. 33, Shuruppak was abandoned before the Old Babylonian period. How could a Shuruppak scribe find the flood story in the Shuruppak archives during the Old Babylonian period when Shuruppak was buried in sand?

The Old Babylonian scribe who translated the archetype Sumerian flood story into Akkadian was not working in Shuruppak. He may have translated copies of the flood tablets stored at Uruk only 32 miles southeast of Shuruppak. Or perhaps he was working at Sippar using the writings about "the beginning, middle, and end of all things" referred to by Berossus.

You say the flood was a river flood, but Gilgamesh and Genesis describe it as an ocean flood.

In the Epic of Atrahasis, written before the Gilgamesh and Genesis versions, the storm caused a river flood: "[Dead bodies] have filled the river like dragon flies... Like a raft they have floated to the riverbank." The corresponding line in Gilgamesh XI changed "river" to "sea". The editor of Gilgamesh XI mythologized the story by changing the river flood into an ocean deluge.

The case for Noah's ark completely fails because of dozens of thorny problems that cannot be salvaged without resorting to the supernatural.

The conventional interpretation of the ark and flood story cannot be salvaged, but the thorny problems disappear if we assume that certain words were mistranslated or misunderstood.

13

Ark and Flood Nonsense

*"The philosophic absurdity that often
marks general beliefs has never been
an obstacle to their triumph."*

Gustave Le Bon, *The Crowd*

It is not possible to document in one chapter all the mistakes, misinformation and nonsense that has been written about Noah, the ark, the flood and "Mount Ararat." Some of these mistakes were made in ancient times. Some of the misinformation is fantasy by twentieth century authors.

Noah's flood is the keystone in the belief system of the young-earth creationists who believe the flood was global and created massive geological changes in the earth's crust. So important is the flood to creationist beliefs that the flood story was explicitly cited as one of the six defining characteristics of "creation science" in the Arkansas Act 590 of 1981, a law that was overturned by the courts.[1] Belief in a global flood is also required by the Statement of Faith of the Creation Research Society, in these words: "The great Flood described in Genesis, commonly referred to as the Noachian Flood, was an historic event, worldwide in its extent and effects."[2]

The most influential modern source of misinformation on the flood is the creationist book *The Genesis Flood* by Whitcomb and Morris[3] first published in 1961. In chapters 1–4 of *The Genesis Flood*, they presented arguments for a global flood and against a local flood theory. Other authors[1,4,5,6] have refuted such creationist theories by showing that each supposed fact would be physically impossible or very improbable. The method used in the present chapter is textual criticism applied to the Genesis text to show that the impossible or improbable story elements were the result of misunderstandings and mistakes made by ancient story tellers. Creationist arguments are printed here in **boldface**:

According to Genesis 7:19–20 all the high mountains under the whole sky were covered with flood water. The waters prevailed above the mountains, covering them 15 cubits deep. The reference to 15 cubits (22 feet) does not mean the water was only 15 cubits deep, it refers to the draft of the ark.

Mountains is a mistranslation of the Hebrew word *hārîm* meaning hills in this context. The King James Version of Genesis 7:19 translates hills correctly. There is no mention of draft or deep or depth in the Hebrew text of Genesis 7:20. The 15 cubits does not refer to how deep the water was, but how much the water rose. The depths would be different at different places. The hills referred to in Genesis 7:20b were less than 15 cubits above the normal high water level during the annual inundation and were therefore covered when the water rose 15 cubits higher as mentioned earlier in the same sentence at Genesis 7:20a. From Noah's point of view, the phrase "under the whole sky" would mean whatever Noah could see from horizon to horizon. Noah could not see beyond the horizon and he would have no knowledge of what was happening thousands of miles away or on other side of the earth. All the high hills that were within his visible horizon happened to be less than 15 cubits high and were therefore covered by the flood. If the flood water had been more than ten thousand cubits deep, the authors of Genesis would have said so. Fifteen cubits is consistent with a local flood.

The flood continued for more than one year. This cannot be reconciled with a local-flood theory. If nothing could be seen but the tops of mountains after the waters had subsided for 74 days, we must conclude that the flood covered the whole earth.

All commentators have assumed that the flood mentioned in Genesis 7:6–17 was the same as the deep "waters" that lasted more than a year. But Noah's encounters with deep water were in two phases: a river flood phase that lasted less than a week and a deep water phase that lasted a year. The river flood washed Noah's barge down into the Persian Gulf and the barge floated about the deep water of the Gulf for a year. The deep water that Noah experienced for a year was not a flood; it was the deep water of the Persian Gulf. The "tops of hills" above the water surface are commonly called islands. If only islands could be seen after the water became more shallow for 74 days, it means only that Noah's barge was still several miles or more from the mainland beyond the horizon. Deep water in the Persian Gulf for more than a year is consistent with a local river flood.

According to Genesis 7:11, all the fountains of the great deep were broken up. The great deep refers to oceanic depths and underground reservoirs. Presumably, the ocean basins were fractured and uplifted sufficiently to pour water over the continents. This continued for five months. Such vast and prolonged geologic upheavals in the oceanic depths cannot be reconciled with a local flood theory. Instead this upheaval was global.

That is a lot of upheaval based on a "presumably." The Hebrew word *baqa* translated as "broken up" in the King James version is translated "burst forth" in the Revised Standard Version and New International Version. The Hebrew word *mayan* for "fountain" can also mean a well or spring which share a common meaning: a source of water. References to sources of sea water breaking or bursting may have meant only that water in the Persian Gulf was bursting onto the shore during a storm. This frequently happens along a seashore during a storm. Noah could not report on oceanic depths because he would have no way of knowing what was happening at oceanic depths. Bursting of Gulf water onto the shore was a local condition.

The Ark was unusually large. For Noah to have built a vessel of such huge magnitude simply for the purpose of escaping a local flood is inconceivable.

It is conceivable that Noah built a large river barge for hauling cargo. When a local river flood occurred, it is conceivable that Noah used the barge as a lifeboat. That may not have been what Noah had planned, but it certainly is conceivable that he used a large river barge to escape a local river flood.

There would have been no need for an ark at all if Noah's intent was to escape a local flood. How much more sensible it would have been for Noah to move to an area that would be unaffected by the local flood. The great numbers of animals could have moved out also. The entire story borders on the ridiculous if the flood was confined to some section of the Near East. The fact that he built the ark "to keep their kind alive upon the face of all the earth" (Genesis 7:3) proves that the flood was global.

The story would be ridiculous only if you accept the myth that Noah knew the flood was coming and built the barge solely as a lifeboat. Alternatively, if he built the barge to transport cattle and grain to market and had no inkling that a flood was coming until the rain began to fall, then using the barge to escape a local flood makes sense. When the rain started falling, it was too late to evacuate to the foothills of the Zagros mountains which were 110 miles away. The phrase "all the earth" did not mean the planet earth, it meant all the ground, all the land in the flooded region known to Noah. He would have had no way of knowing what was happening to the land outside his local region.

The Apostle Peter in II Peter 3:6 refers to the "world that then existed was overflowed with water and perished." Peter's reference to the flood would have no value if the flood were only a local inundation.

Peter received his information on the flood from the same scriptures that we have and was therefore limited by the same ambiguities in the text that we can see for ourselves. Just because Peter referred in broad terms to a world that was overflowed with water, does not prove that the "world" in the original story was anything more than the local world known to Noah. Peter was using the flood story as a metaphor; he was not giving a discourse on geography.

Genesis 7:21–23 teaches that all mankind perished in the flood. Only Noah and his family were left. Since the human race had spread around the planet by the time of the flood, it follows that the flood was global.

If Noah and his family were the only survivors, then they would be the only source of information on the flood. There would be nobody from other parts of the world to report on conditions there. Noah would have had no way of knowing what was happening on the earth beyond his local area. It would have been impossible for Noah to travel all over the earth or even to all the cities of the Ancient Near East checking on whether anyone else survived. Noah and the author of his story cannot be used as a source of information on facts about which they could have no knowledge. The other survivors of the flood near where Noah lived were ignored by the author of Noah's story, because they were beyond the scope of the story. A modern news report about people who survived a local river flood does not mention the billions of people who were not in the flooded area.

There are many places in Genesis where the words "all" and "every" must be understood in the literal sense. The constant repetition of universal terms throughout Genesis 6–9 shows conclusively that the magnitude and geographical extent of the flood was of primary importance in the mind of the writer. Unlike the limited scope of the word "all" in Genesis 41:57: "the people of all the earth came to Egypt to buy grain", the word "all" in Genesis 1–11 deals with universal origins (the material universe, all plants, all animals, etc.) Genesis 1–11 contains many such superlatives which lose their meaning if limited to a local area observed by the narrator.

When a modern news reporter writes that everyone died in an airplane crash, readers are expected to understand that "everyone" does not apply to the entire planet, even if the news item appears on the "World News" page.

Likewise when the narrator of the flood story wrote in Genesis 7:21 that "every man" died, the reader is expected to understand that the scope of "every" applies only to the flooded region. People living outside the flooded region were not included in "every" and were not mentioned, because they were not affected by the flood and were beyond the scope of the story.

Many ranchers in the flooded region survived the river flood by climbing to hills or buildings that were higher than 15 cubits, but most or all of their livestock drowned. In contrast "every beast according to its kind, and all the cattle" that Noah owned or were in his custody were saved in his river barge. In other words, Noah did not leave any of his animals behind.

The scope of Genesis 1–11 is not all global. Genesis 2:14 refers to the river "which flows east of Assyria and the fourth river is the Euphrates." This limits the scope of the story to a local region, the Tigris–Euphrates valley.

Not all species of animal were in the ark. There was need for no more than 35,000 individual animals on the ark. Many of the animals could have hibernated and therefore needed no food or drink. We do not really know how all this was accomplished.

Genesis 7:2 does not say "all animals" or "all land animals." It says "all clean animals." We do not have to guess at how many clean animals there were because Deuteronomy 14:4–5 lists them. Similarly with the unclean animals. About 270 animals would satisfy the totals implied by Genesis 7:2–3. There could have been enough food and drink for 270 animals on Noah's modest size barge and therefore there is no reason to suppose that any of them hibernated.

If we accept the Biblical testimony concerning an antediluvian canopy of waters (Gen. 1: 6–8, 7:11, 8:2), we have an adequate source for the waters of a global flood.

The "canopy theory" was thoroughly discredited by Soroka and Nelson[5] who did the physics calculations to prove that the canopy theory is physically impossible. Which is more likely, that an ancient story teller mistranslated an ambiguous word or that three quintillion tons of water mysteriously appeared and disappeared?

To explain where rain clouds came from, the ancient author imagined that the sky was a large round container, "a firmament" that supported a great reservoir of blue water, the "waters which were above the firmament". The rain gods would open invisible sluice gates in this sky container, releasing water that would be seen as clouds and would fall as rain. To the ancient author, that would explain how clouds were replenished with fresh water and also explain why the sky is blue. We now know that water in the clouds is replenished, not from a reservoir in the sky, but from invisible evaporation of ocean and ground water. The sky appears blue because nitrogen gas in the air scatters blue light from the sun. Mythical theories that ancient people had about sources of rain water and why the sky is blue are not a reliable basis for reconstruction of ancient events.

The ocean basins were deepened after the flood (Gen. 8:3, Psalms 104:6–9) to provide adequate storage space for the additional waters.
The writer of Genesis had no way of knowing whether the ocean basins were deepened or not. Genesis provides no direct evidence that the ocean basins were deepened. The deep waters of Noah's experience did not drain into a deepened basin, the waters became shallow because Noah's barge drifted into shallow water. Psalms 104:6–9 refers to a thunderstorm: "the waters [storm clouds] stood above the mountains…they fled at the sound of your thunder." This is mythic metaphor for a thunderstorm: that the sound of thunder frightened away the water-filled clouds above the mountains.

If the flood was global, then all air-breathing animals not in the ark perished and present-day animal distribution must be explained as migrations from the mountains of Ararat. The kangaroos in the ark migrated in all directions. Some of their descendants reached Australia and only those kangaroos survived. They could have floated across the ocean on natural rafts of vegetation or on boats manned by Noah's descendents.
Genesis does not mention kangaroos. Genesis 7:2–3 specifies seven pairs of each kind of clean animal and one pair of each kind of unclean animal. Deuteronomy 14:4–18 lists the species of clean animals and the species of unclean animals. Kangaroos were not listed and therefore were not in the ark. Hence, there is no indication in Genesis 7:2–3 that the flood was global.

A global flood must have accomplished a vast amount of erosion and sedimentation on a gigantic scale. Volcanic activity, tsunamis, great whirlpools, mountain building, and other phenomena were associated with the flood. The vastness of this geological activity must have been in proportion to the huge depth of the flood.
Such massive changes in the surface of the earth would have destroyed all traces of landmarks in the Euphrates River valley where Noah's ancestors lived (Genesis 2:14) and where Noah lived (according to the Sumerian king list). And after all of this destruction of landmarks, Noah supposedly was able to find his way back to the Euphrates River valley where his descendants lived (Genesis 11) and find the exact spot where some writings were buried (according to Berossus). For Noah to be in the southern Euphrates valley before and after the flood, indicates a local flood in the Euphrates valley.

Flood stories can be found in every part of the world and common to most of them is the recollection of a great flood which destroyed all but a tiny remnant of the human race. Many of these traditions tell of the building of a great boat which saved humans and animals and which finally landed on a mountain. This indicates that Noah's flood was global.

Flooding is experienced in every region of the earth where there are rivers. Myths about flooding can therefore arise independently around the world. Over time, travelers mix these local flood stories together in common tradition. If one story had an unusually memorable story element, such as a boat saving a family from a flood, eventually some other local flood legends would absorb that story element. Similar stories in different parts of the world were the result of travelers and missionaries taking the Noachian story to different parts of the world. No single worldwide flood is needed to account for these flood stories, many of which are unrelated to Noah's story.

Attempts to harmonize Genesis with modern geology by proposing local-flood theories have been discredited. There is no trace of such a local flood in the Euphrates River valley. The flood layer found by Leonard Woolley at Ur was not even in the same century with the flood layers found by Stephen Langdon at Kish.

Just because the Ur flood and the Kish floods were different floods does not imply that neither of them was Noah's flood. One of the Kish floods occurred at about the same time as flooding at Shuruppak and Uruk and could have been Noah's flood, a local flood that occurred about 2900 BC.

A sequel to *The Genesis Flood* was published titled *The World That Perished* by John C. Whitcomb.[7] Whitcomb repeated the same arguments for a global flood and against a local flood that are answered above. In addition he raised the following arguments:

One hundred and fifty days after the Flood began, the waters started to subside and the Ark grounded on Mount Ararat, one of the highest mountain peaks. Another thirty-one weeks were required for the waters to subside. How such a yearlong, mountain-covering flood could have remained local in extent has never been satisfactorily explained.

The Hebrew word for mountain in Genesis 8:4 can also mean hill and is translated as hill in the King James version of Genesis 7:19. A local flood covering a few hills is consistent with Genesis 7:19. Genesis 8:4 says "mountains of Ararat" not "Mount Ararat." If Noah's sons visited one of the mountains of Ararat and story tellers mistakenly assumed the barge had landed there, such a simple error could explain why the mountains of Ararat were mentioned as the landing place. Noah's barge grounded at sea level in an estuary near some low hills of the Euphrates River delta. If Noah's barge was floating about the deep water of the Persian Gulf for a year, then the prior hill-covering local flood need not have been more than a few days.

Mountain peaks several miles high did not exist before the flood. The mountains covered by the flood were less than seven thousand feet high. After the flood began, the mountains rose to their present height and the ocean basins subsided to their present depth. According to Psalms 104:8 "The mountains rose, the valleys sank down."

How would the psalm writer know that? In the same poem he also wrote "You set the earth on its foundations, so that it should never shake" (Psalms 104:5–6). The poet believed that the earth was flat and rested on a shaky foundation. Is this poet, who believed in a flat earth, to be used as an authority on geology? Missing from his poem is evidence to support his statements, examples and identification of which mountains rose, and data on how high they rose and how many years ago and over how many years the mountains rose. This poem is primitive nature myth to explain earthquakes and thunderstorms.

Could Noah have been so ignorant of the topography of southwestern Asia, where the highest mountains of the world are located, as to actually think that the Flood covered "all the high mountains everywhere under the heavens" (Genesis 7:19), when it really covered only a few foothills?

Noah may have known about the Zagros Mountains 110 miles east of Shuruppak. But since he could not see beyond the horizon, he would have no knowledge of whether the Zagros Mountains were flooded or not. He reported only what he could see and he could see only sky and water, because he was several miles from shore. From Noah's point of view, the whole world was flooded and all the high hills (less than 15 cubits high) were covered. Note that the word "hills" is used in the King James Version of Genesis 7:19. "Mountains" is a mistranslation in other versions of Genesis 7:19.

A flood in Armenia 17,000 feet deep while Egypt or India were not flooded would be a more incredible miracle than anything implied by the traditional understanding of a universal flood.

The flood water rose 15 cubits (Genesis 7:20) and had no connection with a 17,000 foot mountain. Mountain is a mistranslation. The flood covered hills not mountains.

There is nothing in Genesis 6–9 to indicate that Noah is giving his personal impressions of the Flood. Instead, it is all seen from God's viewpoint.

Which would be more reliable, Noah's eyewitness testimony or a story which states, without evidence, the beliefs of an anonymous narrator who got the story second hand? Noah's personal impressions are exactly what we need, but do not have.

Genesis 8:4–5 tells us that the ark grounded more than two months before the tops of mountains were seen. Since the mountains were close enough to be seen in the tenth month, they were close enough to be seen before the tenth month if they were not submerged. Since they were submerged prior to the tenth month and the ark was already grounded, the ark must have grounded on the highest mountain. Otherwise Noah would have seen the highest mountain before the ark grounded.

The surface of the earth is curved. There could be many higher mountains that could not be seen because they were beyond the horizon. Moreover, the ark was moving. Land that was not visible in the seventh month could become visible in the tenth month because the ark refloated and drifted closer to the mainland. The observations reported in Genesis 8:4–5 do not imply that the ark grounded on the highest mountain, or any kind of mountain.

So-called Mount Ararat

The mountain in eastern Turkey called *Masis* by the Armenians and *Aghri Dagh* by the Turks, the "Mount Ararat" of popular myth, is an active volcano nearly 17,000 feet high and is a very inhospitable place. The top 3,000 feet is usually covered with ice and snow.

Moore[4] in his satiric article debunking the popular myth of Noah's Ark, describes what would have happened if somehow the ark had landed near the top of this mountain:

> Tired and weak from malnutrition and disease, battered and bruised from being tossed about for a year in the lurching boat, nearly blind from a year's darkness in the depths of the ark, the animals began their exodus by leaping to the rocks below. From here it was a perilous trek down hoof-splitting wastelands of jagged lava, through rushing, boulder-strewn streams and icy snowbanks, with an ever-present danger of landslides and volcanic hot spots. Modern-day Ararat has often bested experienced mountaineers. What were the chances for the miserable wretches from the ark? Tree-dwelling sloths, eyeless cavernicoles, tropical snails, the legless caecilians of Seychelles – these and countless other species would have become extinct on the barren, subfreezing heights of Ararat.

In spite of the physical impossibility of Noah's boat landing on *Aghri Dagh* and the further impossibility of all the animals surviving on the mountain after landing, explorers continue to organize search parties to climb the mountain hoping to find the ark. The expression "mountains of Ararat" in Genesis 8:4 is vague and does not point to a precise landing place. And there is nothing distinctive about *Aghri Dagh* that singles it out as *the* mountain. Ark searchers continue to return to *Aghri Dagh* because it happens to be the highest mountain in that region. As if being the highest would somehow qualify it as the ark's landing place. But being a mountain, any mountain, would actually *disqualify* it as the landing place.

Attention may have been attracted to *Aghri Dagh* by reports from travelers seeing a rock formation shaped like a huge boat 18 miles south of *Aghri Dagh* near the town of Dogubayazit. This rock formation is about 6,300 feet above sea level and is often known as the Durupinar site, named after the Turkish Army Captain who first attracted world attention to the site in 1960.

The Durupinar site is described as an eroded doubly plunging syncline of sedimentary rock and limestone around which a landslide of rocks and mud flowed, thereby producing the pointed boatlike shape.[8] Just as water flows around a rock in a river bed, flowing mud was channeled around the synclinal structure. The central hump in the structure is limestone. Contrary to some claims, petrified wood and fossilized reeds were not found at the site and the rocks have no tree ring structure.

Aghri Dagh first attracted the attention of ark searchers about 1100 CE.[9] About that time someone may have noticed the Durupinar site or a similar boat-shaped rock formation and spread rumors that there was a huge boat there. Later explorers focused on the nearby mountain *Aghri Dagh* as the ark's landing place, because it was the highest mountain near the Durupinar site. *Aghri Dagh* became known as "Mount Ararat" and attracted attention away from Mount Judi south of Lake Van which ancient authors had focused on as the ark's landing place.

Ark enthusiasts hang their hopes on wood that various mountain climbers have reportedly found on *Aghri Dagh*. Trees do not grow on most of the mountain and therefore any wood found there must have been transported from somewhere else. When old wood is found, the climbers uncritically assume that it came from the Ark. But there are many other sources of wood that ark enthusiasts fail to consider. As Bailey[10] explained: "Not only have pieces of wood been brought down from the heights of Aghri Dagh, a considerable amount has been carried *up* it as well." Bailey described several things that were built on the mountain from wood that was carried up onto the mountain, including a house, various huts, several heavy wood crosses, the Monastery of Saint James and the Chapel of Saint Gregory. Later climbers who found wood on the mountain thought they had found remnants of the ark. Even finding large sections of a wooden boat on the mountain would not be incredible, because with enough effort, a group of people could have built a commemorative replica of a boat on the mountain.

Any objects made of wood, especially in the shape of a boat, found on "Mount Ararat" were transported and assembled there during the Middle Ages, and not during the Tigris-Euphrates river flood about 2900 BC forty centuries earlier.

Impossibilities

Creationists paint themselves into a corner by accepting the Genesis flood story literally, mistranslations and all, along with popular misinterpretations that have accumulated over the centuries. By accepting these beliefs, including belief in a global flood, and by reading "all" and "every living thing" too literally, creationists commit themselves to a bizarre assortment of physical impossibilities which are not mentioned in Genesis and have been disproved by people who have taken the trouble to do the physics calculations.[5]

These impossibilities are explained in a well-documented article: "Problems with a Global Flood" by Mark Isaak.[6] The following points are a summary of that article:

1. Gathering all species of animals to the ark from all parts of the world before the flood and redistributing them after the flood would have resulted in extinction of many species. Animals that cannot travel overland, or require special diets, or require special environments such as cold temperature, or require isolation from predators would have become extinct.

2. A boat 300 cubits long and made of wood would not be seaworthy. Wood is not strong enough in such a large boat to prevent separation of the seams in heavy seas. Constant pumping or bailing would be required and the ark would probably break apart.

3. A boat 300 cubits long would not have been large enough to hold all the known species of animals and the much larger volume of food and drinking water for a year in the ark. The logistics of loading all species in the 7 days allowed by Genesis 7:4,10 would have been impractical. Excluding large numbers of species would fail to solve the space problem because the excluded animals would not have been able to survive outside the ark.

4. If all species of animals were aboard the ark, their number and the waste they produced would far exceed the ability of 8 people to care for them. Many animals require fresh foods which would become inedible in the ark. Without refrigeration and dry storage, much of the food that was not consumed by insect pests would be destroyed by bacteria and mold. Without forced air ventilation, the air in the ark would become so hot that many animals would die from hyperthermia.

5. Creationist explanations of where all the water came from and where it went have been shown to be physically impossible. Water falling from

a comet or from orbiting ice or from an orbiting water canopy would be changed to superheated water vapor when it entered the atmosphere. A canopy massive enough to produce water sufficient to cover all the mountains would raise the atmospheric pressure and temperature to lethal levels. Creationists deal with the water after the flood by theorizing that the earth's surface was much flatter before the flood, and after the flood the mountains were pushed up and the ocean basins lowered by subduction. Such theories (without evidence) about rapid subduction of sedimentary ocean floors that were supposedly replaced by heavier (hot!) magma that lowered the ocean floors, fail to explain how the geothermal energy released by such rapid subduction and magma could avoid boiling the oceans and thereby poaching Noah and the animals.

6. If there had been a global flood and geologic upheavals, there would be evidence of it all over the earth. But such evidence has not been found. Tree rings that go back more than 10,000 years and ice cores that go back more than 40,000 years do not show a global one-year deluge. Rock cores from sea bottoms do not show a deluge. A global flood would have produced evidence contrary to the evidence we see.

7. People who believe in a global flood, usually believe that the flood was responsible for creating all fossil-bearing strata. These rocks have been dated by several independent radiometric dating methods and there is worldwide agreement that many of these rocks are hundreds of millions of years old. Modern-looking fossils and human artifacts have not been found in lower level strata. Deep in the geologic column there are formations such as coral reefs, beaches, sand dunes, in-place trees, evaporated salt, and dinosaur footprints, that could have originated only on the surface. A single flood could not have formed such rock formations in only one year.

8. Many plants (seeds and all) would be killed by being submerged for a few months, especially in salt water. Most plants require soil to grow, soil that would have been stripped by the flood. Noah could not have gathered seeds for all plants because not all plants produce seeds, and some plant seeds cannot survive a year before germinating. And Noah could not have distributed them all over the planet Earth.

Some fish require cool clear water, some need brackish water, some need ocean water, some need even saltier water. A global flood would have destroyed most of their habitats. Some species of animals are asexual, parthenogenic, or hermaphroditic and therefore cannot be collected "two of every kind ... male and female."

Many human diseases cannot survive in hosts other than humans. Many other diseases can survive only in humans and in short-lived vectors. For thousands of human diseases to have survived the flood, one or more of the eight people aboard the ark would have to be carrying thousands of diseases.

Since there are other diseases specific to other animals and these diseases must have been somewhere, animals aboard the ark would have to suffer from multiple diseases. This could not happen without killing the hosts. Some diseases such as measles require a community of more than 250,000 people, because the disease needs nonresistant hosts to infect. Such diseases would have gone extinct if only 8 people survived the flood.

9. Genetic variation within animal populations would have been extremely low shortly after the flood, because all of the variation within each species would have come from only a single pair of animals. All the individuals within each species would be very nearly genetically identical. The process which adds variation to populations is very slow, and hence the genetic diversity we see today could not have built up in the short time since the flood.

There are other objections to global flood theories, but the above are enough to prove that a global flood did not happen.

Because "Mount Ararat" was not covered with sea water after the flood subsided, the creationists have a problem of disposing of three quintillion tons of water in only 5 months. Creationists imagine that the ocean basins became much deeper to provide millions of cubic miles of new volume into which the water could drain, thus requiring massive geologic changes in the earth's crust in only 5 months.

Genesis does not describe massive geologic changes. Genesis 8:1b says that a wind blew and then the waters subsided. Anyone who has been on a sailboat knows that wind does not blow the water away from the boat. The wind blows the boat through the water. Sometimes wind blows the boat into shallow water. Creationists ignore the possibility that the water seemed to be rising because the ark drifted into deep water and later the water seemed to be subsiding because the wind blew the ark into shallow water.

If the ambiguous word for hill/mountain in Genesis 8:4 is translated as hill instead of mountain, the global flood becomes a local flood. But this is rejected by creationists as trivializing the flood.

The belief that Noah knew that the flood was coming long before it happened, leads to more absurdities. Creationists argue that building a giant lifeboat to save animals from a river flood makes no sense if Noah knew the flood was coming. He could have evacuated the animals to the mountains at far less cost than building a giant lifeboat. If Noah knew the flood was coming before he built the barge, then the flood was global. The premise is false and the conclusion is false. Noah could not have known the flood was coming until he saw the rain falling, at which time it was too late to move his livestock to high ground. The possibility that Noah's workers built the ark as a commercial barge to transport cattle and grain on the Euphrates River is ignored by creationists.

Creationists believe that the size of the ark was impossibly large (450 x 75 x 45 feet) and was built by Noah and his sons without outside help. This required an impossibly long period of time for construction during which the construction materials would have rotted away and Noah's animals would have died. Construction of a 450 foot boat would also have required considerable skill and knowledge of boatbuilding that was achieved only during the 19th century CE. If Noah had such incredibly advanced knowledge of boatbuilding, then why did he not pass his boatbuilding knowledge to his descendants who reverted to reed rafts?

Creationists believe that Noah lived to an impossibly old age and was 600 years old at the time of the flood. Creationists explain such longevity by further assuming that food, water and air was much more conducive to good health before the flood. The flood ended that paradisiacal state. How then could Noah live an additional 350 years after the flood (Genesis 9:28)? The possibility that the numbers were mistranslated and altered in ancient times is not considered by creationists.

The number of animals that creationists assume were in the ark was also impossibly large. Creationists ignore Deuteronomy 14:4–18 which puts a limit on the number of clean and unclean animals, and instead focus on the overgeneralized words "every living thing … every kind" in Genesis 6:19. This inflates the number of animals to a ridiculous amount that would be impossible for 8 people to care for. It would also be impossible to squeeze all of them into the ark, along with the huge amount of necessary food and drinking water.

"Every living thing" would also include fish which seem unlikely to need protection from a flood until one realizes that fresh water fish would die in the salt water of the ocean. Silt would also be stirred up in the ocean by the massive geologic upheavals that creationists imagine, hence marine fish would also not survive in the ocean. The creationists therefore imagine the ark containing aquariums to save all the species of fish as a result of too literal reading of "every living thing".

Every living thing would include species that lived thousands of miles from the ark. It would be impossible for all of them to travel from the ark to their present habitat. Creationists argue that they could be kept alive by eating food they currently cannot eat, tolerate temperatures and other environmental stresses they currently cannot tolerate, and travel distances they currently cannot travel. This would include polar bears that would die in the high heat of ancient Sumer, kangaroos that would have to cross the ocean to get to Australia, and koalas that can feed only on eucalyptus leaves.

One creationist[11] explained at great length how Noah could have satisfied the special dietary needs of insectivorous bats, soft-billed birds, koalas, pandas, king cobras, three-toed sloths, and various carnivores, without considering the fact that nowhere in Genesis are such animals mentioned. Inclusion of such animals in the ark is based on one word, the word "every" that is repeated in Genesis 6:19, 6:20, 7:4, 7:14, 7:23, 8:17, and 8:19. The possibility that "every living thing" was limited to every living domesticated animal that Noah had in his stockyard is ignored by creationists.

To explain how every living species of animals got to the ark, creationists believe that the animals came on their own volition by some magical instinct. How would the animals know which direction to go to get to the ark? The possibility that a small number of domesticated animals came to the ark because herdsmen brought them to the ark from nearby ranches is not considered by creationists.

Creationists assume that the phrase "under the whole sky" in Genesis 7:19 means all over the planet. They forget that Noah lived at a time when people believed that the earth was flat and therefore "under the whole sky" meant horizon to horizon in all directions from where Noah was standing. Even today when we say "There's not a cloud in the sky," we do not mean over the entire planet. We refer only to the sky we can see from our point of view. Since Noah could not see any land as far as the horizon, it looked to him as if his whole world was flooded. The possibility that there was plenty of dry land that Noah could not see because it was beyond the horizon is not considered by Creationists.

Skeptical reviews of Creationist books may be found in Hughes.[12]

Circular Belief Systems

Clusters of erroneous beliefs reinforce each other. For example, a belief that the ocean rose to cover a mountain top implies that the flood was global and a belief that the Ark grounded in the Ararat region and the fact that Ararat was a mountainous region supports the belief that the ark landed on a mountain. Any attempt to dispute a belief that the ark landed on a mountain carries no weight with a person who knows that Ararat was a mountainous region. One cannot successfully dispute each belief separately because each belief is supported by other erroneous beliefs. Only by casting doubt on the whole system of erroneous beliefs at the same time can the belief system be discredited. But people who subscribe firmly to a belief system are very resistant to looking at the whole system of beliefs from a new perspective. They are not willing to entertain doubts about each separate belief as long as the remaining belief system supports it. When confronted with proof that all of these beliefs are impossible, such true believers simply restate their beliefs.

References

1. Stephen Jay Gould, "Creationism: Genesis vs. Geology" in *The Flood Myth* by Alan Dundes (editor), (CA, University of California Press, 1988), p. 431. [skeptic]

2. Henry M. Morris, *A History of Modern Creationism* (El Cajon, CA, Master Books, 1984). [creationist]

3. John C. Whitcomb and Henry M. Morris, *The Genesis Flood* (PA: Presbyterian and Reformed Publishing Co., 1964). [creationist]

4. Robert A. Moore, "The Impossible Voyage of Noah's Ark," *Creation/Evolution*, 4, 1, issue XI (winter 1983), PO Box 146, Amherst Branch, Buffalo, NY 14226, p. 34. [skeptic]

5. Leonard G. Soroka and Charles L. Nelson, "Physical Constraints on the Noachian Deluge," *Journal of Geological Education*, 31 (1983), pp. 135–139. [skeptic]

6. Mark Isaak, *Problems With a Global Flood*, 2nd edition, Internet web address: www.talkorigins.org/faqs/faq-noahs-ark.html [skeptic].

7. John C. Whitcomb, *The World That Perished*, (Grand Rapids, MI, Baker Book House, second edition 1988), pp. 47–64. [creationist]

8. Lorence Gene Collins and David Franklin Fasold, "Bogus Noah's Ark from Turkey Exposed as a Common Geological Structure," *Journal of Geoscience Education*, 44, 4, (Sept 1996), pp. 439–444. [skeptic]

9. Lloyd R. Bailey, *Noah: The Person and the Story in History and Tradition*, Studies on Personalities of the Old Testament (Columbia, SC: University of South Carolina Press, 1989), p. 113. [skeptic]

10. Bailey, ibid., pp. 104–105, 112–114.

11. John Woodmorappe, *Noah's Ark: A Feasibility Study*, (Santee, CA, Institute for Creation Research, 1996). [creationist]

12. Liz Rank Hughes (editor), *Reviews of Creationist Books*, second edition, (Berkeley, CA: National Center for Science Education, 1992). [skeptic]

13. Ronald L. Numbers, *The Creationists: The Evolution of Scientific Creationism*, (New York: Knopf, 1992). [skeptic]

14

The Source Texts

In this chapter each of the six surviving texts is split into the mythical part that was fiction and the legendary part that may have happened. Corrections in brackets have been made to the legendary parts wherever the original legend was transformed into myth by mistakes and misunderstandings. Arguments supporting these corrections can be found in earlier chapters. Added comments provide theory and limit the scope of words and sentences to what would have been possible, practical, and plausible in 2900 BC.

The Genesis Flood Story[1]

Myth	Legend
6:5 The Lord saw that the wickedness of man was great in the earth and that every imagination of the thoughts of his heart was only evil continually.	
6:6 And the Lord was sorry that he had made man on the earth and it grieved him to his heart.	
6:7 So the Lord said, "I will blot out man whom I have created from the face of the ground, man and beast and creeping things and birds of the air, for I am sorry that I have made them."	
6:8 But Noah found favor in the eyes of the Lord.	
6:9 These are the generations of Noah. Noah was a righteous	

Genesis

Myth	Legend
man, blameless in his generation. Noah walked with God.	
	6:10 And Noah had three sons: Shem, Ham, and Japheth.
6:11 Now the earth was corrupt in God's sight and the earth was filled with violence. 6:12 And God saw the earth and behold, it was corrupt; for all flesh had corrupted their way upon the earth. 6:13 And God said to Noah, "I have determined to make an end of all flesh; for the earth is filled with violence through them. Behold, I will destroy them with the earth."	
	6:14 Make yourself an ark of gopher wood. Make rooms in the ark and cover it inside and out with pitch. 6:15 This is how you are to make it: the length of the
cubits cubits cubits	ark three hundred [spans], its breadth fifty [spans], and its height thirty [spans]. 6:16 Make a tsohar for the ark and finish it to a cubit above; and set the door of the ark in its side. Make it with lower, second, and third [decks].
6:17 For behold, I will bring a flood of waters upon the earth, to destroy all flesh in which is the breath of life from under heaven. Everything that is on the earth shall die.	

Genesis

Myth	Legend
6:18 But I will establish my covenant with you and you shall come into the ark, you, your sons, your wife, and your sons' wives with you. 6:19 And of every living thing of all flesh, you shall bring two of every sort into the ark, to keep them alive with you. They shall be male and female. 6:20 Of the birds according to their kinds, and of the animals according to their kinds, of every creeping thing of the ground according to its kind. Two of every sort shall come in to you, to keep them alive. 6:21 Also take with you every sort of food that is eaten, and store it up. And it shall serve as food for you and for them." 6:22 Noah did this; he did all that God commanded him. 7:1 Then the Lord said to Noah, "Go into the ark, you and all your household, for I have seen that you are righteous before me in this generation.	[Barley, beer and hay were stored in the barge]
	7:2 Take with you seven pairs of all clean animals, the male and his mate; and a pair of the animals that are not clean, the male and his mate; 7:3 and seven pairs of the birds of the air also, male and female,

Genesis

Myth	Legend
to keep their kind alive upon the face of all the earth. 7:4 For in seven days I will send rain upon the earth forty days and forty nights; and every living thing that I have made I will blot out from the face of the ground." 7:5 And Noah did all that the Lord had commanded him. 7:6 Noah was 600 years old	[Noah was 48 years old] when the flood of waters came upon the earth. 7:7 And Noah and his sons and his wife and his sons' wives with him went into the ark to escape the waters of the flood.
7:8 Of clean animals, and of animals that are not clean, and of birds, and of everything that creeps on the ground, 7:9 two and two, male and female, went into the ark with Noah, as God had commanded Noah. 7:10 And after seven days the waters of the flood came upon the earth. 7:11 In the 600th year of	[Seven days after loading of cargo began, the river flood began.] [In the 48th year of] Noah's life, in the second month, on the 17th day of the month, on that day
all the fountains of the great deep burst forth and the windows of the sky were opened.	[rain began to fall from the sky.]

Genesis

Myth	Legend
	7:12 And heavy rain fell upon the earth
forty days and forty nights.	[six days and six nights.]
	7:13 On the very same day,
	[that the rain began to fall]
	Noah and his sons Shem and
	Ham and Japheth, and Noah's
	wife, and the three wives of his
	sons with them entered the ark.
	7:14 They and every beast
	[that Noah had]
according to its kind, and all the cattle according to their kinds, and every creeping thing that creeps on the earth according to its kind, and every bird according to its kind,	
	[and] every bird of every kind [that Noah had],
	7:15 they went into the ark with Noah,
two and two of all flesh in which there was the breath of life. 7:16 And they that entered, male and female of all flesh, went in as God had commanded him; and the Lord shut him in.	
	[And he shut the door.]
forty	7:17 The [river] flood continued [six] days upon the earth and the waters [of the Euphrates River] increased and bore up the ark and it rose high above the
earth	[lowlands next to the river.]
7:18 The waters prevailed and increased greatly upon the earth;	[The water became much deeper because the river washed the barge down into the Persian Gulf]

Genesis

Myth	Legend
	and the ark floated on the surface of the waters.
7:19 And the waters prevailed so mightily upon the earth that all the high mountains under the whole sky were covered.	[The nearest high mountains were beyond the horizon and no land could be seen from horizon to horizon.]
	7:20 The waters rose fifteen cubits higher and covered the hills [that Noah could see].
7:21 And all flesh died that moved upon the earth, birds, cattle, beasts, all swarming creatures that swarm upon the earth, and every man. 7:22 Everything on the dry land in whose nostrils was the breath of life died. 7:23 He blotted out every living thing that was upon the face of the ground, man and animals and creeping things and birds of the air; they were blotted out from the earth.	[And many of the animals died that lived in the flooded region; birds, cattle, wild animals and people who lived in the lowlands died.]
	Only Noah was left and those that were with him in the ark [as far as Noah could see].
7:24 And the waters prevailed upon the earth 150 days. 8:1 But God remembered Noah and all the beasts and all the cattle that were with him in the ark. And God made a wind blow over the earth, and the waters subsided. 8:2 The fountains of the deep and the windows of the sky were closed.	[And the barge was in deep water for 150 days.] [Wind blew the barge into shallow water]. [Rain stopped falling.]

Genesis

Myth	Legend
	The heavy rain from the sky was restrained,
8:3a And the waters receded from the earth continually.	[And the waters became continually more shallow.]
	8:3b At the end of 150 days the waters had abated; and
	8:4 in the seventh month, on the seventeenth day of the month, the ark came to rest
upon the mountains of Ararat.	
8:5 And the waters continued to abate	[And the barge refloated and continued to drift]
	until the tenth month. In the tenth month, on the first day of the month,
the tops of the mountains	[islands] were seen.
	[And the barge continued to drift.]
	8:6 At the end of forty days Noah opened the window of the ark which he had made
	8:7 and sent forth a raven; and it went to and fro
until the waters were dried up from the earth.	
	8:8 Then he sent forth a dove from him, to see if the waters had subsided from the face of the ground.
	8:9 But the dove found no place to set her foot and she returned to him to the ark,
for the waters were still on the face of the whole earth.	[for dry land was still beyond the horizon.]
	So he put forth his hand and took her and brought her into the ark with him.

Genesis

Myth	Legend
	8:10 He waited another seven days, and again he sent forth the dove out of the ark.
	8:11 And the dove came back to him in the evening, and lo, in her mouth a [twig.]
freshly plucked olive leaf. So Noah knew that the waters had subsided from the earth.	
	8:12 Then he waited another seven days, and sent forth the dove; and she did not return to him any more.
8:13a In the 601st year,	[In Noah's 49th year] in the first month, the first day of the month, the waters were dried from off the earth [near the barge at low tide].
	8:13b And Noah removed the covering of the ark and looked and saw that the surface of the ground was dry [near the barge at low tide].
	8:14 In the second month, on the 27th day of the month, the earth was dry [enough at low tide to walk to nearby hills].
8:15 Then God said to Noah 8:16 "Go forth from the ark, you and your wife, and your sons and your sons' wives with you." 8:17 Bring forth with you every living thing that is with you of all flesh – birds and animals and every creeping thing that creeps on the earth – that they may breed abundantly on the earth and be fruitful and multiply upon the earth."	

Genesis

Myth	Legend
	8:18 So Noah went forth, and his sons and his wife and his sons' wives with him.
8:19 And every beast, every creeping thing, and every bird, everything that moves upon the earth, went forth by families out of the ark.	[And every beast and bird in the barge was taken from the barge].
to the Lord	8:20 Then Noah built an altar and took of every clean animal and of every clean bird and offered [cooked] offerings [to a nearby temple] on the altar.
burnt	

8:21 And when the Lord smelled the pleasing odor, the Lord said in his heart, "I will never again curse the ground because of man, for the imagination of man's heart is evil from his youth. Neither will I ever again destroy every living creature as I have done.
8:22 While the earth remains, seedtime and harvest, cold and heat, summer and winter, day and night, shall not cease."
9:1 And God blessed Noah and his sons, and said to them "Be fruitful and multiply and fill the earth."

Gilgamesh

Myth	Legend

The Epic of Gilgamesh Flood Story[2]

8 Utnapishtim said to him,
    to Gilgamesh:
9 "I will reveal to you Gilgamesh
    a hidden story
10 and secret lore of the
    gods I will tell you."

11 Shuruppak – a city you know was
12 located on the Euphrates riverbank –

13 that city was old,
    when the gods in it
14 the great gods decided
    to make a deluge.
15 Anu their father,
16 soldier Enlil their
    counselor,
17 Ninurta their
    throne bearer, [and]
18 Ennugi their canal inspector.
19 Ea, lord of wisdom, was
    present with them.
20 Their words he [Ea]
    repeated to a reed hut:
21 Reed hut, reed hut,
    wall, wall.
22 Reed hut, listen.
    Wall, remember.

23 Man of Shuruppak, son of
    Ubara–^dTutu.
24 Tear down [your] house.
    Build a boat
    [on the same land].

25 Abandon riches,
    seek life.
26 Disregard possessions,
    save life.
27 Take into the boat
    the seed of all
    living things.

Gilgamesh

Myth	Legend
	28 The boat which you shall build
	29 Let its dimensions be measured.
	30 Let equal-size [be] its width and its length.[3]
	31 As [usual in] the *apsû*, likewise cover-over[3] it [with an awning roof].
32 I understood. I said to Ea, my Lord:	
33 "My lord, what you have commanded,	
34 I will obey. I will do it.	
35 [But what] shall I answer [to] the city people and the elders?"	
36 Ea opened his mouth and said,	
37 speaking to me, his servant:	
38 "Tell them this:	
	39 [I learned that the temple of] Enlil hates me.
	40 I dare no longer walk in his land
	41 nor live in his city.
	42 [I will] go down [the river] to the *apsû* [on the shore of the Gulf] to dwell with my Lord [in the temple of] Ea.
	43 He will shower plenty on you;
	44 [an abundance of] birds, a profusion of fish
45 [...] harvest wealth."	
46 [When he orders] bread/dark [in the evening]	
47 [he will] rain down showers of wheat/misfortune.	
48 When the glow of [mor]ning began,	
49 The land was assembled...	
	50 [The carpenter] carried his axe.
	51 [The reed worker] carried his [stone].

Gilgamesh

Myth	Legend
	(lines missing)
	54 The children brought bitumen.
	55 The strong men brought [what] was needed.
	56 On the fifth day I laid out its shape/plan.
	57 One acre its extent,[3] I raised its walls ten dozen cubits each [in length].
	58 The edges [of] its upper part [were] equal-size [and] ten dozen cubits each [in length].
	59 I erected its body [frame] to it. I marked it.
	60 I provided six upper decks.
	61 I divided it into seven [sections].
	62 Its interior I divided into nine [sub-sections].
	63 Wooden water[-resisting] pegs I surely hammered into its interior.
	64 I provided punting poles and laid in supplies.
	65 Six shar of crude-pitch I poured into the kiln [for caulking].
	66 Three shar of refined-pitch [I poured] into the inside.
	67 Three shar of oil the carriers brought.
	68 Besides a shar of oil consumed by "dust",
	69 two shar of oil were stowed by the boatman.
	70 I butchered bulls for [the workmen]
	71 [and] I killed sheep every day.
	72 Beer, oil and wine [I gave]
	73 the workmen [to drink] as if it were river water.
	74 [I made a] feast like the New Year's Day festival.

Gilgamesh

Myth	Legend
	75 I opened [a box of] ointment. I laid down my hand. [I completed my project].
	76 By sunset, the boat was completed.
	77 The launching was difficult. [There was shifting of load]
	78 above and below,
	79 until two-thirds [of the structure was submerged].
	80 [Whatever I had,] I loaded.
	81 Whatever silver I had, I loaded.
	82 Whatever gold I had, I loaded.
	83 All the living beings I had, I loaded.
	84 I sent all my family and relatives aboard the boat.
	85 I sent aboard all the cattle of the field [that I had], the beasts of the field [that I had],
all the craftsmen.	
86 Shamash fixed a time [saying]	
87 "When he orders darkness in the evening, he will rain down misfortune,	
88 enter the boat and close the door."	
89 That time arrived.	
90 He ordered darkness in the evening and misfortune rained down.	
	91 I looked up at the appearance of the weather.
	92 The weather was fearful to behold.
	93 I entered the boat and closed the door.
	94 To Puzur-Amurri the boatman, the sealer of the boat,
	95 I entrusted the great structure[4] with its cargo.

Gilgamesh

Myth	Legend
	96 At the first glow of dawn,
	97 a black cloud arose from the horizon.
98 Adad	98 thundered within it,
99 as Shullat and Hanish went in front	
100 going as heralds over hill and plain.	
101 Erragal	101 [The river flood] tore out the dam posts.
102 Ninurta	102 [The river flood] made the dikes overflow.
103 The Anunnaki raised torches,	[Flashes of lightning]
	104 illuminated the land with their brightness.
105 Adad	105 The fury of [the storm] reached the heavens.
	106 Everything that was bright turned to darkness.
	107 ...the land shattered like...
	108 For one whole day the south wind [blew],
	109 gathering speed as it
	110 passed over the land like a battle.
	111 One person could not see another.
112 People could not be recognized from heaven.	
113 The gods were frightened by the flood.	
114 They fled [and] ascended to the heaven of Anu.	
115 The gods cowered like dogs crouching against the wall.	

Gilgamesh

Myth	Legend
116 Ishtar cried out like a woman giving birth.	

117 The Lady of the gods
    wailed with her
    beautiful voice.	

118 "Alas, the olden days have turned to clay	

119 because I spoke evil
    in the assembly of
    the gods.	

120 How could I speak evil in the assembly,	
121 ordering disaster to destroy my people,	
122 [for] it is I who gave birth to my people.	
123 Like the spawn of fish they fill the sea.	
124 The Anunnaki gods wept with her.	
125 The gods are depressed, they sit weeping.	
126 Their lips burn… together.	
	127 Six days and seven nights
	128 the wind blew, the flood storm overwhelmed the land.
	129 When the seventh day arrived, the pounding storm flood
130 fought a battle	130 [surged intermittently] like a woman in labor.
	131 The sea grew calm; the wind abated; the flood ceased.
	132 I looked upon the sea; [all was] silence.
133 And all of humanity had turned to clay.	
	134 The tideway lay flat as a rooftop.

Gilgamesh

Myth	Legend
	135 I opened the window and light fell on my face.
	136 I was horrified and sat down and wept.
	137 Tears [were] running down my face.
	138 I looked for coastlines in the expanse of the sea.
	139 Twelve[3] times an island emerged.
	140 In country[3] Niṣir the boat grounded.
	141 A mound [in] Niṣir country[3] held the boat firmly, allowing no motion.
	142 A first day, a second day, a mound [in] Niṣir country etc.[5]
	143 A third day, a fourth day, a mound [in] Niṣir country etc.
	144 A fifth, a sixth, a mound [in] Niṣir country etc.
	145 When the seventh day arrived,
	146 I brought out and released a dove.
	147 The dove went out and came back to me.
	148 There was no resting place [that it could see]; it returned.
	149 I brought out and released a swallow.
	150 The swallow went out and came back to me.
	151 There was no resting place [that it could see]; it returned.
	152 I brought out and released a raven.
	153 The raven went out and when it saw the water dried up,
	154 it ate, it flew about, it cawed, it did not return. [The barge grounded again in shallow water. When the ground was dry we disembarked.]

Gilgamesh

Myth	Legend
	155 [Then] I sent forth ... to the four winds and offered a sacrifice.
	156 I placed an offering on top of a hill-like ziggurat.
	157 Seven and seven pots I set out.
	158 Under them I piled reeds, cedar and myrtle.
159 The gods smelled the savor.	
160 The gods smelled the sweet savor.	
161 The gods gathered like flies about the sacrificer.	
162 As soon as the great goddess arrived,	
163 she lifted up the large flies which Anu had made according to her wish.	
164 You gods here, as surely as I shall not forget the lapis lazuli on my neck,	
165 I shall remember these days and never forget them.	
166 Gods, approach the offering.	
167 [But] Enlil shall not come near the offering	
168 because without discussion he sent the storm-flood	
169 and consigned my people to destruction.	
170 As soon as Enlil arrived	
171 and saw the boat, Enlil was furious.	
172 He was filled with anger against the sky gods.	

Gilgamesh

Myth	Legend

173 Has anyone escaped alive?
No man was to survive the
destruction.

174 Ninurta opened his mouth
and spoke to soldier Enlil:

175 "Who except Ea could plan
such a thing?

176 It is Ea alone who knows
every matter."

177 Ea spoke to soldier Enlil:

178 "Oh soldier, you wisest
among the gods.

179 How could you without
discussion bring on a
storm-flood?

180 Charge the crime to the
criminal, charge the
offense to the offender.

181 Be merciful, that he not die;
[but] pull tight that he
may not get loose.

182 Instead of your sending a
flood, better that
a lion had diminished
mankind.

183 Instead of your sending
a flood, better that a
wolf had diminished
mankind.

184 Instead of your sending a flood,
better that a famine had
[ruined] the land.

185 Instead of your sending
a flood, better that a
pestilence had beaten
down mankind.

186 It was not I who revealed the
secret of the great gods.

Gilgamesh

Myth	Legend

187　To Atrahasis I showed a
　　　　dream and so he learned
　　　　the secret of the gods.

188　Now take advise concerning him.

189　Then Ea[6] went aboard the boat.

190　Holding me by the hand,
　　　　he took me aboard.

191　He took my wife aboard and
　　　　had her kneel by my side.

192　Standing between us, he
　　　　touched our foreheads
　　　　to bless us:

193　"Previously Utnapishtim
　　　　was a man.

194　[But] now Utnapishtim and
　　　　his wife are associates; they
　　　　shall be gods like us.

195　Utnapishtim [Noah] shall live
　　　　in the distance at the
　　　　mouth of the rivers."

196　They took us to live in the distance
　　　　at the mouth of the rivers.

Line numbers in different translations of Gilgamesh XI

Line numbers used above are from Heidel (1949). Later translations and transliterations use somewhat different line numbers.

Heidel	Kovacs	Parpola
1–37	1–36	1–37
38–73	37–71	38–73
74–87	72–86	74–87
88–90	87–90	88–91
91–173	91–174	92–175
174–196	175–203	176–204

Atrahasis

Myth	Legend

The Epic of Atrahasis[7]

Atrahasis BE39099 rev ii

44 Enlil opened his mouth to speak
45 And addressed the assembly of
        all the gods.
46 "Come, all of us, and take an
        oath to bring a flood."
47 Anu swore first.
48 Enlil swore. His sons
        swore with him.

Atrahasis RS 22.421

1 When the gods took counsel
        in the lands.
2 And brought about a flood
        in the regions of the
        world.
        [… lines missing …]

6 I am Atrahasis.
7 I lived in the temple of
        Ea[Enki], my lord.

9 I knew the counsel of the
        great gods.
10 I knew of their oath, though
11 they did not reveal it to me.
12 He repeated their words to
        the wall.
13 "Wall, listen [to me] …"

Atrahasis III,i

11 Atrahasis opened his mouth
12 And addressed his lord,
13 Teach me the meaning
        [of the dream]…
14 that I may seek its outcome.
15 [Enki] opened his mouth
16 And addressed his servant:
17 You say, "What am I to seek?"
18 Observe the message that
19 I will speak to you:

Atrahasis

Myth	Legend
20 Wall, listen to me.	
21 Reed wall, observe all my words.	
	22 Destroy your house, build a boat [on the same land].
23 Spurn property and save life.	
	25 The boat which you build
	26 ... be equal ...
	29 Roof it over like the *apsû* [boats]
	30 So that the sun shall not see inside it.
	31 Let it be covered/roofed above and below.
	32 The [covering] should be very strong.
	33 Let the pitch be tough and give [the boat] strength. (continued below)

Atrahasis DT 42(w)

2 ... like a circle ...
3 Let [the covering] be strong above and below.
4 ... caulk the [boat].

5 [At] the appointed time of which I will inform you,
6 enter [the boat] and close the boat's door.

7 [Load into] it your barley, your goods, your property,
8 your family, your relatives,

9 All the wild creatures of the steppe that eat grass [load all you have.]

and the skilled workers.

10 [I] will send to you and they will wait at your door.
11 Atrahasis opened his mouth to speak

Atrahasis

Myth	Legend
12 And addressed Ea [Enki], his lord:	
	13 I have never built a boat...
	14 Draw the design on the ground
	15 That I may see and [build] the boat.
16 Ea drew [the design] on the ground.	
17 "[I will do], my lord, what you commanded."	

Atrahasis CBS 13532

Myth	Legend
2 ... I will explain.	
3 ... [flood] will seize all the peoples together.	
4 ... before the flood sets out.	
5 ... all that there are ...	
	6 ... build a large boat.
	7 Let its structure be ... of good reeds.
	8 ... let it be a very large boat
with the name Saver of Life	
	9 ... cover/roof it with a strong covering.
	10 [Into the boat that] you will make [load all you
	11 have of] wild creatures of the steppe, birds of the heavens,
	12 [... hay that you] heap up.

Atrahasis III,i (continued)

Myth	Legend
34 I will rain down on you here	
35 An abundance of birds, a profusion of fishes.	
36 He opened the water-clock and filled it.	

Atrahasis

Myth	Legend
37 [Enki] told him of the coming of the flood on the seventh night.	[The flood began seven days after loading began]
38 Atrahasis received the command.	
39 He assembled the elders [of the city] to his gate.	
40 Atrahasis opened his mouth	
41 and addressed the elders.	
42 "My god [does not agree] with your god."	
43 Enki and [Enlil] are angry with each other.	
44 They have expelled me [Noah] from [my house (?)]	
45 Since I revere [Enki],	
46 [he told me] of this matter.	
47 I cannot live in [your city]	
48 I cannot walk on the earth of Enlil.	
49 With the gods... [I will dwell.]	
50 [This] is what he told me... [... lines missing ...]	

Atrahasis III,ii

[... lines missing ...]

10 The elders ...

11 The carpenter [carried his axe].

12 the reed worker [carried his stone].

13 [The children carried] pitch.

14 The poor men [brought what was needed].

[... lines missing ...]

[construction details missing]

31 Whatever he had [he put on board].

32 Clean (animals)...

33 Fat (animals)...

Atrahasis

Myth	Legend
	34 He caught…
	35 The winged [birds of] the heavens.
	36 The cattle [of the field] …
	37 The wild [animals of a plain]
	38 [gold/silver] he put on board
	39 … the moon disappeared.
	40 … he invited his people
	41 … to a banquet. …
	42 He sent his family on board.
	43 They ate and they drank.
	44 But he was in and out.
	45 He could not sit, could not crouch,
	46 For his heart was broken
	47 And he was vomiting gall.
	48 The appearance of the weather changed,
49 Adad	49 [thunder] roared in the clouds.
50 As soon as he heard Adad's voice	50 As soon as [Noah heard thunder]
	51 Pitch was brought for him to close his door.
	52 After he had bolted his door
53 Adad was roaring in the clouds.	53 [thunder continued to] roar in the clouds.
	54 The winds became savage as he arose.
	55 He severed the mooring line
	56 and set the boat adrift. [… lines missing …]

Atrahasis BM98977 rev
[… lines missing …]
[The river flood …]
13 It sweeps forward, it kills, it threshes …

Atrahasis

Myth	Legend
14 Ninurta went forth [making] the dikes [overflow].	[The swollen river made the dikes overflow].
15 Errakal tore up [the mooring poles].	[The river tore up the mooring poles.]
16 With his talons [he rent] the heavens.	
17 [And smashed] the land like a pot; he scattered its counsel.	
18 ... the flood set out.	
19 Its might came upon the peoples. [... lines missing ...]	
Atrahasis III,iii [... lines missing ...]	
10 And smashed ...	
11 ... the flood [set out]	
12 Its might came upon the peoples.	
	13 One person did [not] see another.
	14 They were [not] recognizable in the destruction.
	15 [The wind] bellowed like a bull.
	16 [Like] a whinnying wild ass, the winds [howled].
	17 The darkness [was dense], there was no sun [visible].
[... lines missing ...]	
23 ... the noise of the [storm] ...	
24 It was trying ... of the gods.	
25 [Enki] was beside himself,	
26 [seeing that] his sons were	
27 thrown down before him.	
28 Nintu, the great lady,	
29 Her lips were covered with fever.	

Atrahasis

Myth	Legend

30 The Anunnaki, the great gods,
31 Were sitting in thirst and
      hunger.
32 The goddess saw it as she
      wept,
33 The midwife of the gods,
      the wise Mami [spoke]
34 "Let the day become dark,
35 Let it become gloom again.
36 In the assembly of the gods.
37 How did I, with them,
38 command total destruction?
39 Enlil has had enough of
      bringing about an evil
      command.
40 Like that Tiruru, he
41 uttered abominable evil.
42 As a result of my own
      choice
43 And to my own hurt I have
      listened to their noise.
44 My offspring, cut off from me,
45 have become like flies.
46 And for me, as in a house of
      grieving,
47 My cry has died away.
48 Shall I go up to heaven
49 As if I were to live in
50 a treasure house?
51 Where has Anu the
      president gone
52 Whose divine sons obeyed
      his command?
53 He who did not consider, but
      brought about a flood
54 And consigned the peoples
      to destruction?"
      [... lines missing ...]

Atrahasis

Myth	Legend
Atrahasis III,iv	
4 Nintu was wailing...	
5 What? Have they given [birth] to the ... sea	
	6 Like dragonflies they
	7 [the dead bodies] have filled [parts of] the river.
	8 Like a raft they have moved in [floated] to the edge [of the boat].
	9 Like a raft they have moved in [floated] to the riverbank.
10 I have seen and wept over them.	
11 I have ended my lamentation for them.	
12 She wept and her feelings eased.	
13 Nintu wailed and	
14 spent her emotion.	
15 The gods wept with her for the land.	
16 She was surfeited with grief	
17 and thirsted for beer.	
18 Where she sat weeping,	
19 They sat like sheep.	
20 They filled the trough.	
21 Their lips were athirst with fever.	
22 From hunger they	
23 were suffering cramp.	
	24 For seven days and seven nights
	25 came the deluge, the storm.
	26 Where it ...
	27 Was thrown down ... [... 25 lines missing ...]

Atrahasis

Myth	Legend

Legend

[This is where the story may have mentioned opening the door, seeing islands, sending out birds, and grounding]

Atrahasis III,v
[... 29 lines missing ...]
30 To the [four] winds ...
31 he offered [a sacrifice]
32 Providing food.

Myth

34 [The gods smelled] the savor
35 They gathered [like flies]
    about the offering.
36 [After] they had eaten the
        offering
37 Nintu arose to complain
38 against all of them.
39 "Where has Anu the
40 president gone?
41 Has Enlil come to the
        incense?
42 They, who did not consider
        but brought about a flood
43 And consigned the peoples
        to destruction?
44 You decided on total
        destruction.
45 Now their clean faces have
        become dark."
46 Then she approached the
        big flies
47 Which Anu had made and was
        carrying.
48 "His grief is mine.
49 Now determine my destiny.
50 Let him get me out of this
51 distress and relieve me.
52 Truly..."

Atrahasis

Myth	Legend
Atrahasis III,vi	

1 In ...
2 Let these flies be the
3 lapis around my neck
4 That I may remember it
　　　[every] day.
5 [The soldier Enlil] saw
　　　the vessel
6 And was filled with anger
　　　at the sky gods.
7 "All we great Anunnaki
8 Decided together on an
　　　oath.
9 Where did life escape?
10 How did man survive the
　　　destruction?"
11 Anu opened his mouth
12 And addressed the soldier
　　　Enlil:
13 "Who but Enki could do
　　　this?
14 ...
15 I did not reveal the
　　　command."
16 [Enki] opened his mouth
17 [And addressed] the great
　　　gods:
18 "I did it in front of you.
19 [I am responsible] for
　　　saving life ..."
　　　[... 5 lines missing ...]
25 [on the criminal] impose
　　　your penalty.
26 Whoever disregards your
　　　command
27 ... the assembly ...
　　　[... 12 lines missing ...]

Ziusudra

Myth	Legend

The Epic of Ziusudra[8]

143 Anu, Enlil, Enki and
      Ninhursag
144 The gods of the universe,
      had [taken an oath in] the
      name of Anu Enlil.

                                     145   Then king Ziusudra, the
                                         priest …

146 He made …
147 With humble words and
      reverence …
148 Every day he regularly
      stood at [the reed wall].
149 It was not a dream,
      appearing and speaking
      …
150 In the name of heaven and
      earth …
151   … the gods in Nippur …
152 Ziusudra stood at the side
      and listened.
153 "Stand by the wall at my
      left …
154 At the wall, I will speak
      to you, [listen] to my
      words.
155 Heed my instructions.
156 By our [hand] a flood
      [will sweep] over the
      capitals
157 To destroy the seed of
      mankind …
158 The decision, the word of
      the assembly, [is final].
159 By the command spoken by
      Anu Enlil …

Ziusudra

Myth	Legend
	160 The overthrowing of the kingship …
	[… 40 lines missing …]
	[Here is where he builds a large boat. Construction details would be here. He loads the cargo. The storm begins.]
	201 All the destructive winds [and] gales were present.
	202 Then the flood swept over the capitals.
	203 For seven days and seven nights
	204 the flood covered the country
	205 [And] the wind drove the large boat about on the deep water.
	206 The sun came out, illuminating the earth and sky.
	207 Ziusudra opened a window in the large boat
	208 And sunlight entered the large craft.
	209 King Ziusudra
	210 Prostrated himself before the sun-god.
	[The bird scene and the boat grounding are not in the text.]
	211 The king slaughtered an ox and some sheep.
[Here the gods smelled the savor.]	
[… 39 lines missing …]	
251 In the name of heaven and earth, let …	
252 Anu Enlil has sworn by heaven and earth that …	

Ziusudra

Myth	Legend
253 They made the animals come up from the earth.	
254 King Ziusudra	
255 Prostrated himself before Anu Enlil.	
256 [He] gave him life like a god [and]	
257 Elevated him to eternal life like a god.	
	258 Then king Ziusudra
	259 Who protected the animals and seed of mankind,
	260 They caused to dwell in the land of the country of Dilmun,
	261 the place where the sun rises.
	[… 39 lines missing …]

Berossus

Myth	Legend

The Flood Story from Berossus[9]

shars

> Kronos appeared to him in
> a dream and revealed that

> He commanded [him] to set down
> in writing the beginning, middle,
> and end of all things, and to bury
> [these writings] in Sippar, the city
> of the sun[-god];

> and when all was ready, to
> set sail. If asked where he
> was going, he should say:
> "To the gods, to pray for
> blessings for mankind."
> He obeyed and built a
> boat, five furlongs long and
> two furlongs wide. When
> everything was done in
> accordance with directions,
> he embarked with his wife
> and children and his close
> friends.

After the death of Ardates,
his son Xisuthros reigned for
eighteen [years]. In his reign
a great flood occurred and the
story has been recorded as
follows:

on the fifteenth day of the
month Daisios mankind would
be destroyed by a great flood.

[There were tablets buried in
mud at Sippar during the flood.]

[Then he was]
to build a boat;
and to go aboard it with his
relatives and close friends;
to store in it food and drink;
to put in it also living birds
and animals;

[He had a large boat built.]

[He went aboard it with his
wife and children and close
friends.]

Berossus

Myth	Legend
	After the flood had occurred and
as soon as it subsided,	[after the water became shallow]
	Xisuthros released some birds,
	but as they found no food nor
	place to rest, they returned
	to the boat.
	After some days Xisuthros
	again released the birds and
	they returned to the boat
	with their feet muddy. But
	when they were released for
	a third time, they did not
	return to the boat again.
Xisuthros concluded that land	
had appeared. Opening a part of	
the seams of the boat and seeing	
that the boat had grounded upon	
a mountain,	
	he disembarked with [his]
	wife, [his] daughter, and the
	boatman. After prostrating
	himself to the ground, he
	built an altar and sacrificed
	to the gods.
He then disappeared with	[He then departed with his
those who had disembarked	wife, his daughter, and the
from the boat.	boatman.]
Those who had remained in the	[The remaining people from the
boat disembarked when	boat also disembarked.]
	Xisuthros and his companions
	did not return.
They searched for him, calling	
(him) by name.	
	But Xisuthros himself they
	never saw again.
	A voice came from the air,
	telling them they must worship
	the gods;

Berossus

Myth	Legend
and because of his piety, he had gone to dwell with the gods, and his wife and daughter and the boatman shared the same honor. He also told them to return to Babylonia, to go to the city of Sippar as they were destined to do,	[They were told to go to the city of Sippar,] to dig up the writings that were buried there, and to publish them to mankind.
They were located in the	[They traveled on foot to the] country of Armenia.
When they heard this,	they sacrificed to the gods and journeyed on foot by a roundabout way to [Sippar.]
Babylonia. A part of the boat that grounded in Armenia still remains there	[After visiting Mount Judi] in the Kordyaean mountains in Armenia,
and some people scrape off pieces of pitch from the boat to use as amulets. When they went to Babylonia,	they dug up the writings at Sippar.
They built many cities, erected temples, and renewed Babylonia.	

Moses of Khoren

Myth	Legend

Legend preserved by Moses of Khoren[10]

	There was a book about Khsisuthros and his sons, which has not survived to the present, in which they say, is the following portrayal: After Khsisuthros
had floated to Armenia and	
	had landed, one of his sons, named Sim [Shem], went northwest to explore the land. He arrived at a small plain at the foot of an extensive mountain through which a river flowed to the region of Assyria. He lived by the river for two months, and named the mountain 'Sim' after himself. Then he returned to the southeast in the direction from which he had come.
But one of the younger sons separated, with thirty sons and fifteen daughters and their husbands, from their father and took his dwelling place again on the same river bank, after whose name he also named the canton of Taron. But he named the place where he lived "Cronk", because the separation of his sons from him first began at that place. He turned away and lived, so they say, for some time on the borders of the region of Bactria, and one of his sons remained there. The people of the Eastern Lands call the Sem "Zrvan" and the canton	

Moses of Khoren

Myth	Legend
they call "Zaruand" to this day. Often the old peoples from the descendants of Aram relate this matter with loud music, song, and dance.	

References

1. "Genesis" in *The Holy Bible*, Revised Standard Version, (New York, Thomas Nelson and Sons, 1953).

2. Text from the Epic Of Gilgamesh (tablet XI) is adapted from the most clearly expressed phrases in five translations:

Maureen Gallery Kovacs, *The Epic of Gilgamesh*, (Stanford, California: Stanford University Press, 1985), pp. 97–103.

E. A. Speiser, "Akkadian Myths and Epics" in *Ancient Near Eastern Texts*, James B. Pritchard (ed), (NJ: Princeton University Press, 1950), pp. 93–95.

Alexander Heidel, *The Gilgamesh Epic and Old Testament Parallels* (Chicago, University of Chicago Press, 1949/1970).

J. V. Kinnier Wilson, "The Story of the Flood in the Epic of Gilgamesh," in *Documents from Old Testament Times*, D. Winton Thomas (editor), (London: Thomas Nelson and Sons, 1958), pp. 17–26.

N. K. Sandars, *The Epic of Gilgamesh* (Baltimore, MD: Penguin Books, 1964), pp. 105–110.

3. See discussion in appendix A.

4. The tablet literally reads "big house," the common expression for palace, but the sign for house is very similar to the sign for boat, differing only by one wedge. Big house may have been an ancient scribal error for big boat.

5. Lines 142–144 end with the repetition signs KI.MIN meaning ditto or etc.

6. See chapter 5, notes 37–39.

7. W. G. Lambert and A. R. Millard, *Atrahasis: The Babylonian Story of the Flood* (Oxford, Clarendon Press, 1969).

References

8.   Text from the Epic of Ziusudra is adapted from the most clearly expressed phrases in three translations:

Samuel Noah Kramer, "Sumerian Myths and Epic Tales" in *Ancient Near Eastern Texts,* James B. Pritchard (ed), (NJ: Princeton University Press, 1950), pp. 42–44.

Thorkild Jacobsen, "The Eridu Genesis," *Journal of Biblical Literature,* 100/4 (1981), pp. 513–529.

Miguel Civil, "The Sumerian Flood Story" in *Atrahasis: The Babylonian Story of the Flood,* W. G. Lambert and A. R. Millard, (Oxford, Clarendon Press, 1969), pp. 138–145.

9.   Berossus, *Babyloniaka*, flood story fragments, is adapted from the most clearly expressed phrases in three translations:

W. G. Lambert and A. R. Millard, *Atrahasis: The Babylonian Story of the Flood* (Oxford, Clarendon Press, 1969), pp. 134–137.

Alexander Heidel, *The Gilgamesh Epic and Old Testament Parallels* (Chicago, University of Chicago Press, 1949/1970), pp. 116–119.

Gerald P. Verbrugghe and John M. Wickersham, *Berossos and Manetho*, (MI: University of Michigan Press, 1996), pp. 49–50.

10.   Moses of Khoren, flood story legend from Olympiodorus, is adapted from the most clearly expressed phrases in two translations:

Moses of Khoren, *History of the Armenians*, translation by Robert W. Thomson, vol. 4 of Harvard Armenian Texts and Studies, (Harvard University Press, 1978) pp. 79–80 (near end of section 6).

Lloyd R. Bailey, *Noah: The Person and the Story in History and Tradition,* (Columbia, SC: University of South Carolina Press, 1989), p. 194.

15

Epilog

*"The king Ziusudra...elevated to
eternal life, like a god."*
Epic of Ziusudra vi,254-257

You have learned from this book that popular stories about Noah and the flood are derived from a Sumerian myth about a local river flood, and that the ark was just a commercial river barge drifting around the Persian Gulf. There was no global deluge, no submerged mountains, no massive geologic upheavals, no drowning of mankind, no millions of animals, no giraffes, elephants, lions, or kangaroos, no miracles. Noah was just an ordinary executive who boarded a cattle barge when a local river flood overflowed the levees. On the other hand, you have learned several things about Noah that make him a more interesting person. You learned that he was probably a wealthy land owner and that he and his father Lamech were kings of Shuruppak. You learned that Noah's kingship was overthrown by other survivors of the flood and that Noah had to flee to the island of Dilmun where he lived in exile. You learned the exact location of Noah's altar where he made his sacrifice and that temple priests were present at the ceremony. And you learned how the mountains of Ararat got involved.

Most people who read about Noah and his flood, want a fictional story filled with spectacular events, and that is why story tellers over the centuries have indulged their listeners by expanding the scope of the local river flood into a global cataclysm. But in a way, the story tellers who mythologized Noah's story and distorted and suppressed the mundane facts, did Noah a very big favor. For without the myth, Noah's river flood story would have been forgotten millennia ago. The ark story was remembered because successive generations of listeners wanted to hear about a super hero who did miraculous things and knew things that no ordinary mortal could know. They wanted to hear about what the gods were doing and thinking, why they caused the flood, why Noah was warned that a flood was coming, and how one family survived with all the animals of the earth when everyone else died. None of this happened. But by embellishing the river flood story, the poets, story tellers, and editors kept the story alive.

Myth has a greater chance of surviving than history, because myth appeals to a much larger audience. But even myth and popular fiction sooner or later are forgotten. That has not yet happened to Noah. Noah is unique because he is still famous nearly five thousand years after his death.

When the priest of Enki made Noah an honorary god, he said Noah was elevated to eternal life. These were empty words because Noah eventually died. But in a way, what the priest said was true, and far beyond his wildest imagination. Noah was elevated to eternal life, not in body, but in the legend and myth that still lives in the world's literature and in the minds of millions of people. Five thousand years spans the entire period of recorded history. For a man to survive in the collective memory of mankind for nearly five thousand years is more eternal than a mortal man could ever hope for.

I would never have written this book if I thought it would destroy the popular myth of Noah and his ark. Noah's story has survived forty-nine centuries and I would not want to reduce its chances of surviving another forty-nine centuries. The mythic parts of the story were Noah's ticket to immortality and the story will continue to be retold as long as people enjoy hearing myth. But the other side of the story needs to be told too, even if the mundane facts are less than spectacular.

The general population will continue to fantasize about giraffes and elephants marching in pairs down from an ark perched on a mountain top. But as long as the flood story is treated like the Santa Claus story, a popular myth built on a grain of legend, then no harm is done.

But I would not want my efforts to trace the origin of the flood story to be misquoted by creationists as a confirmation of their fantasies. It should be clear from Chapter 13 that I believe most of the Genesis flood story to be fiction. If I were forced to choose between the creationists and the skeptics, I would side with the skeptics. Science is under siege and is continually being chipped away by well-meaning but ignorant people. Rejection of science and logic erodes support for teaching of critical thinking and objective analysis of reality.

That said, it is still possible to analyze the flood story as a literary masterpiece which, like the Santa Claus myth, contains clues about its historic origins. These origins may have included an actual flood and an actual leader of Shuruppak and an actual cattle barge. But the rest of the story may have been the invention of an imaginative story teller. Much of the archetype story reconstructed here may have been fiction that was set in a historic setting. But the same can be said about other famous legends. We may never know how much of Noah's story was fact and how much was fiction. But regardless, forty-nine centuries of story tellers agree on one thing: it makes a good story. Will Noah still be remembered forty-nine centuries from now as the man who saved some animals on his famous ark? Not likely, but who can say?

Ballad of Noah's Ark

In days of old, the poets told
Of Noah, a Sumerian king,
Who built a large commercial barge
For river transporting.

He loaded each year a shipment of beer
With cattle and grain to deliver.
Then his servants escorted this cargo transported
To cities alongside the river.

A rare typhoon occurring in June
Caused destruction, the legends agree.
With flooding so large it washed Noah's barge
On the river down into the sea.

There was no way to know where the water would go
Or that Persian Gulf water would stay.
Noah's problem was he had no way to see
The dry land only ten miles away.

Along on his boat, that was safely afloat,
Were his sons and their wives and his daughter.
They had plenty to eat: bread, beer, eggs and meat,
While awaiting the end of deep water.

After ten months of waiting for water abating
The barge finally grounded on land.
Noah came out all right, but all land within sight
Was tidal marsh, hills, mud, and sand.

Biographers wrote that he landed his boat
On a mountain, but that cannot be.
The barge didn't stop on a high mountain top.
It washed up on the shore of the sea.

But legend forgot this barge grounding spot
And replaced it with mountain locations.
They now say it sat on Mount Ararat,
The result of faulty translations.

My friend, do not fail to learn from this tale.
Be famous in legend and song.
To insure that *your* story is destined for glory
Make sure it is translated wrong.

Robert M. Best

16

Conclusions

"I used to be indecisive, but now I'm not so sure."
— Lily Tomlin

The theories presented in this book are not a monolithic whole to be either totally accepted or totally rejected. Some parts of the theory are more probable or have stronger support in the sources than other parts. The percentages attached to each of the following conclusions are my estimates of the confidence level that each element in the theory is true or not true.

Conclusion:	Confidence Level
1. The ancient flood stories are mostly myth.	100%
2. No one ever lived to be 900 years old.	100%
3. There was no global flood a few thousand years ago.	100%
4. The ocean did not cover high mountains in 150 days.	100%
5. Merchants hauled cattle and grain in river barges on the Euphrates River.	100%
6. A boat floated down the river into the Persian Gulf.	99%
7. A storm caused a Euphrates River flood about 2900 BC.	95%
8. The historic flood of about 2900 BC was the basis for Noah's flood story.	90%
9. This historic flood did not last a year.	90%
10. The numbers in Genesis 5 are ten times too large.	80%
11. The Septuagint Gen 5 numbers are closest to the originals.	80%
12. The flood story was first written in clay about 2600 BC.	70%
13. Noah was a real person who saved animals on a barge.	50%
14. Noah was a fictitious person.	50%

The following confidence level estimates are based on the assumption that Noah was a real person who saved some animals and grain on a river barge during a local river flood.

Conclusion:	Confidence Level
1. Noah was a real person (by definition)	100%
2. Noah's barge did not land on a mountain.	100%
3. "Mount Ararat" (Aghri Dagh) played no roll in Noah's flood.	100%
4. There were many more than ten survivors of Noah's flood.	100%
5. Noah's ark will never be found.	100%
6. Nobody knew a flood was coming until the storm began.	100%
7. Noah's ark was a river barge for hauling cargo.	95%
8. Noah's flood was caused by a thunderstorm.	95%
9. Noah's flood was a river flood lasting several days.	95%
10. Noah hired skilled workmen to build the barge.	95%
11. The river carried Noah's barge into the Persian Gulf.	90%
12. Wind blew the barge into deep water.	90%
13. Wind blew the barge into shallow water.	90%
14. The barge grounded near the shore of the Persian Gulf.	90%
15. Story tellers mistranslated hill or country as mountain.	90%
16. Noah was a chief executive of Shuruppak.	80%
17. There were fewer than 280 animals on the barge.	80%
18. Noah's boatman was on the barge during the flood.	80%
19. Story tellers confused the deep Gulf with a flood.	80%
20. The barge grounded in an estuary.	80%
21. Noah offered a sacrifice at the top of a hill.	80%
22. The barge drifted for several months in the Gulf.	70%
23. Noah's son walked to a mountain after the barge grounded.	70%
24. Noah was a merchant or trade official before becoming king.	60%
25. Noah's barge had hulls using shell-first construction.	60%
26. Genesis 5 was a garbled version of factual records.	60%
27. Noah's barge was dozens of small boats roped together.	60%

28. The barge consisted of quffas lined with wood planking. 50%

29. Noah sacrificed animals on the top of a ziggurat. 50%

30. Temple priests ate Noah's sacrifice. 50%

31. Shem walked to Mount Judi in the mountains of Ararat. 50%

32. The barge grounded, refloated, then grounded again. 40%

33. The barge grounded near the temple of Enki at Eridu. 40%

34. Noah had legal problems after the barge grounded. 40%

35. Noah and his wife lived in Dilmun after the barge grounded. 40%

36. The Genesis 5 numbers were calculated during ED IIIa. 40%

37. "Mount Nisir" should be translated "Nisir Country". 30%

38. The flood occurred when Noah was 48 years old. 30%

39. Noah lived to be 83 years old. 30%

40. The Genesis 5 numbers match the Sumerian king list. 30%

41. Some of the "gods" in the flood story were actually priests. 30%

42. Noah mortgaged his land as security for the cargo. 20%

43. Noah's land at Shuruppak was sold to pay his taxes. 20%

44. Methuselah was evicted from his house. 20%

45. A Shuruppak soldier at Eridu asked "Did anyone survive?" 20%

46. A priest of Enki made Noah and wife honorary gods. 20%

We should not overlook the possibility that the oral traditions recorded in clay by the author of the archetype flood story included fictional linkages between real events and real people. For example, there may have been a real barge loaded with grain and livestock that floated down the Euphrates River during the river flood of 2900 BC, but the owner of the barge may have been an obscure merchant rather than the king of Shuruppak. It may have been a fact that Ziusudra the king of Shuruppak was removed from office at the time of the river flood, but perhaps he did not offer a sacrifice on a ziggurat at the *apsû* temple of Enki at Eridu. And the sons who traveled on foot to Mount Judi in the mountains of Ararat may have been the merchant's sons rather than the king's sons. These are linkages that are possibly false. There is no way to know how many such false linkages are present in surviving editions of the flood story. The legend can be reconstructed, but the historicity of reported acts of the characters is still unproven.

Appendix A

Interlinear Translation of Gilgamesh XI

Standard translations of Gilgamesh XI have been adopted in this book whether possible. However, where the Akkadian text is ambiguous, alternative translations are possible. Selected lines are given below in Akkadian[1] followed by a literal word by word English translation. The corresponding translations in conversational English are given in Chapter 14. Any nonstandard translations below are not essential for my basic theory.

line

29 lu-ú   mìn-du-da   mi-na-tu-šá
    Let-be measured its-dimensions

30 lu-ú   mit-hur ru-pu-us-sa ù   mu-rak-šá
    Let-be equal-size its-width and its-length

31 [k]i-ma   ap-si-i   šá-a-ši   ṣu-ul-lil-ši
    As [usual in the] apsû   likewise roof-over-it [with awning]

56 ina ha-an-ši UD-mi at-ta-di   bu-na-šá
    On   fifth   day   I laid-out its shape/plan

57a AŠ   GÁN   GAM-sa   [text probably corrupt]
     One acre its-extent

57b U   NINDA   TA.ÀM ú-šaq-qa-a É.SIG$_4$.MEŠ-šá.
     Ten dozen-cubits each I-raised   its-walls.

58 U   NINDA   TA.ÀM im-ta-hir ki-bir muh-hi-šá.
    Ten dozen-cubits each equal-size edges its-upper-part.

59 ad-di   la-an-ši   šá-a-ši e-ṣir-ši
    I-erected its-body[frame] to-it. I-marked-it.

60   ur-tag-gi-ib-ši   a-na   6-šú
    I-provided-upper-deck with sixfold [rooms]

61 ap-ta-ra-as-su   a-na   7-šú
    I-divided [its width?] into sevenfold [sections]

62	qer-bi-is-sú ap-ta-ra-as a-na 9-šú
	Its-interior I-divided into ninefold [subsections]

139	a-na 12 TA.ÀM i-te-la-a na-gu-ú
	At twelve times emerged island

140	a-na ^{KUR} ni-ṣir i-te-mid ^{GIŠ} eleppu
	In (country) Nisir grounded (wooden) boat

141a	KUR-ú ^{KUR} ni-ṣir ^{GIŠ} eleppu iṣ-bat-ma
	Mound (country) Nisir (wooden) boat held-tight

141b	a-na na-a-ši ul id-din
	that its-movement not allowed

156	áš-kun sur-qin-nu ina UGU ziq-qur-rat KUR-i
	I-placed [an] offering on top-of [a] ziggurat hill-like

Discussion

Eleppu (boat) is feminine and the suffixes –*šá* refer to the boat as "her," but to avoid confusion the boat is referred to here as "it".

Line 30

Use of the word "equal-size" (*mit-hur*) at line 30 regarding the width and length and references to 120 cubits at lines 57 and 58 has led commentators to assume that the poet was describing a boat shaped like a cube or a step-pyramid. Line 30 literally reads "Let equal-size [be] its width and its length." This is usually interpreted to mean the width was equal to the length, i.e. the deck was square. The ancient editor of Gilgamesh tablet XI may have believed the deck was square, but he may have misunderstood his source text. The word *mit-hur* is singular where the plural *mit-hur-ū* would be expected. This suggests that in the Sumerian archetype flood story, line 30 may have been separate clauses: "Let its width be equal and let its length be equal" meaning that the barge had equal widths and also had equal lengths, i.e. the sides were straight and parallel. Unlike sailboats and marsh boats, the barge did not have a variable width and curved sides that converged to a pointed bow and stern. If one measured the widths at the bow and at the stern and at other places in between, all the width measurements would be equal to each other. Likewise with the length measurements which would also all be equal to each other. Since Gilgamesh XI does not explicitly state the width of the boat, but merely that it is equal, there is a real possibility of misunderstanding. Genesis 6:15 gives explicit dimensions in which the width is not equal to the length. The rectangular decks had square corners in a carpentry sense and were not square in a geometric sense.

Line 57a

The first phrase in line 57 is ▻— ⸗⸗ ⸗ ⸗⸗ according to Parpola.[2] Since there are no genitive endings, this is not a prepositional phrase and it is usually translated "One IKU its extent." The sign ⸗⸗ can be read as IKU, but in Sumerian it could also be read as GÁN (*eqlu* in Akkadian) meaning field.[3] Translators reject this reading because GÁN is not the common Sumerian sign for field and would be possible only in nonliterary (legal) texts from the third and very early second millennium BC.[4] Within the orthography used in literary texts from the first millennium, ⸗⸗ can only be read as the area measurement IKU, which implies that the preceding sign ▻— is the numeric value **one**. ⸗ is GAM in Sumerian (*kippatu* in Akkadian) and can mean circle, loop, circumference, or entire extent. Since one IKU of area (14400 square cubits) is consistent with a square 120 cubits by 120 cubits which is suggested by line 58, all recent translations treat the first phrase in line 57 as an area measurement: "One IKU its extent."

A square deck 120 cubits by 120 cubits is not consistent with the dimensions given in Genesis 6:15. Since both Genesis 6 and Gilgamesh XI are surviving editions of a Sumerian archetype flood story,[5] either Gilgamesh XI,57–58 is corrupt or Genesis 6:15 is corrupt. Genesis 6:15 gives numeric values for the length and width, but Gilgamesh XI does not give a numeric value for the width, saying only that it is equal. The ratio of length to width in Genesis 6:15 is six (5/2 in Berossus) which is plausible for an actual barge, but a square deck 120 cubits by 120 cubits is not plausible. This suggests that lines 57–58 of Gilgamesh XI are corrupt. There are many ways such corruption could have occurred. The editor of Gilgamesh XI may have wanted to exaggerate the size of the barge, just as he exaggerated the river flood into an ocean deluge. Alternatively, he may have copied lines 57–58 from a corrupt copy of Atrahasis or the Sumerian archetype flood story.

As discussed in Chapter 8, the archetype flood story was probably first written in clay in Sumerian during the Early Dynastic IIIa period. During this period, syllabic writing was sufficiently developed to record speech, but was often ambiguous because case endings were often omitted and had to be supplied by the reader. When these early tablets were copied or translated, different scribes would often supply different endings, depending on their differing interpretations of the ambiguous text.[6]

The Sumerian equivalent of line 57 may have begun with the phrase GÁN GAM MA where GÁN meant 'field' and GAM meant 'curve'. The case marker MA was very ambiguous[7] and could be a genitive marker, a locative marker, a nominalizer, etc. Assuming that MA was a locative marker, the scribe would have translated the previous two signs as a prepositional phrase "On a field curve..." Sumerian did not have prepositions and hence the scribe would have added the Akkadian preposition *i-na* at the beginning of the phrase. But he apparently forgot to provide a genitive case ending and the resulting phrase would not have looked like a prepositional phrase to later scribes, even after *i-na* was changed to ▷— *(ina)*.

During the Old Babylonian period, the signs GÁN and GAM were rarely used as logograms in literary texts.[4] A scribe apparently copied (not translated) these archaic signs because they had acquired new meanings which made sense in Akkadian. GÁN was read as *iku* (acre) and GAM was read as *kippatu* (circle, extent) in Akkadian, which may have been how they were read by the Old Babylonian scribe who produced the Akkadian translation of the flood story (Atrahasis version) that was added to the Gilgamesh epic.

If we assume that the text of lines 57–58 is corrupt and that genitive endings should be present in line 57a, the ambiguous sign ▷— can be read as the preposition *ina* meaning in, at, on, etc. Lines 56 and 57 both begin with ▷— and it is generally agreed that ▷— in line 56 is the preposition *ina*. In a text originating in the third or early second millennium, the sign ▷⤢ can be read in Sumerian as GÁN meaning field, although a different sign was used for field during the Old Babylonian period. The field mentioned at line 57a was probably the same field where a house was demolished (this house was mentioned at line 24) to clear a construction site on which to build the river barge.

Line 57b

Line 57b does not give the height of the walls as 120 cubits. It literally reads "120 cubits each I raised its sides/walls." The Akkadian root of *šaqqa* is *šaqu* which means to grow high, to rise, to move upward.[8] There is no additional indication of whether the 120 cubits was height or length and therefore the text is ambiguous. It could mean each wall was raised to a height of 120 cubits, or it could mean the raised walls were each 120 cubits long. It is more plausible to treat the 120 cubits as a measurement of wall length rather than wall height, because a boat as high as its length would be roll over in the water if anyone were foolish enough to build such a boat. Other texts that specify wall measurements often omit an indication of whether the number means length or height. An example[9] from an unrelated house building tablet: "he shall build the wall (of the house) and raise it (to the customary height, making it) four ninda and two cubits (long)." The word long or length is implied, because this measurement (about 83 feet) was obviously wall length.

Some scholars[10] argue that the ark in Gilgamesh XI had a ziggurat (step pyramid) shape and that line 61 refers to seven levels stacked one above the other. Even if the Babylonian scribe who edited Gilgamesh XI believed the boat had such a very improbable shape, without explicit numeric dimensions and an indication of what the "seven" refers to, the scribe could be mistaken about the shape of the boat.

Line 58

Line 58 is literally "120 cubits each equal-size edges its upperpart". The word for equal-size (im-ta-hir) has an inflectional infix t signifying reciprocity, i.e. not just "equal" but "equal to each other." This probably meant that the lengths of the left edge and the right edge of the upper part were equal to each other and equal to 120 cubits, i.e. the superstructure was symmetrical.

Line 59

In line 59 ad-di means 'I erected' or 'I placed',[11] la-an-ši means 'its body',[12] and e-ṣir-ši means 'I drew it' or 'I marked it'.[13] In shell-first construction, framing was built inside the hull after the hull shell was completed. The "body" being erected in line 59 probably refers to framing. The marking may refer to construction lines that a story teller saw boatbuilders mark on the inside of a hull to indicate the position of each frame member.

Line 60

Line 60 reads "I provided an upper deck/story sixfold." The verb ur-tag-gi-ib-ši means to provide with an upper story or upper floor and is based on the root rugbu meaning attic, roof, story.[10,14] Scholars usually translate this as six decks, because each deck could be "upper" relative to a lower deck. But just as building a house with six roofs implies that the roofs are arranged horizontally in six different side-by-side positions, building an upper deck sixfold implies that one upper deck was built in six horizontal sections. A barge with six or seven decks stacked vertically would have been impractical in 2900 BC.

Lines 61–62

Lines 61–62 indicates that the interior of the barge was divided into seven [sections] and nine [subsections], which suggests that the barge consisted of 63 separate pontoons arranged in a horizontal rectangular array of 7 columns abeam and 9 rows from bow to stern. This would be practical to build, unlike a barge with seven or nine sections built vertically.

Line 139

In line 139, XII TA.ÀM is distributive[15] and means twelve each or twelve times. A variant text of Gilgamesh XI has fourteen rather than twelve. Some scholars translate this as a distance of 12 leagues, but there is no indication that distance is meant. No unit of measurement is given.

Lines 140–145

Gilgamesh XI,141a reads "KUR-*ú* ^{KUR}*ni-ṣir* held tight the boat." *Niṣir* is transliterated as a proper name, because of the two KUR signs that precede *niṣir* and the absence of a case ending on *niṣir*. The first KUR is followed by a phonetic complement -*ú* which indicates that KUR-*ú* is to be read in Akkadian as *šadû*, not *mātu*. Since *šadû (shadû)* can mean mountain as well as hill, and scholars knew the Biblical expression Mount Ararat, it has become customary to translate KUR-*ú* ^{KUR} *niṣir* in lines 140–144 as Mount Niṣir or Mount Nimush.[16] But since this noun phrase was probably derived indirectly from the archetype flood story written in Sumerian, this KUR may originally have meant land or country or hill. KUR seldom meant mountain in Sumerian.[17] Because the complement -*ú* has no meaning in Sumerian, the Babylonian scribe who translated the Sumerian archetype flood story into Akkadian apparently added the sign -*ú* to KUR because he interpreted KUR to mean hill/mountain and not land/country. Or the editor of Gilgamesh XI may have added -*ú* to KUR to exaggerate hill or mound into mountain.

The second KUR is a determinative indicating that *niṣir* is the name of a hill or land or country (or in Akkadian, a mountain). Thompson[18] read this determinative as *mātu*, an Akkadian word for country. KUR-*ú* ^{KUR}*ni-ṣir* can be translated "mound [in the] country *Niṣir*".

The country *Niṣir* may have acquired its name from the root *niṣirtu*. With reference to localities, *niṣirtu* had the "connotation of hidden, inaccessible, secluded," and also meant arcane and secret.[19]

The semantic ranges of the words *apsû* and *niṣirtu*[16] overlap somewhat. Although the word *apsû* sometimes meant an underworld ocean god, a mythical primeval sea, aquifers, or an arm of the Persian Gulf, *apsû* also had the connotations of "not seeing within", "mysterious and secret", "which no one can look into", "impenetrable", and "a place of secrets".[20]

Hence, "country *Niṣir*" or "country *Nimuš*" can be identified with *apsû* country, a marshy area near Eridu that was considered secluded, inaccessible, mysterious, and/or secret. In Gilgamesh XI,42 the flood hero said "I will go down [the river] to the *apsû* to live with Ea, my Lord" which would be at the temple (*apsû*-house) of the god Ea/Enki in the city of Eridu. In the original story, the mound in "country *Niṣir*" on which the barge grounded, may have been a sand bar in a secluded, inaccessible, marshy estuary that was part of the *apsû*, an arm of the Persian Gulf, near Eridu.

Line 156

In line 156, *ziggurat* KUR-*i* is a construct-genitive phrase in which KUR-*i* can be interpreted[21] as an adjective: "I placed an offering on top of a hill-like ziggurat." Until recently, scholars who interpreted KUR-*i* as mountain assumed the location of this offering was a desolate mountain top. They treated *ziggurat* in Gilgamesh XI,156 as a metaphor for peak,[22] because a mountain would not have a ziggurat, a temple tower. But recent scholars have interpreted ziggurat literally as ziggurat.[10, 23] The flood hero sacrificed on top of a ziggurat, a man-made hill-like structure at the temple of Enki in the city of Eridu.

References

1. Transliteration is from Simo Parpola, *The Standard Babylonian Epic of Gilgamesh*, (Helsinki, Finland: University of Helsinki, 1997), pp. 109–111. Line numbers follow Heidel (1949) and Thompson (1930).[18]

2. ibid., p. 58, line 57.

3. Rene Labat, *Manuel D'Épigraphie Akkadienne*, (Winona Lake, Indiana: Eisenbrauns, 1988 reprint of 1976), p. 87, sign 105.

4. Prof. Walter Farber, personal communication.

5. See Chapter 2 herein.

6. C. B. F. Walker, *Cuneiform*, (Los Angeles, CA: University of California Press, 1987), pp. 15–16.

7. Prof. John L. Hayes, personal communication.

8. John A. Brinkman, and others (editors), *The Assyrian Dictionary* (Chicago: Univ. of Chicago, 1980), CAD, vol. Š-2, p. 22, upper left column.

9. CAD, vol. I–J, op. cit., p. 36, under *igāru*, bottom left.

10. Steven Holloway, "What Ship Goes There: The Flood Narratives in the Gilgamesh Epic and Genesis...," *Zeitschrift für die alttestamentliche Wissenschaft*, 103 (1991), pp. 328–355. See also Kovacs,[23] p. 99, note 3.

11. CAD, vol. N-1, op. cit., p. 83, lower right.

12. CAD, vol. L, op. cit., p. 80, left middle.

13. CAD, vol. E, op. cit., pp. 346–348.

14. Wolfram Von Soden, *Akkadisches Handwörterbuch* (Wiesbaden, Germany: Otto Harrassowitz, 1965), p. 993.

15. Labat, op. cit., p. 99, sign 139.

16. The cuneiform sign (Labat's 374) for *ṣir* and *muš* is the same sign and is used both at line 9 (secret) and lines 140–145 (proper name) in Gilgamesh XI. Reading *ni-ṣir* as *ni-muš* does not affect my arguments.

17. Prof. Åke Sjöberg, personal communication.

18. R. Campbell Thompson, *The Epic of Gilgamesh*, (NY: AMS Press, Clarendon Press, 1930), p. 63, lines 140–141; also Labat, p. 167, sign 366.

19. CAD, vol. N2, op. cit., p. 276.

20. Margaret Whitney Green, *Eridu in Sumerian Literature*, Ph.D. dissertation, (University of Chicago, 1975), pp. 166–167. In CAD, vol. A2, pp. 194–195, *apsû* is defined as deep water where birds and fish live.

21. Profs. David I. Owen and David Marcus, personal communications.

22. CAD, vol. Z, op. cit., p. 131, lower right.

23. Maureen Gallery Kovacs, *The Epic of Gilgamesh*, (Stanford University Press, 1985), p. 102.

Appendix B

Chronological tables

The following chronologies in solar years were constructed from the numbers in Tables IV and V in chapter 7. No attempt has been made to correct for truncation errors that resulted from representing one-quarter and three-quarters as .2 and .7 in the data. Also no attempt has been made to correct for cumulative errors caused by fractional years in a Sumerian king list being added to the Genesis 5 numbers.

Era Year	Sumerian kings	Approximate year BC
0.0	Nameless king X reigning	3113.0
30.5	Nameless king Y began reign	3082.5
80.0	Nameless king Z began reign	3033.0
98.2	Alulim began reign	3014.8
117.0	Aloros began reign	2996.0
124.7	Alalgar began reign	2988.3
134.5	Alimma began reign	2978.5
146.7	Enmenluanna began reign	2966.3
153.0	Enmengalanna began reign	2960.0
161.2	Dumuzi the shepherd began reign	2951.8
171.2	Ensipazianna began reign	2941.8
179.2	Enmenduranna began reign	2933.8
197.7	Sukurlam (Lamech) began reign	2915.3
202.7	Ziusudra (Noah) began reign	2910.3
212.4	the six-day flood	2900.6

Table IX Chronology of modified Sumerian King List data

If these names are not mythical, they are the kings of Sumer during the Jemdet Nasr period (c3200–2900) based on the fact that the list ends with Ziusudra who was king of Shuruppak at the time of the 2900 BC river flood, at the end of the Jemdet Nasr period.

Era Year		Approximate year BC
0.0	Adam born	3113.0
23.0	Seth born	3090.0
43.5	Enosh born	3069.5
62.5	Kenan born	3050.5
79.5	Mahalalel born	3033.5
81.0	Adam died	3032.0
96.0	Jared born	3017.0
102.2	Seth died	3010.7
112.2	Enoch born	3000.7
122.0	Enosh died	2991.0
128.7	Methuselah born	2984.2
141.5	Kenan died	2971.5
145.5	Lamech born	2967.5
148.7	Enoch died	2964.2
157.0	Mahalalel died	2956.0
164.2	Noah born	2948.7
180.2	Jared died	2932.7
ca. 197.	Shem born	2916.0
208.7	Lamech died	2904.2
212.4	the six-day flood	2900.6
213.4	Noah left the ark	2899.6
213.6	Methuselah died	2899.4
214.2	Arpachshad born	2898.7
247.2	Noah died	2865.7

Table X   Chronology of modified Genesis 5 data

Appendix C

Possible textual corruption of Genesis 8:3a

Genesis 8:3a is usually translated "and the waters receded from the earth continually" from the Hebrew "*vay-yashubû ha-mayim me^cal ha-arets haloch va-shob.*" The Septuagint, the Peshitta, and Targum Onqelos concur in this traditional interpretation. But as discussed in chapter 4, after the barge grounded, the water was only several feet deep. If this water had continued to subside, soon the barge would have been surrounded by dry land.

The first four words translate literally "and-they-returned the-waters away-from-upon the-earth." The masculine plural "they" refers to the waters. The second word יָשֻׁב *(yshb)* is usually pointed *yashubû* (they returned), but can also be pointed *yesh^ebû* (they remained/stayed/waited/sat/dwelled) from the root *yashab*.[1] Apparently it made no sense to pre-Septuagint scribes copying this ambiguous Hebrew word for the waters to be both staying/ remaining and continually receding. And so they erroneously assumed that the root was *shub* (to return) which was strengthened by the *shob* at the end of the sentence.[2] But the original meaning of this word was probably *yesh^ebû* (they remained). Later, in Genesis 8:5 the waters decreased/abated, but in Genesis 8:3a the waters remained.

The compound preposition *me^cal* literally means away-from-upon, but in combination with *yesh^ebû* describes a static condition, not movement. The waters remained/waited/stayed upon the earth away-from dry land.

The next two words *haloch va-shob* are usually translated "receded continually" (RSV) or "receded steadily" (NIV). The early scribes interpreted this phrase as a continuing action because *haloch* (to go forward) used with a second infinitive absolute *shob* (to return) can mean the returning action was going continually. Gesenius[2] gives examples of continuing and coordinated actions from Gen 8:5, Gen 8:7 and I Sam 6:12. *Shob* does not mean recede; it means to return. Literally *haloch va-shob* mean to-go-forward *(haloch)* and–to-return *(va-shob)*. In modern Hebrew, *haloch va-shov* means a round trip; you go forward to a place and then you return. Sea water going forward and returning is often called ebbing and flooding; the tide goes out and then the tide comes in. In Hebrew these would be coordinated actions.

If the first word was *yesh^ebû* (they remained) and not *yashubû* (they returned), then Genesis 8:3a should be translated as coordinated actions: "and the waters remained upon the earth, ebbing and flooding."

1.   Robert Young, *Young's Analytical Concordance to the Bible*, (Nashville: Thomas Nelson Publishers, 1982), appendix p. 54.

2.   A. E. Cowley (ed), *Gesenius' Hebrew Grammar* (Oxford: Clarendon Press, 1910), pp. 342–344.

Bibliography

Alster, Bendt, "Dilmun, Bahrain, and the Alleged Paradise in Sumerian Myth and Literature" in Potts (editor), *Dilmun: New Studies.*

Adams, Robert McCormick, *Heartland of Cities.* Chicago: University of Chicago Press, 1981.

Bailey, Lloyd R., *Noah: The Person and the Story in History and Tradition,* Studies on Personalities of the Old Testament. Columbia, SC: University of South Carolina Press, 1989.

———. *Genesis, Creation, and Creationism.* New York: Paulist Press, 1993.

Barber, Richard, *King Arthur Hero and Legend.* New York: Boydell Press, 1986.

Barr, James, "Archbishop Ussher and Biblical Chronology," *Bulletin of the John Rylands Univ. Library of Manchester,* 67(2). Great Britain, 1985, pp. 575–608.

Barre, Lloyd M., "The Riddle of the Flood Chronology," *Journal for the Study of the Old Testament,* 41 (1988), pp. 3–20.

Berossus, quoted by Syncellus, 53–56 and Josephus, *Antiquities of the Jews* I, 3, 6. See also: *Berossos and Manetho* by Verbrugghe and Wickersham.

Bibby, Geoffrey, *Looking for Dilmun.* New York, Knopf, 1969.

Brinkman, John A., and others (editors), *The Assyrian Dictionary.* Chicago: Oriental Institute of the Univ. of Chicago, 1980.

Brookes, Ian A., "A Medieval Catastrophic Flood in Central West Iran" in *Catastrophic Flooding,* L. Mayer and D. Nash (editors). Boston, MA: Allen & Unwin, 1987, pp. 225–246.

Campbell, Antony F. and Mark A. O'Brien, *Sources of the Pentateuch.* Minneapolis: Fortress Press, 1993.

Campbell, Joseph, *The Masks of God: Oriental Mythology.* New York: Penguin Books, 1962, pp. 119–130.

Casson, Lionel, *Ships and Seamanship in the Ancient World.* NJ: Princeton University Press, 1971.

Civil, Miguel, "The Sumerian Flood Story" in *Atrahasis,* W. G. Lambert and A. R. Millard. Oxford: Clarendon Press, 1969, pp. 138–145.

Clinton, Henry Fynes, *Fasti Hellenici, Vol III, The Civil and Literary Chronology of Greece*, monograph 119 in Burt Franklin Research and Source Works Series (1965), pp. 349, 358.

Cohn, Norman, *Noah's Flood*. New Haven, CT: Yale University Press, 1996.

Cornwall, P. B., "On the Location of Dilmun", *Bulletin of the American Schools of Oriental Research*, 103 (Oct 1946), pp. 3–10.

Crawford, Harriet, *Sumer and the Sumerians*. London: Cambridge University Press, 1991.

Cryer, Frederick H., "The Interrelationships of Gen 5,32; 11,10–11 and the Chronology of the Flood (Gen 6–9)", *Biblica*, 66 #2 (1985), pp 241–261.

Davila, James R., "The Flood Hero as King and Priest," *Journal of Near Eastern Studies*, 54, 3 (July 1995), pp. 199–214.

De Graeve, Marie–Christine, *The Ships of the Ancient Near East*. Leuven, Belgium, 1981.

Dundes, Alan, (editor), *The Flood Myth*. CA: University of California Press, 1988.

Emerton, J. A., "An Examination of Some Attempts to Defend the Unity of the Flood Narrative in Genesis, Part II", *Vetus Testamentum*, 38, 1 (1988), pp. 1–21.

Englund, Robert K., "Hard Work ... Labor Management in Ur III Mesopotamia", *Journal of Near Eastern Studies*, 50 (1991), pp. 255–280.

Friberg, Jöran, "The Third Millennium Roots of Babylonian Mathematics" Research Report. Sweden: University of Göteborg, Department of Mathematics, 1979, pp. 10, 20, 41–46.

———. "Numbers and Measures in the Earliest Written Records", *Scientific American*, 250 (February, 1984), pp. 78–85.

Gardner, John and John Maier, *Gilgamesh*. NY: Knopf, 1984.

Garrett, Duane A., *Rethinking Genesis*. Grand Rapids, Michigan: Baker Book House, 1991.

Gelb, Ignace J., Piotr Steinkeller, Robert M. Whiting, *Earliest Land Tenure Systems in The Near East: Ancient Kudurrus*. Chicago: Oriental Institute of the Univ. of Chicago, 1989.

George, A. R., *House Most High*. Winona Lake, Indiana: Eisenbrauns, 1993.

Gould, Stephen Jay, "Creationism: Genesis vs. Geology" in *The Flood Myth*, Alan Dundes (editor). CA: Univ. of California Press, 1988, pp. 427–437.

Green, Margaret Whitney, *Eridu in Sumerian Literature*. Ph.D. dissertation, University of Chicago, 1975.

Greenhill, Basil, *Archaeology of the Boat*. Middletown, CT: Wesleyan University Press, 1976.

Haites, Erik F., James Mak and Gary M. Walton, *Western River Transportation*. Baltimore, Maryland: Johns Hopkins University Press, 1975.

Haldane, Cheryl Ward, "Boat Construction in Ancient Egypt" in *The Pharaoh's Boat at The Carnegie* by Diana Craig Patch. Pittsburgh: Carnegie Museum of Natural History, 1990.

Hasel, Gerhard F., "Genealogies of Gen 5 and 11 and Their Alleged Babylonian Background", *Andrews University Seminary Studies*, 16, (1978) pp. 361–374.

Heidel, Alexander, *The Gilgamesh Epic and Old Testament Parallels*. 2d edition. Chicago: University of Chicago Press, 1949.

Heinrich, E. and Seidl, U., *Die Temple und Heiligtümer im alten Mesopotamien*. Berlin: 1982. Illustrations are in vol. 2.

Heyerdahl, Thor, *The Tigris Expedition*. NY: Doubleday, 1981.

Holloway, Steven, "What Ship Goes There: The Flood Narratives in the Gilgamesh Epic and Genesis...", *Zeitschrift für die alttestamentliche Wissenschaft*, 103 (1991), pp. 328–355.

Hossain, Mosharaff, *Floods in Bangladesh*. Dhaka, Bangladesh: Universities Research Centre, 1987.

Ifrah, Georges, *From One to Zero: A Universal History of Numbers*. NY: Viking Penguin, 1985.

Jacobsen, Thorkild, *The Sumerian King List*. Chicago: University of Chicago Press, 1939.

———. "Formative Tendencies in Sumerian Religion" in *The Bible and the Ancient Near East*, George E. Wright (editor), Essays in Honour of W. F. Albright. NY: Doubleday, 1961.

———. "The Eridu Genesis", *Journal of Biblical Literature*, 100/4 (1981), pp. 513–529.

Jaroff, Leon, "Phoney Arkaeology", *Time*, July 5, 1993, p. 51.

Jones, Charles W., *Saint Nicholas of Myra*. Chicago: University of Chicago Press, 1978.

Jones, Dilwyn, *Boats*. Austin, TX: University of Texas Press, 1995.

Josephus, *Complete Works, Antiquities of the Jews* I, 3, 6. Grand Rapids, MI: Kregel Publications, 1974.

Kidner, Derek, *Genesis*. Chicago: InterVarsity Press, 1967.

Klein, Ralph W., "Archaic Chronologies and the Textual History of the Old Testament", *Harvard Theol Review*, 67 (1974), pp. 255–263.

Kovacs, Maureen Gallery, *The Epic of Gilgamesh*. California: Stanford University Press, 1985, pp. 97–103.

Kramer, Samuel Noah, "Dilmun, The Land of the Living", *Bulletin of the American Schools of Oriental Research*, 96, (Dec 1944), pp. 18–28.

———. "Enki and Ninhursag" in *Ancient Near Eastern Texts*, James B. Pritchard (editor). NJ: Princeton University Press, 1950, p. 38.

———. "Sumerian Myths and Epic Tales" in *Ancient Near Eastern Texts*, James B. Pritchard (editor). NJ: Princeton University Press, 1950, pp. 42–44.

———. *Enmerkar and the Lord of Aratta*, Museum Monograph. Philadelphia: University of Pennsylvania, 1952.

———. *The Sumerians*. Chicago: University of Chicago Press, 1963.

———. "Reflections on the Mesopotamian Flood", *Expedition*, 9, 4 (summer 1967), pp. 12–18.

Labat, Rene, *Manuel D'Épigraphie Akkadienne*. Winona Lake, Indiana: Eisenbrauns, 1988.

Lamberg–Karlovsky, C. C., "Dilmun: Gateway to Immortality", *Journal of Near Eastern Studies*, 41, 1 (January 1982), pp. 45–50.

Lambert, W. G., "A New Look at the Babylonian Background of Genesis", *Journal of Theological Studies*, N.S. 16 (1965), p. 299.

Lambert W. G., and A. R. Millard, *Atrahasis: The Babylonian Story of the Flood*. Oxford: Clarendon Press, 1969.

Landström, Björn, *Ships of the Pharaohs: 4000 Years of Egyptian Shipbuilding*, NY: Doubleday, 1970, pp. 27–29.

Langdon, S., "The Chaldean Kings Before the Flood", *Journal of the Royal Asiatic Society* (1923), pp. 251–259.

Larsen, C. E., "The Mesopotamian Delta Region: A Reconstruction of Lees and Falcon," *Journal of the American Oriental Society*, 95 (1975), pp. 43–57.

Larsson, Gerhard, "The Chronology of the Pentateuch: A Comparison of the MT and LXX," *Journal of Biblical Literature*, 102 (1983) pp. 401–409.

Laymon, Charles M. (editor), *The Interpreter's One-Volume Commentary on the Bible*. Nashville: Abingdon Press, 1971.

Longman, Tremper III, *Fictional Akkadian Autobiography: A Generic and Comparative Study*. Winona Lake, Indiana: Eisenbrauns, 1991.

Malamat, Abraham, "King Lists of the Old Babylonian Period and Biblical Genealogies," *Journal of the American Oriental Society*, 88 (1968), pp. 163–173; reprinted in *I Studied Inscriptions from Before the Flood*, Richard S. Hess and David Tsumura (editors). Eisenbrauns, 1994, pp. 183–199.

Mallowan, M. E. L., "Noah's Flood Reconsidered," *Iraq*, 26 (1964), pp. 62–82.

McGovern, Patrick E., et al, "Neolithic Resinated Wine," *Nature*, 381 (6 June 1996), pp. 480–481.

McGowan, Chris, *In the Beginning*. Buffalo, NY: Prometheus Books, 1984.

Moore, Robert A., "The Impossible Voyage of Noah's Ark," *Creation/Evolution*, 4, 1, issue XI (winter 1983). PO Box 146, Amherst Branch, Buffalo, NY 14226.

Moses of Khoren, *History of the Armenians*, translation by Robert W. Thomson, vol. 4 of Harvard Armenian Texts and Studies. Harvard University Press, 1978, pp. 79–80.

Murphy, C. C. R., "What is Gopher Wood?", *Asiatic Review*, N.S., 42 (January 1946), pp. 79–81.

Nissen, Hans J., *The Early History of the Ancient Near East*, translation by Elizabeth Lutzeier. Chicago: University of Chicago Press, 1988.

Nissen, Hans J., Peter Damerow, Robert K. Englund, *Archaic Bookkeeping*. Chicago: University of Chicago Press, 1993.

Noegel, Scott B., "Fictional Sumerian Autobiographies," *Journal of the Association of Graduate Near Eastern Students*, 4/2 (1993), pp. 46–55.

Numbers, Ronald L., *The Creationists: The Evolution of Scientific Creationism*. New York: Knopf, 1992.

Oppenheim, A. Leo, "The Seafaring Merchants of Ur," *Journal of the American Oriental Society*, 74 (1954), pp. 6–17.

Oppenheim, A. Leo, *Ancient Mesopotamia*. Chicago: University of Chicago Press, 1977.

Parpola, Simo, *The Standard Babylonian Epic of Gilgamesh*. Helsinki, Finland: University of Helsinki, 1997.

Parrot, André, *The Flood and Noah's Ark*. London: SCM Press, 1955.

Pellegrino, Charles R., *Return to Sodom and Gomorrah: Bible Stories from Archaeologists*. NY: Avon, 1994.

Postgate, J. Nicholas, *Early Mesopotamia*. London: Routledge, 1992.

Potts, Daniel T., (editor) *Dilmun: New Studies in the Archaeology and Early History of Bahrain*. Berlin: Berliner Beiträge zum Vorderen Orient 2, 1983.

Powell, Marvin A., "Ancient Mesopotamian Weight Metrology" in *Studies in Honor of Tom B. Jones*, M. A. Powell & Ronald H. Sack. Neukirchen–Vluyn; Butzon & Bercker Kevelaer, 1979, p. 86.

———. "Masse und Gewiechte" (in English), *Reallexikon der Assyriologie*, 7, pp. 457–517, especially 494–495.

Raikes, R. L., "The Physical Evidence for Noah's Flood," *Iraq*, 28 (1966), pp. 52–63.

Roux, Georges, *Ancient Iraq*. NY: Penguin Books, 1992.

Ryan, William and Pitman, Walter, *Noah's Flood: The New Scientific Discoveries About the Event That Changed History*. NY: Simon & Schuster, 1999.

Sandars, N. K., *The Epic of Gilgamesh*. Baltimore, MD: Penguin Books, 1964, pp. 105–110.

Schmandt–Besserat, Denise, *Before Writing: From Counting to Cuneiform*, Vol. I. Austin, Texas: University of Texas Press, 1992.

Scott, Bob, "What's Causing All the Floods?" in *Storm, the World Weather Magazine* (September 1993), pp. 22–24.

Short, A. K., *Ancient and Modern Agriculture*. San Antonio, Texas: Naylor Company, 1938.

Skinner, John, *A Critical and Exegetical Commentary on Genesis*. Edinburgh: T&T Clark, 1930.

Sollberger, Edmond, *The Babylonian Legend of the Flood*. London: British Museum, 1971.

Soroka, Leonard G. and Charles L. Nelson, "Physical Constraints on the Noachian Deluge," *Journal of Geological Education*, 31 (1983), pp. 135–139.

Speiser, E. A., "Akkadian Myths and Epics" in *Ancient Near Eastern Texts,* James B. Pritchard (editor). NJ: Princeton University Press, 1950, pp. 93–95.

———. "Authority and Law in Mesopotamia," *Supplement to the Journal of the American Oriental Society,* 17 (July–Sept 1954), pp. 8–15.

Stigers, Harold, *A Commentary on Genesis.* Grand Rapids: Zondervan, 1975.

Teeple, Howard M., *The Noah's Ark Nonsense.* Ann Arbor, Michigan: Edwards Brothers Inc., 1978.

Tigay, Jeffrey H., *The Evolution of the Gilgamesh Epic.* Philadelphia, PA: University of Pennsylvania Press, 1982.

Tov, Emanuel, *Textual Criticism of the Hebrew Bible.* Minneapolis: Fortress Press, 1992.

Ullendorf, Edward, "The Construction of Noah's Ark", *Vetus Testamentum,* 4 (1954), pp. 95–96.

Veenker, Ronald A., "Gilgamesh and the Magic Plant", *Biblical Archeologist,* 44 (Fall 1981), pp. 199–205.

Verbrugghe, Gerald P. and John M. Wickersham, *Berossos and Manetho.* Ann Arbor, Michigan: University of Michigan Press, 1996, pp. 49–50.

Wenham, Gordon J., "The Coherence of the Flood Narrative", *Vetus Testamentum,* 28 (1978), pp. 336–348.

———. "Method in Pentateuchal Source Criticism", *Vetus Testamentum,* 41, 1 (1991), pp. 84–109.

Wilson, J. V. Kinnier, "The Story of the Flood in the Epic of Gilgamesh", in *Documents from Old Testament Times,* D. Winton Thomas (editor). London: Thomas Nelson and Sons, 1958, pp. 17–26.

Wolff, Hans Walter, "Problems Between the Generations in the Old Testament," in *Essays in Old Testament Ethics,* James L. Crenshaw and John T. Willis (editors). New York: Ktav Publishing House, 1974, pp. 77–95.

Woolley, Leonard, "The Flood" in *Myth or Legend.* NY: G. E. Daniel Capricorn Books, 1955, pp. 39–47.

———. *The Sumerians.* New York: W. W. Norton, 1965.

Young, Davis A., *The Biblical Flood.* Grand Rapids, MI: Wm. B. Eerdmans Publishing Co., 1995.

Young, Robert, *Young's Analytical Concordance to the Bible.* Nashville, TN: Thomas Nelson, 1981.

Creationist and "Arkologist" Books
(not recommended)

Berlitz, Charles, *The Lost Ship of Noah*. NY: Ballantine Books, 1987.

Balsiger, David and Charles E. Sellier Jr., *In Search of Noah's Ark*. Los Angeles, CA: Sun Classic Books, 1976.

Berlitz, Charles, *The Lost Ship of Noah*. NY: Ballantine Books, 1987.

Bright, Richard C., *The Ark, A Reality?*. Ranger Associates, 1989.

Crouse, William, *Ararat Report*, 1996, P. O. Box 2667, El Cajon, CA 92021.

Cummings, Violet, *Has Anybody Seen Noah's Ark?*. Creation Life, 1982.

Fasold, David, *The Ark of Noah*. MA:Knightsbridge Pub., 1990.

Montgomery, John Warwick, *The Quest for Noah's Ark*. Bethany House, 1974.

Morris, John D., *Noah's Ark and the Ararat Adventure*. Master Books, 1994.

Morris, Henry M., *A History of Modern Creationism*. El Cajon, CA: Master Books, 1984.

Navarra, Fernand, *Noah's Ark: I Touched It*. Logos International, 1974.

Sellier, Charles E. and David W. Balsiger, *The Incredible Discovery of Noah's Ark*. NY: Dell Publishing, 1995.

Snelling, Andrew A., "Amazing 'Ark' Expose", *Creation Magazine*, 14, 4, (Sept–Nov 1992), pp. 26–38.

Thomsen, Paul, *The Mystery of the Ark: The Dangerous Journey to Mount Ararat*. Wolgemuth and Hyatt, 1991.

Whitcomb, John C. and Henry M. Morris, *The Genesis Flood*. Philadelphia, PA: The Presbyterian and Reformed Publishing Co., 1964.

Whitcomb, John C., *The World That Perished*. Grand Rapids, MI: Baker Book House, 1988.

Woodmorappe, John, *Noah's Ark: A Feasibility Study*. Santee, CA: Institute for Creation Research, 1996.

Glossary

abeam	sideways, from one side of the boat to the other
Adad	storm god
Aghri Dagh	= "Mount Ararat"
Akkad	a city in northern Babylonia where Sargon I ruled
Akkadian	a semitic language of Mesopotamia
ANE	Ancient Near East
apsû	fresh water, marsh lands, primeval sea, temple at Eridu, god of subterranean waters, arm of the Persian Gulf
Armenia	a kingdom in eastern Turkey that included the Ararat region
Ashurbanipal	the last great king of Assyria (668–627 BC)
Atrahasis	= Noah in the Epic of Atrahasis, "exceedingly wise"
Babylon	a large city at 32°33′ N, 44°24′ E in middle Mesopotamia
ballast	heavy material in the bottom of a boat to improve stability
barge	a rectangular flat-bottomed boat for hauling cargo and propelled by towing or punting
Berossus	a Babylonian priest who wrote a history of Babylonia about 281 BC
bilge	the lowest point of a boat's inner hull
bow	front end of a boat
braces	diagonal poles to make a boat frame more rigid
bulkhead	a vertical partition separating compartments in a boat
CE	common era, same as AD
coracle	a quffa-like boat with a hull covered with animal skins
cubit	the length of a man's forearm, about 20 inches in Sumer
cuneiform	wedge-shaped writing used on clay tablets
deckbeam	horizontal board supporting deck planks and joists
Dilmun	a commercial seaport on an island in the Persian Gulf
draft	the distance from the bottom of a boat to the water line
dunnage	loose padding to support cargo in a boat and to prevent damage from adjacent cargo
Ea	god of fresh water and wisdom = Enki
Enki	god of fresh water and wisdom = Ea
Enlil	a Sumerian nature god whose temple was at Nippur
Eridu	a city at 30°52′ N [30°49′ N ?], 46°3′ E in southern Mesopotamia
Erragal	= Nergal, underworld god of war and pestilence
exilic	related to the Babylonian exile of the Jews in 606–536 BC
frame-first	boat construction method, internal frame built before hull

freeboard	the part of a hull above the water line
Gilgamesh	a Sumerian king of Uruk (about 2660 BC), deified hero in literature
Gilgamesh XI	the eleventh tablet of the twelve tablets of the Epic of Gilgamesh, the tablet containing the flood story
Gudea	a king of Lagash (2141–2122 BC)
Hammurabi	a Babylonian king (1792–1750 BC)
haček	the ˇ mark over an s to indicate sh sound
har	Hebrew word for hill or mountain
inundation	annual (shallow) flooding of the river valley
J	a hypothetical scribe who wrote Yahweh (Jahweh in German spelling) for the Hebrew God in the Pentateuch.
joist	horizontal board supporting a floor or deck planks
Josephus	Jewish historian (38–101 CE)
Khsisuthros	= Noah in the flood story recorded by Moses of Khoren
Khufu	Cheops, the Egyptian king who built the great pyramid and reigned about 2590–2566 BC
Kish	a city at 32°33' N, 44°39' E in middle Mesopotamia
KJV	King James Version (of the Bible)
KUR	Sumerian word for hill, land, country
lapis lazuli	a dark blue stone used in jewelry and art work
Lucianic	a version of the Septuagint edited by Lucian before 311 CE
lugal	great man, king, chief executive
Masis	= "Mount Ararat"
Masoretic	the standard Hebrew Old Testament from which most Bible translations are made; transmitted by the Masoretes, a group of Jewish scribes after 70 CE
matting	mats of woven material
Mesopotamia	the land between the Tigris and Euphrates rivers
Moses of Khoren	legend collector and author of a history of Armenia about the eighth century CE
Mount Ararat	a mythical mountain erroneously identified as Aghri Dagh
Mount Judi	a 7,000 foot mountain in southeast Turkey
neap tide	a tide of minimum range occuring twice each lunar month
Nebuchadrezzar	two Babylonian kings (1124–1103 and 604–562 BC)
Nineveh	a city at 36°24' N, 43°8' E in northern Mesopotamia
Ninurta	god of the stormy south wind
Nippur	a city at 32°10' N, 45°11' E in middle Mesopotamia
Nisir	see Appendix A
NIV	New International Version of the Bible
Old Kingdom	period in Egypt, about 2686–2181 BC.

P	a hypothetical Priest who wrote part of the Pentateuch
Pentateuch	the first five books of the Bible
pitch	asphalt, bitumen, naturally occuring tar from crude petroleum
place value notation	same number signs in each column, like decimals
planking	planks, wood boards that form the hull or deck of a boat
pontoon	a boxlike flat-bottomed boat
punting	to propel a boat by pushing with a long pole
Puzur Amurri	or Puzur Illil, Noah's boatman
quffa	a woven reed boat like a large waterproofed basket
R^{jp}	a hypothetical scribe who combined texts from J and P
regnal year	a year calculated from the beginning of a king's reign
RSV	Revised Standard Version of the Bible
š	haček over s indicates sh sound
ṣ	dot under s indicates ts sound
Samaritan	text of the Pentateuch written in Old Hebrew script about 150 BC.
Septuagint	text of the Pentateuch translated from Hebrew into Greek at Alexandria about 280 BC, later to include the remainder of the Old Testament, often abbreviated LXX
sexagesimal	a number system based on 60, alternating 6 and 10
shadû	Akkadian word for hill or mountain
sheathing	waterproof woven material covering the outside of a boat
shell-first	a boat construction method, the hull (shell) is built before the frames
Shem	Noah's eldest son
Shuruppak	a city at 31°45' N, 45°34' E in southern Mesopotamia
sign value notation	different number signs in each column, like Roman
Sippar	a city at 33°3' N, 44°18' E in middle Mesopotamia
spring tide	a tide greater than average range, twice each lunar month
stern	rear end of a boat
Sumer	an ancient group of city-states in southern Mesopotamia
Sumerian	a language of southern Mesopotamia, first written language
superstructure	a boat structure built above the main deck
truss	a rigid frame assembled with diagonal members
Ur	a city at 30°56' N, 46°8' E in southern Mesopotamia, Urim
Urartu	= Ararat, an ancient kingdom in eastern Turkey centered around Lake Van
Uruk	a large Sumerian city at 31°18' N, 45°40' E, north of Ur. Gilgamesh was king of Uruk.
Utnapishtim	= Noah in the Epic of Gilgamesh, "he found life"

Xisuthros	= Noah in the flood story recorded by Berossus
Zagros	a mountain range east of the Persian Gulf, in western Iran
ziggurat	a raised platform or step pyramid near a temple
Ziusudra	= Noah in the Epic of Ziusudra, "long life"

Numbers and units of measurement

ban	unit of capacity, about 9 liters
bariga	unit of capacity, about 54 liters
dish	the number 1 in the sexagesimal system
gar	*ninda*, unit of length, 12 cubits, 20 feet
gesh	the number 60 in the sexagesimal system
geshu	the number 600 in the sexagesimal system
gur	unit of capacity, two bushels
iku	unit of area, 0.918 acre
kùš	cubit, about 20 inches
ninda	*gar*, unit of length, 12 cubits = 20 feet
shar	*šar*, the number 3600 in the sexagesimal system
sila	unit of capacity, about 0.9 liters
u	the number 10 in the sexagesimal system

Archaeological periods in Mesopotamia (years are approximate)

Ubaid period	5300–4000 BC	
Uruk period	4000–3100 BC	
Jemdet Nasr period	3100–2900 BC	(Noah)
Noah's river flood	2900 BC	
Early Dynastic I period	2900–2750 BC	ED I
Early Dynastic II period	2750–2600 BC	ED II (Gilgamesh)
Early Dynastic IIIa period	2600–2500 BC	ED IIIa
Early Dynastic IIIb period	2500–2350 BC	ED IIIb
Old Akkadian period	2334–2250 BC	(Sargon I)
Classical Sumerian period	2250–2112 BC	
Ur III period	2112–2004 BC	
Isin and Larsa periods	2017–1763 BC	
Old Babylonian Period	1894–1595 BC	(Hammurabi, Amazaduga)
Middle Babylonian (Kassite)	1570–1155 BC	
Second Dynasty of Isin	1157–1026 BC	
Neo–Assyrian period	980–627 BC	
Neo–Babylonian Period	625–539 BC	

Index

Order Form

Please send ____ **copies of**
    Noah's Ark and the Ziusudra Epic
ship to:

Name _____

Address _____

City, state _____ ZIP _____

☐ Check enclosed

Credit card number: _____

☐ Visa   ☐ Mastercard   expires _____

Signature _____

Print credit card name _____

Mail orders to:
    Enlil Press
    5100 S. Cleveland Ave. 318–325
    Fort Myers, FL 33907–2136

Prices:
    $38.73 for first book and
    $29.05 for each additional book (25% discount)

Fax orders to: (941) 368–7480
Internet orders: www.noahs-ark.cc/sales